Leaving the
House of Ghosts

Leaving the House of Ghosts

Cambodian Refugees in the American Midwest

SARAH STREED

McFarland & Company, Inc., Publishers
Jefferson, North Carolina, and London

Library of Congress Cataloguing-in-Publication Data

Streed, Sarah.
    Leaving the house of ghosts : Cambodian refugees in the
American Midwest / Sarah Streed.
      p.   cm.
    Includes bibliographical references and index.

    ISBN 0-7864-1354-9 (softcover : 50# alkaline paper)

    1. Cambodia—History—1975–1979.   2. Political atrocities—
Cambodia.   3. Refugees—Middle West.   4. Cambodian
Americans—Middle West.   I. Title.
DS554.8 .S76 2002
959.604'2—dc21

                   2002008468

British Library cataloguing data are available

On the cover: (foreground) Sam and Sokhary You with their newborn
son, 1981 *(photograph by Catholic Relief Services); (background)* The
1980 exhumation of the "killing fields" of Choeung Ek *(photograph by
Professor Ben Kiernan, director of the Genocide Studies Program, Yale
University)*

Manufactured in the United States of America

*McFarland & Company, Inc., Publishers
  Box 611, Jefferson, North Carolina 28640
    www.mcfarlandpub.com*

For my husband, Roger, and our children,
Alec, Drew, Sarah, Brian and Theron

Acknowledgments

This book could not have been written without the unflagging support of my husband, Roger Luhn, and the innumerable hours he spent reading and critiquing. He obtained medical articles for me to read when pertinent. Most of all, he took care of our children and ran the household around the clock while I was finishing various drafts—and never once indicated in any way that this was more than should be expected of a mate.

I owe an enormous debt to David Chandler, professor emeritus of history at Monash University in Melbourne, Australia, and author of many books on Cambodia. Scholar extraordinaire in all things Cambodian, he gave his time to read my manuscript and check for historical and factual accuracy. This book would not be what it is without him.

I would also like to express my gratitude to my mother and father, Jack and Joan Streed, who took in three Cambodian refugees twenty years ago and have given of themselves to those in need throughout their entire lives. I would especially like to thank my mother for her weeks of cumulative babysitting over the years in order for me to write and my father for his pertinent advice as well as for encouraging me when I first came up with the idea for this book. My sister Ellyn Bullock read previous drafts and gave me helpful counsel; she gave me legal counsel as well. My brother Erik Streed shared his expertise on fishing and current events. My brother Stephen Streed read and critiqued the essays. All of my family were generous enough to freely share their memories with me for which I am grateful.

Roger and I are lucky enough to have solid and lasting friendships with several incredible people. I would like to thank Tori Jacobs and Dana Marks who have offered support and encouragement throughout the years. Patrice Coffin and Laura Nordstrom were always willing to help—even if it meant child care in a pinch. Glenn Skoy scanned in the entire first draft after my computer crashed and I thought all was lost. Lucy and Jeff

Heegaard remained interested in my book—year after year—and gave me the idea for the essay on surviving.

C.E. (Buzz) Poverman, author and professor, yet again gave me excellent advice at a crucial juncture in my writing life. Sophea Mouth was an invaluable guide through the labyrinthine ways of Cambodian culture and customs. Pat Dillon read an early draft of the first essay and told me how to fix it. Mark Salisbury, of Salisbury Studios, got most of the photos ready for publication. Also, a special thanks to the librarians of Stoughton Public Library who good-naturedly searched for my countless requests, especially Marilyn Granrud and Jane Groshan.

Last, but not least, to the survivors who told me stories: Thank you. Without your courage there would be no book.

Contents

Map of Cambodia. Reprinted with permission from *Cultural Survival Quarterly* (Volume 14, Number 3: 1990).

Introduction

I have a mental exercise I do every now and then to remind myself of the changeability of life—how little we know of what's ahead. I take a photograph from years ago: Two toddler girls sit on an old woman's lap. One of the girls is blond with blue eyes; the other is a dark-haired, dark-eyed Cambodian. The girls are just one month apart in age, and the lap they are on is their great-grandmother's, "Grandma Elinore." Two beautiful girls, dark and light, salt and pepper in the same container. I take this photo and ask myself: Could I ever have imagined that one day Roger and I would be the parents of both these girls, as well as three others?

The answer is, of course, no, I could and never would have imagined. There is a sort of satisfaction in this, in knowing that I can't imagine what lies ahead, because it takes the onus of trying to control uncontrollable events out of my hands. I can react, I can try, but I cannot make sure that things turn out the way I'm planning because that is not within my power. There is comfort in that.

When my foster brothers arrived at our house in Excelsior, Minnesota, in the early 1980s and faced my siblings, parents and myself as their new family, they were teenagers, but ancient in the ways of the world—having survived the autogenocide, escaped to refugee camps in Thailand and emigrated to America as refugees. Much later—about eight years—I became interested in writing down their amazing stories. As background, I began to read as much as I could about the time of Pol Pot and his Khmer Rouge.

The more I read and the further I explored, the more it was clear that there was a dearth of literature on the subject. There were fine books of scholarship, some autobiographies and a few journalistic accounts—usually mixed with the American struggle in Vietnam—as well as some oral histories, but virtually no literary compilations. Ruminating upon my foster brothers' undesired roles in that horrifying portion of history prompted

1

me to think that perhaps I could put together some sort of literary record of their lives and that time.

I began to interview survivors: my foster brothers, one brother's wife, another's friends. The project grew. I wanted to do more than record the stories that chance had placed near me; I wanted stories that together would paint a complete picture of Pol Pot's brutal experiment in Communism from 1975 to 1979. This meant that I rejected some very worthy stories because I had already interviewed a survivor who had been in that same part of the country, or of the same social class, or had the same general story of escape across the border.

The stories gushed from the survivors' mouths in a torrent; each interview easily took anywhere between three to twelve hours. Again and again I was told that they didn't want to "lose" their stories, that they were glad someone was writing them down. After recording the interviews, I transcribed them much as they had been told to me in the taped narratives. Upon reading these I found that the stilted language and idiosyncratic grammar obscured the stories. I also felt it would be confusing for a reader to follow multiple stories in the first person. So I rewrote the stories in the third person, careful to retain the teller's phrasing, point of view and understanding of events. At this point, several selected readers told me it was too overwhelming to read these stories one after another without anything to break them up; thus I arrived at the present format of stories interspersed with essays on the topic.

A problem arose as I worked on the book. Pol Pot's reign of terror was experienced by many survivors when they were children. For example, my foster brothers were children of five and seven when the Khmer Rouge took over the country and fifteen and seventeen when they came to the United States. Their stories present the boys as victims of something they couldn't understand because they were children at the time.

As I encountered these occasional conflicts between recollections of childhood trauma and what had been written in a book of historical or scholarly research on Cambodia, I was in a dilemma. I wanted to convey accurate information to the reader, but what constitutes accurate information in a story? Often stories are impressionistic rather than factual—so is history, for that matter. Scholars comment on the reality versus the mythology of events, but mythology arises from narrated, or recounted, stories: Sinn or Noeun or Sophea or Samantha saw such and such and felt such and such. I was inclined to cut what I perceived as incorrect facts and information, but also felt I had to try and preserve narrative integrity—preserving history as the survivors experienced it. In order to verify the authenticity of what I was hearing, I checked innumerable details and facts with published accounts from other survivors, and I consulted with certain scholars personally. In the end, I was able to write the stories and feel confident that they both preserve narrative integrity and can also be verified historically.

The book could have been written in a much shorter period of time; however, I was only able to work on it for so long before my emotions overwhelmed me. I vividly remember writing about how Sinn and Noeun were wrenched from their families and put into labor camps around the age of five, then shutting down my computer and grabbing the car keys to pick up my own still-innocent five-year-old son from childcare. Or encouraging my ectomorphic daughter to eat more breakfast and then working on the paragraph in Prum's story where her mother gives her the last grains of rice. Or writing about Sokhary You giving birth on the mountain without doctor or hospital and only a rusty scissors to cut the umbilical cord, then recalling the delivery of our third child—involving pitocin induction, shoulder dystocia and meconium—and realizing that neither he nor I would have made it without hospitals and modern medicine. It was at times like these that it became too much; I had to stop writing, I couldn't go on.

A few months ago I was driving home alone, without any of our five children—a rare occurrence—while thinking about my writing. As I made a rather sharp turn onto our street, one of the children's history books slid from the floor in the back of the minivan to the area next to me between the two front seats. I glanced down at the title, "American History," and it struck me that our two adopted children of Cambodian ethnicity probably wouldn't be able to find their history in it. Our three birth children can look in a history book and read about how two hundred years ago their ancestors came over on a boat from Sweden, but the American history of our two adopted children starts twenty years ago with refugee camps springing up in Thailand in response to the huge numbers of refugees fleeing Cambodia. I realized that, in a sense, I was writing a book of history for Khmer-Americans.

And so to reach the beginning of the story, and the history of Cambodian immigration to the United States, we must leap across continents and back in years—to a small southeast Asian country on April 17, 1975, when adolescent boy and girl soldiers, looking ominously alike in their short, close-cropped haircuts and black pajama-like uniforms, marched into the major cities of Cambodia, waved their AK-47s in the air, and ordered everyone to leave their homes and possessions to go to the countryside.

1

The Cambodian Autogenocide and Its Aftermath

On April 17, 1975, after five years of civil war, the Khmer Rouge guerrillas invaded the major cities of Cambodia and forced the inhabitants on a mass exodus to the countryside. Their invisible leader, Pol Pot, established a reign of terror to bring about his dream of an agrarian society where work was done by hand without corruptive former influences. When this brutal experiment in Communism was ended in 1979 by the Vietnamese capture of the capital city, Phnom Penh, an estimated 1.5 million Cambodians were dead and hundreds of thousands more began to flee the country.

The survivors of the autogenocide poured across the border into Thailand, which was ill equipped to handle the huge influx. In the spring of 1979, when Thai soldiers tried to force 40,000 refugees back into Cambodia by pushing them across a valley filled with landmines, the world took note. By November 1979, Khao-I-Dang, the second colossal holding camp, had been opened; less than two months later it held 130,000 refugees, the largest number of Khmer outside of Cambodia. Various organizations around the world began to attempt to deal with the human fallout: enormous numbers of refugees, orphans and wounded coming from one small country in Southeast Asia.

In 1981, I was attending a college outside of Chicago, away from home in Minnesota. With the exception of the brother next down from me, Erik, who was also away at college, the rest of the family remained where I had grown up, near the "big lake," Minnetonka, the birthplace of Minnetonka Moccasins and Tonka toys. The two youngest children of the family, Ellyn and Steve, were in high school and living at home, while my parents, Jack and Joan Streed, both taught school. My father

The 1980 exhumation of the "killing fields" of Choeung Ek on the outskirts of Phnom Penh was one of the first concrete proofs to the outside world of what had happened in Cambodia between 1975 and 1979. Fifteen thousand people, mainly from Tuol Sleng prison, were killed in these 129 mass graves. (Photograph by Professor Ben Kiernan, director of the Genocide Studies Program, Yale University.)

taught English at Minnetonka High School, the same high school my siblings and I attended; my mother taught preschool in a neighboring town.

Refugees from the autogenocide in Cambodia were just beginning to trickle into the area and many of the ESL (English as a Second Language) students at Minnetonka High were teenagers who had survived those terrible years as children. As a high school student, Ellyn volunteered in the ESL class and from there one thing led to another: The teacher of the class gave our family's name to Lutheran Social Services; a social worker from Lutheran Social Services called my parents to inquire about the possibility of our family sponsoring some refugees; my parents talked it over and decided that, yes, we could be sponsors.

A few weeks later, Lutheran Social Services told my parents that they had two unaccompanied minors—brothers who had survived and escaped to a Thai refugee camp—in need of sponsoring. At some point when both Erik and I were home my parents broached the subject with us children. Our reactions ranged from enthusiasm to mild hostility. Ellyn and I were positive, my brothers were more hesitant, especially Steve, who, as the youngest and years away from leaving home, was committing to the most.

Deciding to go ahead, my parents met with Lutheran Social Services to discuss our family's role in the boys' lives. They made it clear that while they felt comfortable providing a home and some emotional support, we were not trying to replace the boys' Cambodian parents or families. It was then decided that the two brothers would come and live with our family as foster children.

This story of how our lives were about to change forever with the addition of two boys who had survived the autogenocide is just one of many such stories. The Refugee Act of 1980 was a piece of humanitarian legislation that allowed for the resettlement of 50,000 Cambodians each year through 1983. From 1980 to 1982 American families opened their homes to more than 60,000 Cambodian refugees, part of 152,000 refugees total accepted for resettlement. My family gave three of those refugees a home.

I was returning home for the summer break after my junior year at college. I took Amtrak from Chicago to Minneapolis, where my mother waited at the station. For months I had been hearing snippets of information about the two Cambodian boys now living with my family, how they had turned out to be cousins instead of brothers and were attending Minnetonka High School. While my parents and siblings had borne the brunt of incorporating two new members into the family, taking one or both boys along to the movies, friends' houses, fishing and swimming, I remained secure in my collegiate world, not really bothering to keep track of what was going on "back home."

The day of my return was one of those beautiful summer days in Minnesota that make everything seem right. The sun glinted off tiny Galpin Lake as we drove up. I noticed the blooming flowers surrounding my parents' house—making it look snug and cottagey amidst the trees—as my mother parked the car on the driveway. I got out, took my suitcase and book bag from the trunk, and started up the brick serpentine walk.

Someone came out of the house. From behind me my mother said, "Sarah, this is Noeun*." (She pronounced it "Noo-en.")

*pseudonym

He was small and dark with a wide grin.

"Sar-ah, my sees-ter." he said, "You look like peec-ture."

I laughed and his grin grew bigger. Although at that point I had no idea of what he had been through, I was struck by how young and small he was: a mere boy. It would be years before I would put together that he had arrived fresh from the horrors of the Pol Pot autogenocide and that he had lost most of his family, except for his cousin Bunna, who now came out the door.

Although the same age as Noeun, he was much smaller and had none of Noeun's charm. Emaciated, with a big head drooping down on a slender stalk of a neck, he never once raised his eyes to meet mine, even during the introduction. I immediately liked Noeun very much, but was puzzled by Bunna.

In 1983, Sinn Lok, another survivor, became a part of our household. Unlike Noeun, whose father had been an officer in Lon Nol's army, Sinn's father had been a farmer in the country. This fit with the pattern of refugee emigration from Cambodia to the United States: the first group to find U.S. sponsorship were the soldiers—along with their families—of American-backed Prime Minister Lon Nol. Until the autogenocide, these Cambodians had often been urban dwellers with fairly sophisticated lifestyles. After this first wave of refugees had been absorbed, the next wave began, mostly the families of farmers and laborers from the countryside that had lived simple, yet plentiful lives in prewar Cambodia.

Sinn was a handsome boy, but quiet and taciturn. He had been a few years younger in age when the killing started and seemed to adapt more slowly than Noeun and Bunna had. However, he gradually built up a circle of friends—most from the school volleyball and church softball teams he was on—and settled in. In high school, he got a steady job at a cabinet-making shop and soon acquired superb woodworking skills; so much so that he was promoted with a raise and was able to buy a used Honda Accord.

Over time, when I was home, I listened, asked questions, and heard the stories of Pol Pot and his Khmer Rouge. I was amazed that these boys—so mild and unassuming—had experienced such terrible things. Caught in the torturing maw of history, somehow they had managed to survive the autogenocide that resulted in the deaths of approximately 1.5 million of Cambodia's seven million people.

In four years Pol Pot nearly succeeded in his goal of obliterating the Cambodian social fabric and culture: destroying irrigation and transportation systems, electricity, schools, hospitals, monks and temples, markets, families, and in general, all human bonds. He carried out his goal of achieving a perfect Communist country and a "pure" Khmer civilization by smashing the bases of economic survival and instituting the great new society of *Angkar,* the "Organization," where individuals became part of one great collectivization growing rice.

Pol Pot was the leader of the Khmer Rouge, a group of left-wing guerrillas so named by Prince Sihanouk, the ruling monarch since Cambodia's independence from France in 1953. The term means "Red Cambodian" in French: "rouge" is French for red and "Khmer" is the word Cambodians use for both the Cambodian racial or ethnic group as well as their language. After the Khmer Rouge invaded Phnom Penh in 1975, signaling the start of Communist rule, a man with the given name of Saloth Sar emerged in 1976 as prime minister and party secretary under his *nom de guerre* of Pol Pot. In Cambodia, Pol Pot is a common name that draws no attention to the bearer, much like John Smith in the United States. Even his scattered family members didn't know who this "Pol Pot" was; thus, he could accomplish his ignominious deeds without recompense.

Pol Pot and his Khmer Rouge committed crimes from 1975 to 1979 which were documented by a 1979 U.N. Human Rights Commission as "the worst to have occurred anywhere in the world since Nazism." Like Hitler, Pol Pot was meticulous in his record keeping: when Vietnamese photographers discovered Tuol Sleng—the Khmer Rouge secret interrogation and torture facility—in 1979, they also found over 5,000 mug-shot photographs of prisoners, over 4,000 "confessions" as well as entry and execution records, interrogators' notes and countless other documents stored in nearby houses.

Also like Hitler, Pol Pot was in search of a "pure" nation and tried to eliminate all racial minorities; the Khmer Rouge attempted to eradicate the Chams, Laotians, Chinese, Thais, Germans, French, Americans and anyone else who was not pure Khmer. In so doing, Pol Pot completely disregarded the fact that Cambodian people are a mixture of racial stocks. Also, in a pernicious twist, he targeted his own people, inducing French author and journalist Jean Lacouture to coin the term "autogenocide."

As I listened to my foster brothers' accounts of the Pol Pot years, I began to wonder about the United States' involvement with Cambodia during this time. I knew, vaguely, that Cambodia was connected with the Vietnam War in some way, and, perhaps like other shameful aspects of that war, had been pushed aside and hidden.

I began to read, and then to ask my foster brothers about what I read.

What I discovered appalled me. First, the historical context: In 1969 with Richard Nixon one year into his presidency and the United States still embroiled in the Vietnam War, U.S. B52s bombed inside Cambodia for the first of many times, ostensibly in order to destroy North Vietnamese supply routes and eradicate Communist base camps. As Cambodia was a neutral country, at first the bombings were kept secret from the American public and Congress by the use of code names, e.g., "Operation Breakfast," and last-minute changes in strike coordinates given to unsuspecting pilots.

In March 1972 Hanoi launched an enormous offensive into South Vietnam and by April it seemed that the South Vietnamese might be driven out, leaving Nixon to face failure and defeat a few months before the U.S. presidential election. In January 1973 both the United States and North Vietnam signed the Paris peace agreement, committing also to end military action in Cambodia. When in February 1973 this cease-fire ended, the U.S. resumed bombing, culminating in three times as many tons of conventional explosives falling on Cambodia as fell on Japan during World War II. Since the U.S. Air Force was no longer bombing over Vietnam and Laos—due to the Paris agreement—and because the Air Force did not use forward air controllers to choose their targets, the bombs were concentrated on the countryside and there were many civilian casualties.

In 1970, longtime monarch Prince Norodom Sihanouk was overthrown by his prime minister, General Lon Nol, possibly with the complicity of American intelligence. Whatever the means, Lon Nol was immediately recognized by the American government as the new head of state. (However, the U.S. placed so little value on Cambodia—other than as peripheral to Vietnam—that during the four years the U.S. and Cambodia were allies in a war together, Nixon never once asked to meet with Lon Nol. Cambodia, on the other hand, had complete—albeit naive—confidence that the U.S. would protect and care for the country.)

From 1970 to 1974, the U.S.—committed to aiding Lon Nol's corrupt and money-loving government so they could fight the Communists—proceeded to dump goods, ammunition, advisors and money into the country, fostering unprecedented corruption, especially in Phnom Penh. During this time the countryside languished and became increasingly under the control of the Khmer Rouge. Up until 1970 the Khmer Rouge had been under 4,000 in number and not a powerful force. Then, in the United States' sixty-day invasion, the Vietnamese Communists at the border were pushed into the interior, where they helped the Khmer Rouge expand. Civil war ensued, with the Khmer Rouge guerrillas fighting Lon Nol's soldiers.

In retrospect, I could see the inexorable progression of events: first, selective American aid to a tiny country in Indochina, then saturation bombing of that same country resulting in the destruction of a previously fragile neutrality, thereby making it possible for a murderous tyrant heading the Khmer Rouge Communist guerrilla army to invade the capital and seize control of the flimsy, U.S.-backed government of Lon Nol.

This meant that the refugees my family had taken in had become refugees in the first place as a result of American policy. My family's actions seemed somewhat akin to putting a landmine in a neighbor's back yard, and then, upon hearing an explosion, quickly running over to drive the neighbor to the emergency room. Of course, these perplexities and misgivings concerning my own country's policies are similar to what many Americans have felt and continue to feel about all of U.S. involvement in Vietnam.

When Roger and I got married in 1986, Noeun and Sinn were the hosts at the wedding. In dark suits with pink rose boutonnieres and the pink dotted ties I had given to all my brothers for that special day, they stood at the door of the church and greeted the guests while handing out programs. It was a morning wedding with an outdoor lunch reception held afterwards in my parents' yard.

There is a photograph in my wedding album that I still treasure: Noeun and Sinn standing on the green lawn, suit coats off but ties still on, white shirts and teeth gleaming at the camera. So much has happened since then, but that photograph captured one step along the way of an enormous journey that began in 1982, when two boys escaped the killing fields of Cambodia to end up on a green lawn in Minnesota.

The survivors of the Cambodian autogenocide from 1975 to 1979 who have settled here are Americans now. Their children are being born on this soil and taking their place in the next generation. They are adding their stories of immigration and survival to the huge mass of stories that have formed this country—stories of fleeing war, deprivation, famine and loss to live in a country of peace, plenty and safety, or the possibility thereof. And as U.S. citizens, they have the prerogative to add their chapter to the book of American history.

2

The Race for Survival:
The Story of Noeun Nor

The Nor* family lived in Phnom Penh, the capital city of Cambodia. Mr. Nor, smart and competent, worked hard and supported his family in a secure middle-class life-style. Noeun* was the oldest boy and one of five children. He had an older sister, two younger brothers and one younger sister. When Noeun was a baby, Mr. Nor was a mechanical engineer working on ships in the coastal city of Sihanoukville. This work required him to be away a great deal, so he came home only one night a week, usually on the weekend. Mrs. Nor stayed home to take care of the children.

Education was very important to Mr. Nor so the children went to school when they turned five—even the girls, which was unusual in Cambodia. Noeun's older sister attended a government school and Noeun began attending kindergarten at a prestigious private school when he was five years old. Noeun's younger brother was registered to begin at this same school when he turned five.

Mr. and Mrs. Nor were ardent supporters of Prince Norodom Sihanouk, who had ascended the throne in 1941 and won the country's independence from France in 1953. Mr. Nor continually made reference to the prince and how he was trying—and would succeed in the end—to get a better life for the Cambodian people. The entire family was aware of political events, educated and informed.

When Sihanouk was abroad in 1970, he was overthrown in a bloodless coup and one of his former generals, Lon Nol, was made prime minister. There was great instability in the country; the Vietnamese Communists and Khmer Rouge occupied a third of the country and were fighting Lon Nol for control; it was a civil war. Noeun remembers, as a

*pseudonym

Bicycle traffic on a street in Phnom Penh in 1992. (Photograph by Susan Cook and from the personal collection of Susan Cook, Brown University.)

child, seeing his father and others growing worried and discouraged over two events in 1971: Lon Nol's stroke followed by a two-month sojourn in Hawaii and the attack of the Vietnamese Communists on the Pochentong airport. The blow to Mr. Nor's morale at this time was so great that Noeun never again heard his father express confidence in the war's outcome.

Lon Nol's government was marked by unprecedented corruption, aided by the flow of U.S.-made goods and money into the country. Noeun recounts anecdotes he remembers from the Lon Nol time: "Someone buys a picture for five dollars, sells it to another for ten dollars, then that person sells it back to the first person for fifteen and on and on. Or, when Lon Nol's people collected taxes, they'd collect ten dollars, but by the time it reached the government, nine dollars were gone. Only one dollar was left for the tax, the rest had disappeared."

By the time Noeun was in kindergarten, Mr. Nor had joined the air force and was serving as a military pilot based in Phnom Penh. He was specially selected to enroll in training classes taught by American soldiers;

he and other chosen pilots were taught to fly fighter jets and drop bombs. By 1973 he had risen to the rank of captain in the national armed forces of Lon Nol.

The United States resumed and intensified bombing in Cambodia in late February 1973 in an effort to defeat the Khmer Rouge, the guerrilla soldiers of the Communist Party of Kampuchea, or Cambodia. The Khmer Rouge had been replacing the Vietnamese Communists and were becoming stronger and more organized; they kept fighting and pressing towards the capital. By the end of 1974 they had cut off all roads to Phnom Penh. The U.S. airlifted rice and ammunition into the capital in February and March, but then Congress voted to stop aid to Cambodia.

On New Year's Day 1975, the Khmer Rouge launched a rocket and artillery barrage on Phnom Penh, to capture the capital and close down Pochentong airport. They surrounded Phnom Penh and camped at the perimeter of the city, cutting off all escape.

Rocket fire set buildings alight near the airport and many people died; the fuel depot caught on fire and a thick cloud of smoke rose into the air. Captain Nor was trapped at the airport but, fortunately, wasn't wearing his uniform—just a T-shirt for working on the planes—and in the confusion was able to run home to his family.

Later, Noeun described the scene, based on what his father had told him: "Airplanes, gas and missiles exploding like popcorn—the airport burned for a week."

On April 17, 1975, when Noeun was seven years old, the Khmer Rouge captured Phnom Penh and thus controlled the country. Adolescents dressed completely in black, carrying AK-47s, and wearing Ho Chi Minh sandals—old tires cut in shape of the foot and held on by string— quietly walked into the city. Their faces were grim as they repeated that everyone must leave. When people asked, the soldiers said Sihanouk was now king. (He was really a puppet for the Communist Party. The myth that Sihanouk was in power would be put to rest for good on April 2, 1976, when the Khmer Rouge announced a new government with Pol Pot as prime minister.)

Captain Nor quickly put on ragged clothes so that the soldiers wouldn't recognize him or his former position in Lon Nol's army, then the family left with just what they could carry. Noeun, a strong boy, carried five pounds of rice on each shoulder, his mother also carried some, his brother and one sister carried five pounds each. Captain Nor pushed a wheelbarrow full of clothes, bedding and the two babies.

The streets were packed with masses of people leaving Phnom Penh.

Although the Nor family didn't know it yet, all of Cambodia's major cities were being forcibly evacuated on the same day. April is the cruelest month in Cambodia—dry and hot—so the evacuation occurred at the worst possible time. In later years, this walk out of the cities would become known as the "death march" because of the number that expired along the way due to heat, crowding, and lack of food and sanitary conditions.

The Nor family walked for a week until finally reaching a village in the country where they were permitted to stay. The village had previously been taken over by the Khmer Rouge; the original villagers were referred to as "old people" and were considered to be better than the people from the city, or the "new people." The new families were separated into groups.

After some days in this village, the Khmer Rouge told the new people that they had to move again. They divided the families into groups and then moved the groups into different provinces, like Kompong Chhnang, Battambang, and so on. The Nor family and others were moved to Battambang Province in the north—known as the Rice Bowl Province before the war because of the abundant rice crops. The Nor family was ordered to live in the little village of Rien Kae Sie.

Some new people began to disappear. They were taken away and never seen again. "*Bat kluon,*" the ones left whispered to each other: "taken away" or "disappearing body." People knew, even though no one ever stated it directly, that the ones taken way were killed. After a while, Noeun understood that the Khmer Rouge were killing people even though he never saw anyone killed in front of him.

People were careful while walking because suddenly the ground could slip and they would see they had been walking on dead bodies. One time Noeun put his foot down and it went through a hole. There was a terrible smell and he realized that he had put his foot through a corpse.

Noeun tried to figure out the reasoning behind the killings, but only came up with twisted logic. As near as he could tell, the Khmer Rouge—or the Communists—were poor and hated rich people. They hated people with light skin because light skin indicated a city life—farmers were dark skinned from working in the fields all day under the sun. Sometimes new people with light skin rubbed dirt on it to get darker, trying to look like old people.

The Khmer Rouge first took away and killed the officers and soldiers from Lon Nol's army. Then they killed all the rich people they could find. They killed anyone with education; they took away those who were rumored to have been doctors, lawyers, professors, teachers and students—even police officers. They looked for people with glasses because glasses meant you were educated, or at least a student. If they didn't like someone, they said, "You're a doctor," and took the person off and killed him. They killed the film stars, actors and actresses, and the pop music stars, including Mao Sareth, the most famous woman singer in Cambodia.

After a while they had killed so many people that things got crazy and they just kept on killing. They killed anyone they wanted to. It was like using drugs. They killed a few, then more and more, until they were addicted and couldn't stop. If they got tired of doing the killing themselves, they took children and trained them to be killers. After these children knew how to kill, the Khmer Rouge said to them, "Your mother is no good. Your father is no good." Then the children went and killed their parents.

They trained Noeun to kill, but he never killed anyone. Once they told him to go kill his parents, but he didn't do it. When they asked him to kill his parents, he said, "oh, I don't know," and walked away.

Occasionally, it was a test. One time, some Khmer Rouge approached him and said, "If we tell you to go kill your family, will you do it?"

Noeun answered no, but the soldiers didn't kill him. It was a kind of a game the soldiers were playing with Noeun, but a dangerous one. Sometimes it was play, sometimes not—and it was hard to know which was when.

The Khmer Rouge suddenly appeared one morning after the Nor family had been living in Rien Kae Sie for five months. Casually they looked around and picked the strongest boys—like Noeun—and divided these children into several groups. Noeun's brothers were put in another group but his sisters were left with Mrs. Nor. Without any further talk they marched Noeun's group out of the village to a central place where it was combined with other groups made up of the strongest children from other villages.

Noeun and his new group were marched to a labor camp where they were added to an enormous group of a thousand boys and told to start digging. Their job—to be done without any machinery—was to dig miles of canals around the dried-up rice fields and then pile the dirt in levees on either side to keep the water in during planting. The days were long; the boys arose at six o'clock in the morning, worked until two, had a tiny bit of rice, went back to work until nine in the evening, jumped in the lake to get clean, then laid down on straw mats to sleep.

The first few days Noeun was constantly near tears because he missed his family so much, especially his mother. He was eight years old.

The boys kept on working. The work was immeasurable; if they finished one canal, they started another. They dug canals around rice fields, then worked in the rice fields. After a year of working like this, Nouen sought out the Khmer Rouge.

"I miss my mother," he said. "Can I go and see her?"

"No," the soldiers said, and waved him back to work with their guns.

Noeun went back to work. Now, instead of getting a tiny bit of rice at lunch each day, each boy was given a cup of thin broth with a few kernels of corn floating in it. The Khmer Rouge took a big pot of water, put in one ear of old corn and boiled it over a fire for a long time. If Noeun counted the corn in his cup, he counted about ten kernels—that was per day for fifteen hours of work.

One evening when the boys finished digging a canal faster than usual, rather than give them a much needed rest, the Khmer Rouge moved them to another camp. They reached the new camp at midnight; it was a dark night with a cloudy sky and no moon. Exhausted from marching all night on top of digging all day, the boys found any spot on the ground and went to sleep. Noeun saw a stone, all smooth, in the field, so he put his back against it and went to sleep.

Upon awaking in the morning, Noeun saw that he had been sleeping against a skull. Boys began waking up and in the daylight they could see bones and skeletons strewn everywhere: It was a killing field—a field where the Khmer Rouge had killed Lon Nol soldiers.

The Khmer Rouge came and told the boys to dig a canal around the field and fill it with water. After the boys did this, the water mixed with the soil around the bones, and during the dry season the Khmer Rouge ordered this water to be let out of the canal into the rice fields to fertilize the young rice plants.

There was no water to drink at this camp other than the water in the canal. The Khmer Rouge used this water to cook for the boys and to make the corn soup. Various people tried to boil the water in order to get rid of the germs, but there was still the smell. The boys stayed at this camp for a month, then moved again.

A year after he had asked the first time, Noeun asked again if he could go see his mother. Again the Khmer Rouge refused. Noeun couldn't help it, he began to cry. He felt so terribly sad and lost and alone.

The soldiers said, "Why are you crying? Do you want to sleep under the ground?"

Noeun said, "No, but I want to see my mother. I don't know how she feels right now. I don't know where she is."

A female Khmer Rouge soldier said, "Our leader is taking care of her. You don't have to worry."

A week later, after the boys finished their work at nine o'clock in the evening, Noeun waited until the other boys went to bed, then snuck out of the labor camp and started running. He had decided that he had to see his mother; he didn't care what would happen. He missed her so much. It had been two years since he had last seen her. He ran all the way to Rien Kae Sie—about twenty-five miles—in four hours.

He arrived at the village in the middle of the night. No one was around and the village square was deserted. He remembered the particular hut his family had built so he went and looked inside but didn't see his mother, or anyone else from his family. He was afraid to wake up someone from another hut and ask because they would inform the Khmer Rouge that he had left the labor camp. He also knew that he had to be back by dawn or he would be missed. So he looked around one last time, cried in disappointment, and ran four hours back to the labor camp. He didn't sleep at all that night.

Boys began to die from starvation and overwork. Every day boys around Noeun died; boys were working and dying.

Sometimes a boy fell down, but wasn't yet dead, so the Khmer Rouge said, "This person is useless."

Noeun watched as they kicked the boy until he was dead—or hit the boy with an ax to kill him.

Usually after killing a boy, the Khmer Rouge turned to the others and said, "To keep you is no profit, to kill you is no loss."

Sometimes a soldier looked at a certain boy, didn't like him, and took him away to kill. It was whatever they wanted or how they felt at the time. If they wanted to kill someone, they killed him.

Noeun fell down a few times himself, but for some reason wasn't killed. One time he was so tired he was walking in a kind of trance and his eyes couldn't see. He collapsed, but managed to get back up. Two times that same day he fell down, but got back up. Each time he thought the Khmer Rouge were going to kill him but they didn't.

The second time a soldier even came over to help him up and asked, "Do you feel all right?" These were the same soldiers that were killing everybody else! Noeun was left alive without knowing why.

Some of the Khmer Rouge guards were nice and some were cruel—like if a boy wasn't walking fast enough they kicked him in the back. Or if they gave a boy an order and the boy looked at them, they took the end of a gun and hit the boy across the face. No one ever did that to Noeun, but then Noeun never looked at any of them. Whatever they said, he did. He knew that he couldn't fight them, that he couldn't win.

Noeun tried again to see his mother a year later. He ran at night to Rien Kae Sie and again didn't see any of his family; however, on the way back to the labor camp, he caught a glimpse of his cousin Bunna work-ing in another field. He didn't stop, but made a mental note as to where Bunna was. He still didn't know where his mother, father, or any of his siblings were, but he had located a cousin.

One afternoon Noeun left his work group to go in search of some-thing to eat: tiny crabs in the canal water, kernels of rice lying around, anything. He was hunting in a nearby field when he heard some shouted orders and climbed to the top of the levee to see what was happening.

There, only 100 yards away, was his father with his hands tied behind his back. Some Khmer Rouge with machine guns were shouting at him to move faster. The appearance of Captain Nor was so unbelievable and frightening that Noeun couldn't breathe. He hadn't seen his father for several years, hadn't known anything about what had happened to him, and suddenly there he was in front of him like an apparition. With mind racing, Noeun guessed that when he had been put with the group of boys, his father had been taken to another labor camp and made to work, until maybe, on this particular day, he wouldn't work for the Khmer Rouge anymore.

Noeun crouched behind the levee and watched as the Khmer Rouge untied his father's hands, then pointed their guns at his head and told him to dig his own grave. After he had finished, they asked him some-thing that Noeun couldn't hear because of the noise of the water running through the canal.

The newly dug grave was in a clump of saplings. The Khmer Rouge stretched out Captain Nor's hands and retied each one to a small tree so he was standing stretched out and cruciform. Noeun tried to close his eyes but couldn't. Thoughts were rushing through his head: Is he hurting? Is he scared? He felt he should rush out to try and help his father but knew if he did so, he would be in the grave with him. So he stayed where he was, hidden behind the levee.

A Khmer Rouge soldier cut open Captain Nor's chest with a knife, reached in his hand and pulled out the liver. Captain Nor screamed shrilly and terribly, his eyes rolling wildly. After what seemed like an eternity to Noeun but was probably not more than a several minutes, his father's screams ceased, his head dropped and Noeun knew his father was dead.

The Khmer Rouge soldiers were squatting around the body, passing around Captain Nor's liver to eat. They ate for a few minutes, then stood up with Captain Nor's blood still on their hands and lips. The Khmer Rouge thought that if you ate the liver from a live man, it gave you courage. Jokingly, they said you had to eat the liver of a living man, the liver of a dead man didn't taste good. Often they drank whiskey as they ate livers. Some Khmer Rouge made a habit of eating livers, but not all Khmer Rouge did this. Some were normal people following orders, but some were like these soldiers: cruel and inhuman with bloodshot eyes.

The Khmer Rouge left. Somehow Noeun made it back to his group and began to work, despite his reeling thoughts. He wondered if at any minute those same soldiers were going to come for him. He replayed in his mind his father's death over and over again: How did he feel? Was he scared? Did he suffer much? He couldn't get his mind off these questions. But he told himself that if he had tried to help his father, he would also be dead. All he could do was try and find his mother so that he could tell her about her husband's death.

A few months later Noeun got a cut that didn't heal, but instead kept getting bigger and bigger. He was starving. His hair had fallen out and his knee and head were the same size. When he tried to get up, he had to get his butt up first, or he would fall back down because he was so weak.

Because he was still able to work, the Khmer Rouge put him in a "hospital" instead of killing him. The hospital was a wood and bamboo shelter where the patients slept on iron beds. There was no medicine; the patients were given grass. But somehow a nurse got some real medicine to give to Noeun so that he got better. He returned to the labor camp.

Toward the end of 1978, rumors began circulating among the boys that the Vietnamese were going to invade Cambodia and fight the Khmer Rouge. In general, Cambodians felt happy at this prospect.

People said, "The Vietnamese are not going to be hard like Pol Pot."

Traditionally, there was a history of hatred between the Cambodians and Vietnamese. Cambodians viewed the Vietnamese as dissatisfied and obnoxious and the Vietnamese saw Cambodians as lazy, but vicious when roused. This history arose from the cultural and linguistic differences between the two countries.

But after the Pol Pot regime, Cambodians hated Pol Pot and the Khmer Rouge, even though they were fellow Cambodians. They tried to help the Vietnamese target Pol Pot and the Khmer Rouge, saying, "Pol Pot stood right here. He bombed over there."

Many people escaped at night since the Vietnamese were going to invade anyway. Noeun also escaped and ran to the camp where he had seen his cousin Bunna.

He found Bunna and whispered, "Bunna, we have to run."

Bunna asked, "Why?"

Bunna was very sick and weak. Noeun was also weak but could still run. The two boys waited outside the camp until they saw a few other people running, then Noeun put his arm around Bunna and half-dragged him down the road.

Later, refugees who had stayed longer in Cambodia told Noeun what had happened to the others. When the Khmer Rouge realized the Vietnamese invasion was inevitable, they told everyone to dig huge holes because the Vietnamese were going to bomb. Then they forced the people into the holes and buried them.

Noeun and Bunna reached the jungle, where they ran at night and stayed in hiding behind the trees during the day. Many Cambodians were hiding in the jungle at this time, but no one let anyone else see them because they didn't know who to trust. Each night Noeun and Bunna ran a few miles farther. Occasionally they went into a village to try to find food—corn or potatoes. When it was impossible to go into a village, Noeun killed animals to eat. He did all the killing because Bunna was too weak. Noeun killed anything edible—rabbits, snakes, fox, and fish. After he had killed an animal, he put a stick through the middle and roasted it over a fire.

One morning Nouen made a bed of grass in a hollow under a tree and helped Bunna to lie down. Once Bunna had been safely tucked away, he went out hunting for food. Almost immediately, he spotted a cobra, as big around as his arm. When the cobra saw Noeun, it reared up so it was as high as his head and made a noise like the hiss of an angry cat. Noeun remembered his grandfather telling him that when cobras are up looking, they're just looking, but when they lower their heads, they're ready to strike. He grabbed a stick from the ground, waited until the cobra looked down, then quickly stepped aside. The cobra struck— whoosh—and Noeun hit him square with the stick held in both of his hands, like he was swinging a bat at a baseball. The cobra fell down dead.

Noeun took the snake back to Bunna very carefully because he knew the venom inside the snake was still poisonous. Upon reaching Bunna, he held up the cobra, stepped to the side, and said, "Hey Bunna, you want to watch?" Bunna looked, Noeun cut the throat and the venom squirted into a tree. The boys laughed together. It was fun—but also frightening.

Another time Noeun and Bunna heard some rustling in the grass and thought Khmer Rouge were nearby, so Noeun built a makeshift nest up in a tree. They stayed up there that night and in the morning when Noeun climbed down, there were a pair of wild Indochinese tigers growling and stalking around the trunk. He climbed right back up and he and Bunna stayed high in the tree, shaking, while the tigers walked round and round the bottom. The boys were petrified with fear because they knew how fierce these tigers were—they would just as soon kill you as look at you. After an hour of circling, the tigers left.

Noeun saw to it that they made their way north through the jungle, moving little by little until they were in the Siemreap Oddar Mean Chay Province. He saw the Angkor ruins in the distance and thus knew they were heading toward the Thai border.

One night they slept under a tree and Noeun awoke in the morning with something tickling his bare chest, something foreign and smooth. It was a snake coiled on his stomach. Noeun recognized it as a python that squeezes its prey to death. He didn't breathe, moved a slight bit, waited, moved a slight bit again until the snake slithered away. Noeun had almost wet his pants. He didn't understand why the snakes were attracted to him; they never came near Bunna.

It was frightening to live in the jungle but Noeun felt that he at least had a chance. He knew that if he had stayed with the work group in Battambang he would be dead. In the jungle it could work one of two ways: he could have good luck or he could be killed. So he took that chance. Other people had the same chance but were too scared to take it. However, Noeun also knew that without luck he and Bunna could have died in the jungle and nobody ever would have known.

Just before crossing the Thai border, Noeun was shot, probably by a Khmer Rouge soldier trying to prevent them from escaping. The bullet hit him in the neck and he fell. When he regained consciousness, Bunna was leaning down over him packing dirt on the wound to stop the bleeding. It wasn't a bad wound, but it scared the both of them. (Noeun still bears the scar—a slash going from the neck across one cheek and ear.)

Nouen and Bunna crossed into Thailand two months after entering the jungle. Once they were actually across the border they didn't know what to do, so they sat down on a road. A Red Cross doctor came along in a car, saw that Noeun had been shot, loaded both boys into the car and brought them to a hospital.

The hospital at the Khao-I-Dang refugee camp in Thailand was packed with Cambodian refugees who had been shot or had stepped on landmines. Every morning the doctors went outside the hospital compound searching for people who had been hurt and brought them back to the hospital for treatment.

Noeun recovered from his wound after a month. It was 1979. The Red Cross didn't know what to do with Noeun and Bunna so they put them in "coma comprea"—the Khao-I-Dang orphanage, where they stayed for three years.

In some ways, the orphanage was very good for Noeun and Bunna: they attended school, studied, and had enough food to eat. But in other ways it was difficult, especially for Noeun. He had nightmares every night, mostly about his father. In the nightmares Noeun was running and running; he didn't know what from or toward, but it was bad.

One night as the boys were getting ready for bed, another boy started teasing Noeun and said, "Oh, Noeun's going to run again tonight." The boys that slept near Noeun heard him talking and crying in his sleep.

After a year or so the problem seemed to abate. Noeun felt happier and even occasionally forgot about his father's death. But he still had problems with the other refugees: Vietnamese, Laotian, Hmong. Once he gambled at cards with a group of Vietnamese men. Noeun won, but the others didn't give him money. After a fuss, they gave it to him, but then wanted it back. Noeun refused and two of the men came after him. There was a fight and Noeun almost killed them both.

Noeun also took karate at the orphanage—four hours every day for three years. He became a black belt. He was trying for one higher belt but failed the second test: three men against one. He always won two on one, but couldn't win three on one.

In 1982 some staff members approached Noeun and Bunna and said they had found a sponsor for them in the United States of America, a group called the Lutheran Social Services. Noeun and Bunna were given complete physicals—every day for a week doctors checked them for various diseases—and they both passed.

On April 7, 1982, Noeun and Bunna flew from Thailand to San Francisco, stopping only in Japan to refuel. Noeun had been on a plane many times because his father was a pilot, but Bunna had not. Consequently, Noeun felt fine and ate steadily while Bunna vomited continuously throughout the flight.

When the plane touched down in the United States, Noeun felt safe and happy. Out loud, in Khmer, he said, "I'm born again."

He knew he never wanted to return to Cambodia.

The next day the boys flew on to Minneapolis, where a representative from Lutheran Social Services met them and brought them to a temporary foster home while things were being readied with the permanent foster family.

The boys immediately began school at an American high school. Noeun didn't know what to do, all the students were talking so fast. He could only say "hello" over and over again. When people responded with "hi," he wondered what they were saying.

After several weeks Noeun and Bunna went to live with the Streeds, the permanent foster family, in Excelsior, Minnesota. Noeun felt nervous about meeting his new siblings Ellyn and Steve. He was told Sarah and Erik were away at college but would soon be home for the summer. Everyone in the family spoke fast, especially Ellyn.

Ellyn and Steve took Noeun and Bunna along when they went out with their friends—movies, parties, the beach and so on—but Noeun remained nervous. It was about a month before he felt comfortable with his new family.

Noeun sometimes found life in America to be hard. He tried to forget about the old things but they kept coming back. He was often depressed and surly and couldn't control his temper. There was something dark inside him from being hurt so much in Cambodia. He began to realize it was more than simple anger, sometimes he could control it but sometimes he couldn't. Sometimes under the effort of trying to control it, his whole body shook for an hour. Occasionally he went to bed with his body shaking and woke up calm in the morning.

In the fall, Noeun began attending Minnetonka High School. He did fairly well at his studies but occasionally got into trouble with the other students. One time another Cambodian refugee threw a book at him and they began to fight verbally. The shaking started and Noeun swore. The other boy swore back. That day after class, they met at a park and fought. Noeun won. He never lost.

In 1983, Noeun met Prum Nath*, another Cambodian refugee, at Minnetonka High. They were friends for a year at school before they began dating. Noeun liked her and felt they were compatible.

Nouen and Bunna asked Lutheran Social Services for help in locating any surviving members of their families. At the end of 1983 they were told both boys' mothers were in Khao-I-Dang. Later, they also located one of Noeun's brothers and the younger sister. The older sister and another brother were still missing.

Mrs. Nor and Bunna's mother came to the United States in 1984. They went to live with other relatives in Boston. Noeun, Bunna and Prum went to visit them. As soon as possible, Noeun got his mother alone and told her about Captain Nor's death. Mrs. Nor said that she had already heard about it from one of Captain Nor's friends and Noeun should try to put it from his mind. Bewildered, he tried to understand how his

*pseudonym

mother could say something like that to him. He reasoned that she hadn't seen it with her own eyes and that's how she could tell him to try and forget. Noeun knew this was impossible; he would never forget as long as he lived.

He also tried to tell his new nephews about the war and they didn't believe him. He told them that he had only a tiny bit to eat and had to work real hard and they said, "No, it's not true." Noeun realized that little children in America couldn't believe something so terrible could happen.

After graduating from Minnetonka High, Noeun began vocational training. He had once hoped to be a pilot like his father but realized during his vocational-technical school classes that it would never happen.

"It's too late for me," he told the Streeds, "My mind is messy, it's not cleared out. At Vo-Tech, I'm in the middle of learning and something hits my mind—a bad thing from Thailand or Cambodia, something about my mother, brother, sister, back then. Ten, fifteen minutes later, I think, 'Oh I'm in school' and try to pick up and study again."

He became resigned to the fact that he didn't have the concentration required to do an extremely specialized job. He often thought how if there hadn't been a war in Cambodia he probably would have been a pilot. As a child he hadn't been scared of anything; he had climbed trees like a monkey.

Noeun and Prum returned to Boston in 1989 to get married. They had the traditional Cambodian wedding ceremony with a monk officiating, surrounded by family and friends. They had dated for five years. Prum's foster parents flew in from Minnesota for the wedding. Although not legal under U.S. law, many Cambodian refugees mark their marriages this way—with a Cambodian ceremony and a monk present.

After a few weeks, Noeun and Prum returned to Minneapolis while Bunna stayed on in Boston. Noeun had a job with the Plastic Injection Molding factory in Minneapolis and had worked his way up at the factory until he was in charge of the calibration of the machinery, something only a few employees were asked to do. It was the highest position possible without an engineering degree. He was proud of this job, because he had been selected out of many employees.

The year following their marriage Noeun and Prum had a baby daughter, and a little over a year after that, a son. Immediately Noeun placed his lost hopes and dreams onto his children. He was determined his children were going to get the education they needed in order to succeed.

He told Prum, "Don't worry. As long as I'm alive, I'll work. Our kids will go to grade school, then to high school. When they graduate from high school and want to go to college, I'll tell them, 'Daughter, son, just study. Don't worry about money. I'll support you.'"

He also told Prum, "I'll buy them whatever they want, a car, whatever, as long as they study. But if they don't study, if they just hang around and skip school, I'll beat them. I don't care if I go to jail; I'm not going to let them fool around or do drugs. If they need a spanking, they'll get it."

Noeun worked all the time. He worked double shifts, night shifts and overtime on weekends and holidays. Prum also began working in a local data entry firm when the children got a little older. Because of Noeun's heavy work schedule—with Prum's salary helping out—they were able to purchase a brand-new house in a development in Chaska, Minnesota.

Often, Noeun should not have made it. He recounts the times:

> So many times I should have died. A lot of people were just like me, but they were killed. Those few times that I fell down, I felt like I was already dead. A few times the Khmer Rouge told me to kill my family and I said no, but it just passed by. A few times I fell down on the ground, but got back up. A few times the soldiers saw me fall, but didn't kill me. Then in the hospital I was so sick, but that one nurse gave me real good medicine. In the jungle I met a lot of wild animals, but they just walked away. I got shot and yet I'm still alive. Over and over again, somehow I was saved.

In 1997, Noeun was living in a new country with a family, a new house, and a good job. He had survived Pol Pot and the Khmer Rouge; he had survived the years of hard labor, of starvation and disease. He had escaped from the horrors of Cambodia and fled to Thailand—and from there to America.

"I feel proud that I'm still alive," he said to the Streeds one evening in 1997. "I feel proud because I made it. It was like I was running a race, and I won. That's what it feels like."

3

The Weaker Brother

Erik and I returned home from college for the summer of 1982, putting our family together for the first time in its newly enlarged state of six children plus parents. We had many fun times together that summer, like the time Erik taught Noeun and Bunna "Satisfaction" by the Rolling Stones. All summer long the two of them warbled the rock classic around the house before they could even speak a coherent sentence of English.

It was also a summer of adjustment. There was the time—now enshrined in our family's treasury of famous stories—when Bunna approached Dad about having his own bedroom.

"Dad, I need own room," he said, "Too many in room now. No good."

"That's not going to be possible, Bunna," said my father. "There are no more rooms in the house."

Bunna didn't pause at all but said decisively, "But Dad, you have big living room—why not make two rooms?"

Erik and Steve bore the brunt of the difficult adjustments since they shared a room with Noeun and Bunna. There were three bedrooms in the house which naturally divided up into one for my parents, one for the girls and one for the boys. Literally having nowhere else to put them, my parents bought another set of bunk beds and installed Noeun and Bunna in the downstairs bedroom with Erik and Steve. That made four adolescent males—two of them having come through a genocide—in one basement bedroom and that was too many.

One evening when Bunna and Noeun had gone with our parents to a Lutheran Social Services function, the four birth children gathered, impromptu, to talk.

"It's not working," Steve said. "I don't trust them. Bunna is always asking for things from Mom and Dad that we don't have, and Noeun, well, have you seen him shake when he gets angry? One of these days he's going to kill one of us in our sleep."

Bunna standing on the ice of Galpin Lake in the early 1980s. (Photograph from the personal collection of Sarah Streed.)

"It's not that bad," Erik answered, who, unlike Steve, was home for the summer and didn't have two years left until high school graduation. "Just leave them to their friends and Cambodian parties. I don't think they would actually kill anyone, they're just kids."

"But Noeun has killed someone," Steve responded. "He told me about it one time—playing cards with soldiers or something, and getting in a fight and killing one. Yesterday he got mad over some little thing and threw a Coke can at me. I think he's got it in him."

After some more discussion we decided that I, being the eldest, was going to approach our parents about the situation and mention Noeun and his temper. I remember that my mother became worried but left it to my father to decide if anything truly needed to be done. My father pooh-poohed the idea that Noeun—or either of the boys—could be dangerous. Things went along much as they had before.

Relations between Steve and Noeun were finally to explode years later, after Steve had moved out but had returned for a visit. He and Noeun had words, then the tenuous thread holding their mutual hostility in check snapped, and they were rolling around on the floor, bumping into my mother's refinished furniture, with my dad futilely trying to pull them apart and my mother screaming for him to call the police. The fight ended when Steve and Noeun, by being separated, agreed to an uneasy truce. Their relationship has been distant, but cordial, ever since.

Very clear differences between the two "brothers" emerged. In physical appearances alone, Noeun's handsome face and macho "I can do anything" pose contrasted dramatically with Bunna's scrawny, pock-marked visage that constantly looked on the verge of tears.

It became apparent these differences were more than skin deep in the months that followed. Noeun attacked his life in America with cheerful determination and good will. Although subject to attacks of fierce anger and dark thoughts, he never wavered in his goals to obtain an education, find a job, and make a new life for himself. Bunna, on the other hand, whined continuously and copiously; even now I can't remember his face in a smile. Whereas Noeun told us stories about his life in Cambodia, Bunna's only interaction with us was to demand one material possession after another. Noeun always acted like the protective big brother around Bunna, even though I think Bunna was slightly older and they were not truly brothers.

I remember being puzzled as to why two boys, the same age and social situation—the same extended family, in fact—ended up in such different states after the autogenocide. Many years later, I arrived at my answer: Bunna would have been dead and never even made it to America except for Noeun. Not just once, but over and over again, Noeun had saved Bunna's life. To put it simply: Noeun was the survivor; his was the personality and the force, the ability to tackle a new life, that had gotten them through. Bunna, although physically a survivor because of Noeun, had the personality and manner of one who had been defeated. I think Bunna was aware that except for Noeun he would have died many times over, and didn't know how to reconcile that with his life as a survivor in America.

Despite Noeun's temper, it was Bunna who had the harder time adjusting to American, and more specifically, our family's, mores. He simply couldn't believe that once ensconced in an American family, on American soil, he wasn't going to have everything he wanted. Whereas Noeun quickly adapted to our family's rather Spartan—by American standards—existence, realizing that my parents were of the variety that were richer in compassion than money, Bunna never quite understood the distinction.

His litany was heard daily around the house—a steady drone in the background:

"Why you no have big TV? Americans suppose have big TV, lots TV."

"I need car. How go places, have fun, no car?"

Each month my parents received an amount of money from social services to use for food, clothes, school supplies, and so on, for their two foster children. On the day my mother told me to take Bunna shopping to buy him a shirt, I got his chant full bore: "I want this; this no good, need that."

Loose at the mall, Bunna was insatiable. We bought the polyester, psychedelic button-down shirt that he chose, but then, contrary to the custom in our family, he kept wanting and asking.

"Sarah, I need many shirt, many pant, at school I am only one with few clothing."

"But Bunna, we don't have enough money. Mom gave me enough to buy one shirt. Besides, you have just as many clothes as all of us kids."

"Yes, but your family not good. American supposed be rich, many clothes, like Dallas TV."

"But Bunna, not all Americans are rich. Mom and Dad don't have a lot of money."

"They have too a lot, they just not spend. Beside I so cold all the time, just shiver all day in school."

"Bunna, we're going home. We bought the shirt, now come on."

To give Bunna credit, at school he was surrounded by some kids from very wealthy families and he probably couldn't figure out why the Streed family didn't have as much as these classmates. He and Noeun went to Minnetonka High School with Ellyn and Steve, the same high school where my father taught English and that Erik and I had attended. The high school was in a very prosperous Minneapolis suburb on Lake Minnetonka, so even though our family of six, and then eight, lived on a schoolteacher's salary, we attended the same school as the children of parents high in the echelons of corporate America: Dayton's, Pillsbury, General Mills and 3M.

I was gone for part of the following year and for a while Bunna and Noeun faded into names that cropped up in conversation or voices that answered the phone. I do remember hearing that Noeun and Bunna had had some sort of falling-out and were not speaking to each other. This went on for a year or so and none of the siblings could figure out why; my parents, if they knew, weren't saying. In retrospect, I think it was probably over a woman: namely, Prum.

Noeun and Bunna both hung out with a group of young Cambodian survivors in the area. One of these was a very pretty, very shy, girl named Prum. It was obvious they both liked her and for a while it was unclear who she liked back. She finally committed herself to dating Noeun, saying that she thought of Bunna like a brother.

Years later, Prum referred indirectly to this conflict, telling me, "It was hard at first because Bunna like me. I like him too, but think of him like brother."

The following summer I was again home, although some of my siblings were not. During the year, both Noeun and Bunna had tentatively located their birth mothers in Khao-I-Dang refugee camp. They had sent letters to a friend in Cambodia who got in touch with the women; then Noeun and Bunna had received a grainy videotape of women looking vaguely like their mothers in the mail. Since it had been so many years and so much had happened, everyone was slightly worried that two strange women were posturing as their mothers in order to extort money from two American boys. Later, it would turn out that these women were indeed their birth mothers and they ended up resettling in the Boston area.

After a few weeks at home, I realized things had changed for Noeun. He was gone a great deal, working, and on the rare occasions when he was home he often had Prum with him.

One sunny morning I came out the kitchen door with a big jar of water holding tea bags to make sun tea. Noeun was lying on a lawn chair, reading. I set the jar on the rock wall in the sun and turned to go back in. It struck me that I hadn't seen Prum around in quite some time—I hesitated next to the lawn chair—had they broken up? I hoped not. Prum seemed nice and kind, and was obviously devoted to Noeun. Surely he hadn't gone and dumped her?

"Hey Noeun," I said casually, forcing him to look up from his magazine, "Where is Prum today? I haven't seen her in a while."

"She's working," he said. "She works a lot now."

Then, as the real inquiry behind my words struck him, he grinned—the same I-can-do-anything grin that so characterized his personality—and said, "You think I take my hand away from Prum, hey, Sarah?"

I stumbled over some explanation—"I hadn't seen ... I had thought..."

He laughed, and then I laughed with him.

More time passed. Bunna and Noeun, who had come to the States somewhere around the age of fifteen, were men going to vocational school, working and generally making their way in the world. I was living in Morocco as a Peace Corps volunteer, teaching English in a high school in a village sixty miles south of Casablanca.

On a stopover from his own travels, my brother Erik came to visit me in Morocco. In a sad conjunction of fate, during his visit I received a letter from Ellyn back in the States. In it, she said that Bunna had died. After locating his birth mother and birth sisters in Boston, he went to visit them and one night during the visit, he simply went to sleep and never woke up.

"Remember how Bunna was always so worried about his future?" my sister wrote. I did, and felt the same grief and bewilderment she did. How could someone, after surviving so much, just die in their sleep after finally reaching a safe place?

Of course, I shared the letter with Erik. Shocked and shaken, we sat in my apartment, the shutters open to the dust and heat of the alley below, talking desultorily of Bunna and how this could have happened. How could his life end upon reaching the promised land of the United States? Eventually we spoke affectionately even of his foibles: Bunna, such a pest with his constant demands for more.

Then we both thought of Noeun—he would be heartbroken! Thinking of Noeun's desolation galvanized Erik and I into action. We decided to send a telegram to him, which meant a trip down the dusty streets to the post office. We purchased a telegram sheet and leaned over the wooden table for long time in our mutual effort to offer comfort to Noeun from so far away. After putting down some words, knowing they were inadequate but the best we could do, we signed it and paid the money to have it sent, then returned to my apartment feeling sad and ineffectual.

Back in the States, my mother—upon the news of Bunna's death—flew out to Boston, where for three days she sat and wept with Bunna's birth mother, sometimes holding her hand. She told me later that the pain of seeing Bunna's birth mother weep over the loss of her biological child was almost greater than she could stand.

By 1981, before Bunna died, there were enough mysterious deaths among southeast Asian refugees to occasion an article in the U.S. Centers for Disease Control Morbidity and Mortality Weekly Report, which noted that the deaths constituted a distinct phenomenon. The mystery deaths were given the acronym SUND, or Sudden Unexpected Nocturnal Death. SUND occurred in young, healthy men at night when they were asleep. When the families were interviewed, they recounted that nothing untoward had happened to the young men in the twenty-four hours preceding death.

This was exactly as it had been with Bunna; he had been sleeping, and in fact, was visiting his remaining birth family after finally locating them after years of searching. But I remained haunted by his untimely death. Why had he died after reaching the United States, especially after finding his birth mother and sisters and joining them in Boston? My mind wouldn't let it rest. I would worry about Bunna's death for a period of time, let it drop, then pick it up again.

The experts seemed to be as mystified as I was, concluding that the actual cause of death remained unknown. Eventually I decided that Bunna had come through so much that upon reaching the other side, his spirit gave out. At a certain point—even after arriving at a safe place and finding part of his birth family—he just let go. However, I wasn't completely satisfied; this speculation only put my mind at ease partway.

In 1988, another Morbidity and Mortality Weekly Report updated the 1981 report on SUND, using data from deaths that had occurred in the meantime. In addition to previous data, the report stated that most deaths occurred within the first two years after arrival in the United States. But once again, the cause of death remained unknown.

Then on August 29, 2000, Michael L. Tan wrote on SUND—using the Filipino term "bangungot" for the syndrome—in the *Philippine Daily Inquirer*. He spoke of the various reports of SUND in various populations. He briefly discussed the lean medical findings, and then wrote a paragraph that made sense on the cause of Bunna's death for the first time:

> An area that has been neglected in this nightmare death research is the role of mental health. Notice how, in all the countries with this syndrome, the ones who are most often affected are males going through the stress of migration or being away from home: Filipino sailors out at sea, Thai construction workers in Singapore and Southeast Asian refugees in North America. Since males in these cultures often have to put up a facade of stoic strength, even during very difficult times, they may not be able to express their anxieties openly. Suppressing these emotions could make them more susceptible to this sudden death syndrome.

At last, for me, an explanation of Bunna's mysterious death. I recollected very clearly that he had been experiencing much stress in his life while suppressing his true emotions. The copious whining and fretting, the excessive worry about his future, were what he expressed; the anxiety of living in a new country, the worry as to how he could carve a future out of completely unknown territory—that was what he was truly feeling.

Bunna had made it to the United States because of Noeun. Nouen had spotted Bunna in another labor camp and come to find him when the

Vietnamese were invading. Noeun had physically held Bunna up while they ran-walked miles to the jungle. Noeun had laid Bunna on a towel and gone to hunt food. Noeun had fed Bunna and moved him through the jungle, protecting him from tigers and snakes. When Noeun was shot on the Thai border, the doctor in the car had stopped to take Noeun to the hospital and Bunna came along. When any sponsoring American families were inquiring, they were told, "There are two brothers who come together and can't be split up." We Streeds were told this, accepted the package deal and Noeun and Bunna came to live with us. A few years later, Bunna, the weaker brother, died and Noeun, the stronger brother, was unable to save him this one last time.

4

Tricked Twice:
The Story of Sinn Lok

The Lok family were rice farmers in the small village of Onlongpay, which lay in Kompong Speu Province of southern Cambodia. Sinn and his six siblings lived comfortably with their parents in a house surrounded by fruit trees planted by their ancestors: mango, papaya, breadfruit, and banana. The villagers honored the many trees, not only for their age and beauty, but for the shade, food, and shelter for the birds they provided.

With the arrival of the monsoon season in May and June, Cambodia bloomed. Bright green grass appeared overnight in the countryside, trees threw forth leaves followed by buds, flowers sprang up in the fields. Most importantly, the rice began to grow. The rains fell and covered the rice fields. They kept falling until only the green tips of the four- to six-foot-high plants peeked above the muddy water. Flooded fields and swollen creeks stretched as far as the eye could see. The birds sang all day long, but were especially loud in the morning.

During the rainy season the Lok parents and older children worked in the rice fields, planting, tending and then harvesting rice. During the rainy season of 1972, Sinn—the third child down and the first boy—was too young at four years old to help in the rice fields, so he was given the job of taking care of the family ox. He was to take the ox up the mountain in the morning so the animal could graze on higher ground, then bring the ox back before nightfall. The first time he approached the swollen river with the waters rushing past in a torrent, he felt afraid to cross because he didn't know how to swim. So he remained on the banks with the ox all day and returned home at dark with the hungry animal.

Sinn's father could tell he hadn't taken the ox up the mountain but didn't say anything. That night, Sinn went out and picked grass until his arms were sore in order to feed the animal. The next day he crossed the

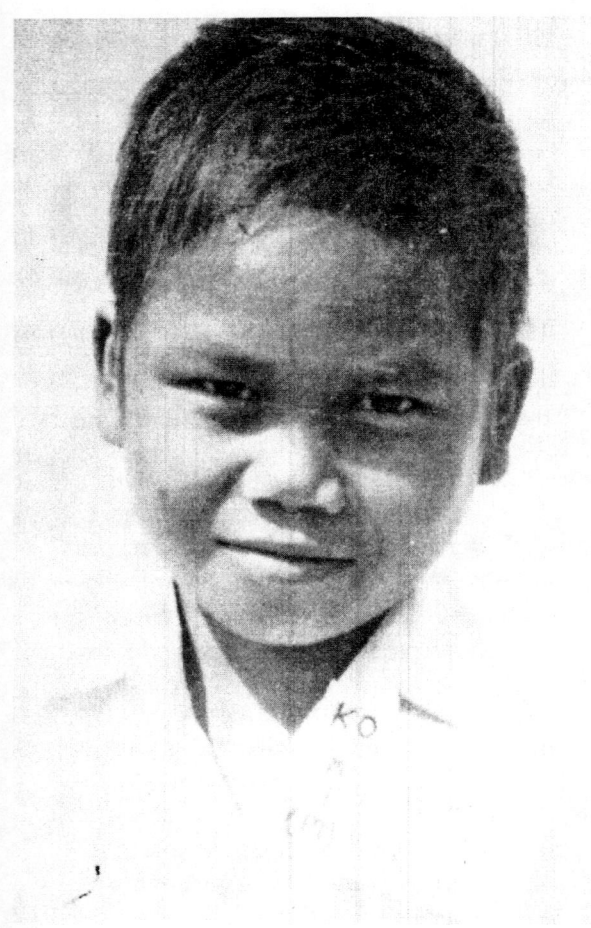

Identification photograph of Sinn Lok taken at a refugee camp on the Thai border. (Photograph from the personal collection of Sinn Lok.)

river with the ox and continued to do so every day until the rainy season was over.

Towards the end of September and the beginning of October, the rains slowed and the waters receded. The rice ripened and the color of the fields changed from green to orange and yellow. The sun shone day after day until the rice was harvested and the once flooded fields turned to dry dust. The sun kept shining all through the dry season from December to April, until the dirt burned Sinn's bare feet, and the single tarred road connecting the villages softened.

During the dry season the Lok family and the other villagers tended to their second crop: sugar. They cut the tips of the sugar palm flowers to allow the sap to flow into bamboo containers and boiled this sap to get sugar which was stored in huge clay jars. The Lok family sold sugar at the weekly market; they sold a great deal and this second crop got them through the dry season.

War shattered the peasants' peaceful village existence in 1973. Planes flew low dropping bombs and the Lok family and others frantically ran to hide in big holes they had dug as crude bomb shelters. No one knew who was fighting who but rumors said the United States was bombing Cambodia; these rumors were borne out by the American markings the villagers could see on the planes as they dipped down over the village.

Sometimes a bomb hit the village and a few houses burned down. The villagers said to each other that American planes dropped the bombs because they didn't like Cambodia.

War changed village life in other ways, too. As the Khmer Rouge guerrillas gained control over rural areas, they planted landmines. Advancing toward the capital, they mined whole expanses of land—forests, fields—as they went. A bull from Sinn's village stepped on one of these landmines and was blasted with shrapnel. Amazingly, the bull lived, but his bellowing was heard for miles. All the villagers knew immediately what had happened and were glad it was a bull and not one of them. They wanted to keep away from the mines but it was impossible; they could encounter mines anywhere: in a field, along a road, on the way to find greener pastures for an ox.

In 1975, when Sinn was six years old, he went to play with the other children at the Buddhist temple. On the way home he happened to hear on a radio that the war was over. He ran home and saw villagers crowded around another radio, listening intently. Upon hearing that the war had ended, everyone grew happy and excited, but then agreed that it was too soon to celebrate; they would wait and see what would happen.

At first, life did not change drastically. *Angkar* or the "Organization"—the name the Communist party of Cambodia used to conceal its Communism from outsiders—was the new ruler. The soldiers let families stay together and told the villagers to continue working in the fields. The pattern of planting and harvesting rice didn't seem any different. Then people began disappearing—*bat kluon*—and although no one said so out loud, everyone knew it was connected with *Angkar*.

Angkar separated the families. Children were put in groups of 100 and worked in teams; Sinn was put in a group away from his parents and siblings. His mother and father remained in the village with a sister who was too young to be in a work group. Occasionally Sinn received permission and came home for a few days to visit. His parents never voiced their discontent because they were afraid—like everyone else—that the *chlop*, or official informer, would hear and report back to the Khmer Rouge and then they too would "disappear."

Sinn worked near his village, then was put in another group that moved from village to village in the area. In Cambodian culture it was not the custom to hug; sometimes people shook hands or bowed to each other, but that was all. So when Sinn went home for what would be his last visit, his mother didn't hug or touch him as he left. After he had returned to the work group, *Angkar* never granted him permission to leave again.

After a while Sinn realized that he had seen his family for the last time. He was very sad but didn't cry, just spent his waking hours thinking of his mother, father, and home in the village. In accordance with the mores of the confused, war-torn world he lived in, he eventually became accustomed to life without parents.

Sinn was working one day when a Khmer Rouge soldier came to the fields and announced that the children were invited to another village for a party. Most of the children didn't want to go but were afraid to say no; no one ever talked back or refused the Khmer Rouge because they might end up "disappearing." All the children went to the party.

At first there was a party, complete with food, music and dancing. Then the Khmer Rouge soldiers began picking out children and pairing them up, boys with boys and girls with girls. They put Sinn in a group with twenty other children, chose a leader, and designated the group as a new work group.

The children immediately began doing field-work: clearing, irrigation, plowing and planting, often in the rice fields. Sinn was working with his group when he spotted his cousin working in another group next to him. Suddenly, one of the boys in the other group hit a landmine with his hoe and it blew up. Nobody was hurt in Sinn's group but several died in the next group and Sinn's cousin lost a finger. He was taken to a Khmer Rouge hospital where Sinn visited him the next day. The cousin never came back to rejoin the work group.

When the dry season came, the boys were given other work instead of being allowed to rest. The work never ceased. The group remained in the area where Sinn had been born, but Sinn never glimpsed any of his family.

A teenage boy was appointed chief cook to make sure the children were fed their near-starvation rations. Some of the children got sick from overwork and lack of food and then "disappeared."

Sinn's work group was moved again and again until they were far from Sinn's village. The Khmer Rouge were capricious with the children; sometimes they took a child from one group and moved him to another group. Sinn's group traveled all the way from his village in the south to Siemreap Oddar Mean Chey Province in the north. At each stop along the way the children worked long and hard.

The group kept working and moving. Sinn couldn't keep track of the stops, just moved when the Khmer Rouge said and did what they ordered. One time his group was camped on top of a mountain, harvesting tea and many of the children began insisting that they had seen something: a ghost, an animal, a scary man, a stranger, or a soldier. The children grew so frightened talking about it that the Khmer Rouge finally moved them off the mountain.

The Khmer Rouge told the children that some of them would be transferred to Phnom Penh. Everyone wanted to go to the capital city—including Sinn, who wanted to be closer to his parents and village—so the leaders said they could take only the biggest children. They told the children to line up and began picking the ones who could go to Phnom Penh.

Sinn was one of the smaller ones in the group so he stood on a coconut to make him taller. The ruse worked and he was chosen, but instead of going to Phnom Penh the children were taken by truck to the Tonle Sap Lake and put on a huge boat with four hundred other children. The boat was on the lake for two days and two nights. When it landed back on shore the children were taken off and marched right back to Siem Reap. The children tried to figure out why they had been put on the boat in the first place; some said it was so they would become lost and not be able to run away and rejoin their families.

This was the second time Sinn had been tricked. The first time had been when the Khmer Rouge told the children they were going to a party but put them in work groups instead. After being tricked twice, Sinn resolved that he would never trust anyone again.

The Khmer Rouge marched Sinn's work group five miles north to Angkor Wat—the immense, majestic temple built between 1110 and 1135 by the Khmer Empire. Sinn and the others were told to get to work cleaning up the temple grounds, so they began pulling grass away from the buildings and cutting down trees whose enormous roots had overgrown the statues.

While the children were working on Angkor Wat, rumors abounded. Most said that the Vietnamese were going to invade. Some said either the Soviet Union or Vietnam had dropped a bomb on Pochentong Airport in Phnom Penh.

Shortly after, invading Vietnamese soldiers reached Angkor Wat. There was pandemonium. The children, who up until that point had been working steadily, stopped. Sinn and a few others huddled under a shelter close to the river and tried to stay out of the Vietnamese soldiers' way.

That night Sinn and some others went to a potato field to dig up potatoes to eat. One of the boys hit a landmine while digging and was instantly blown to pieces. The other boys simply stared. It had happened so fast. Sinn didn't understand how the mine could have been under the potato. Why hadn't the person who planted the potato been blown up? How did the mine stay intact through all of the planting and weeding, and then blow up when the boy dug up the potato? Sinn and the other boys stopped digging up potatoes and went back to the shelter near the river.

A few children—Sinn included—talked of how they had heard that Thailand and freedom were nearby. The next day these children got up and ran. No one stopped them. When they got tired, they walked, then ran again, then walked.

They ran—walking when they got tired—for days, only halting to eat one meal a day. No one wanted to take the time to stop any more than that. The children got so tired that they slept as they were walking. Several times Sinn fell asleep while walking, then tripped and jumped awake.

Everyone was on the lookout for landmines. There were so many kinds that you couldn't possibly be aware of what to look for, but people tried, nonetheless. The PMN type were buried in the ground or covered with twigs. The POMZ type had a thin tripwire to watch for a few inches above the ground. The ball-mines were often used with the POMZs. Mostly, people understood that they were impossible to avoid; they just walked on and hoped.

When they reached the jungle, the children tried to stay on the narrow trail, feeling this was safer. The only problem was that when they stopped to rest, they had to get off the trail to sit in the shade of a tree, and then sometimes, people tripped the mines. Once, Sinn's group overtook a mangled man being carried on a stretcher. When Sinn asked, the man carrying the stretcher said that his friend had stepped on a mine.

After several weeks the children approached the Thai border; they could see the soldiers guarding it. They stayed in the area but couldn't cross. They could hear fighting in the distance. The children moved back and forth along the border and decided that if the fighting ever came nearby, they would take a chance and run for Thailand.

By this time the group was like a family. Two older children—around seventeen years old—had emerged as the "parents" or leaders. They took care of the others, told them what to do and cooked the food.

While living near the border, the children merged with other groups trying to escape into Thailand. A kind of transient village was formed with old and young making a camp together. The unwritten policy was that the group cooked and shared together any food they could find but each person was responsible for his or her own water, carried in containers made out of bamboo stalks.

After a year no one had been able to cross into Thailand and people began to run out of food and water. The elderly people in the group were getting sick and many died at this time. The children buried them. One day Sinn carried his water in the bamboo stalk all day long but didn't get thirsty. Several people asked him for water and he gave them some of his. Later on that night he became very thirsty but his water was gone. He went to the same people that had drunk his water earlier and asked for some of their water but they refused.

The group happened to be camped near an empty well so Sinn went down to the bottom of the well to get some water. There wasn't any water at the bottom—just damp dirt—so he ate the dirt. He became very sick. His body began to swell—mostly his legs—and he had constant diarrhea. He worried that he was going to die, or worse, that he would be put in the "death house."

Everyone knew of the "death house" and viewed it with disgust and horror. If someone was put in, they didn't come out. The Khmer Rouge said it was a hospital and a house for the sick, but everyone knew that if you went in, you didn't get better, you died. Sinn didn't know if people were actually killed inside the house, but it was referred to as "the death house." One boy that Sinn knew was sick only for a day when the Khmer Rouge came to take him to the "death house." The boy screamed and screamed, "I don't want to go; I don't want to die." But the soldiers picked him up and took him to the house anyway. He died the next day. Sinn lived in constant fear but for some reason no one came to take him to the "death house." He thought that perhaps it was because he was still taking care of himself.

No one took care of anyone else; everyone was on their own. So even though Sinn was so sick, he tried to take care of himself. He gathered wood and built a fire to warm himself. People said salt caused swelling, so he stopped eating salt.

People were dying all around. Sinn had been slightly friendly with another boy who was also sick. One night they ate a meal together then went to sleep next to each other. The next morning when Sinn woke up, the boy was dead. Sinn was very sad. They hadn't been friends exactly—because no one had friends during that time—but Sinn had known him and they had been in the same group.

Some of the group unknowingly cooked some poisonous mushrooms and gave some to Sinn. After Sinn ate the mushrooms, he began sweating profusely and went blind for twenty minutes. He urinated constantly. But then he remembered that the people from his village used to say, "Take MSG for poison; it will make you throw up and you will get better." The leaders kept MSG to put in the food so Sinn got some, put it in his water and drank. In a few minutes he was past the crisis. He was very sick, but still alive.

Sinn found some old, hard corn kernels, cooked and mashed them, then ate the paste. He also ate *may sror*—a substance like rock salt, but extremely sweet. There were packages left from before the war that were traded from person to person. Sinn procured a package and sprinkled this on a corn patty. He knew the *may sror* was good protein but couldn't eat it alone; it was too sweet.

Several times the group attempted to cross the border but didn't succeed. One time they slipped in close, but then a Vietnamese soldier appeared. People tried to run across the border, but no one knew exactly where it was, or even if they had already crossed it.

Again, while a group was trying to cross the border a soldier appeared, but this time Sinn and a few others got cut off from the others. None of them were carrying food so for a night and the following day, no one ate anything. They were afraid to move for fear of running into a soldier so they sat for a day and a night in the rain. The following morning they found their group and were reunited.

They tried to stay close to the river. They lived by eating snails and sometimes by stealing food from Thai farmers. At first, Sinn decided not to steal food because he knew people were shot for that, but then he became so hungry that he was willing to try stealing. He and some others left the camp and went deeper into the jungle. They glimpsed some Thai farmers through the trees and Sinn turned and ran all the way back to the camp.

Everyone lived in perpetual fear. One night as the group was gathered around a fire, there were noises—someone was coming! People ran in all directions, tripping and falling in their haste to get away. Mothers jumped up and ran, leaving their babies behind.

People ran so far away that they couldn't find their way back. The mothers tried to return to their babies, but lost at night in the jungle—it was an impossible task. Around noon the next day—almost without realizing it—Sinn crossed the border into Thailand. The moment that he realized he was in Thailand he felt a short-lived sense of safety and well-being. Then, almost immediately, he grew anxious and worried about what was to come.

Sinn and three others were too sick to walk so they lay down by the border. Someone from the refugee camp came along and took them to a temporary hospital set up in a tent. Sinn watched from his cot as people died all around him. Every hour, as he lay there, someone stiffened up and died.

Slowly, over days, he felt better until he was able to get up and walk. He lay in his cot only part of the time. Once, as he was lying down, he heard gunshots so close that they sounded like they were right in the hospital. Everyone that could, got up and ran. As Sinn was running out, a nurse stopped him and put a load of medicine in his arms. Hurriedly, she tried to give him instructions on how to take it, but he couldn't understand. He just grabbed the medicine and left.

Later, in the jungle, Sinn heard that everything was back to normal and they could all return, but he was too afraid to go back. He and two other boys chose to stay in the jungle. Sinn took the medicine the nurse had given him all at once.

The three boys couldn't find food so they decided to return to the hospital. Sinn walked back, climbed into his cot, then became sick from all the medicine and vomited for several hours.

One morning many buses drove up in front of the hospital. The nurses told Sinn and the other patients that they were moving. Sinn got on the bus and sat by four other boys from the hospital.

The bus drove to Sa Kaeo, a huge refugee camp on the Thai border. The buses stopped in front of a big tent. Sinn and the other boys got off and stood talking about their situation: They didn't have any food, they didn't have parents, they didn't know anyone and they didn't know what to do next. Should they stay together? Go their separate ways?

As they were discussing their options a lady came out of the tent and spoke to them in Khmer: Where were they going? They didn't know. Did they have families? No, they didn't. She took them into the big tent, which turned out to be a children's hospital.

The children's hospital tent was located in the middle of the refugee camp which was surrounded by a big fence. More and more refugees entered the camp. The staff wouldn't let any refugees go back out once they were in because they feared the people outside would attack them for food. Children inside the fence had plenty of food, but no parents; children outside the fence had parents but no food.

Sinn remained at the children's hospital. More children kept arriving each day; the staff kept giving the children food and medicine. The staff was French, German, and American. Some worked for the Red Cross.

One time the Thai prince and his wife came to the children's hospital, accompanied by many buses. The staff told the children that anyone who wanted could go with the prince and his wife. Sinn didn't trust the staff and thought this was a ruse.

"I'm not going," he told the boy in the cot next to him, "It's a trick to take us all back to Cambodia."

He stayed in his bed and watched as children boarded the buses and drove off.

Even after he was better, he continued to stay at the children's hospital. There was nowhere else to go, nor anything else to do. He didn't know anyone so he just sat. He didn't think about anything except food. He wondered if the hospital staff would continue to feed him, and what he would do if they stopped. Mostly, he pondered the question: Who will feed me if the people at the hospital stop? Sometimes the Thai people gave out money to the children, so he hoarded this in case he would ever need to buy food.

Sinn stayed at the hospital for several years and outlasted many volunteers who took care of the children. First, there was a French lady volunteer who gave the children clothes and fed them a lot of food. When she left, a Korean man took her place. He was followed by a series of Thai nuns. The nuns were followed by two American women, about thirty years old; they were kind to the children and treated them fairly. Sinn felt sad when they left to return to Washington, D.C., but didn't think of saying goodbye or asking for their addresses.

"I don't think they'll remember me," he told another boy. "There are so many children here. I am just one of a huge group."

After a while schools were set up in the camp and Sinn attended school daily. Every day children were picked to go to other countries: Australia, America, France.

One morning a list of ten names was called, and Sinn's was among them. These children were taken outside the camp, where a man asked Sinn: "What do your parents do? How many children in your family? What is your first name? Your father's name? When is your birthday?" Sinn was afraid when the man asked these questions. After the man had finished, he didn't tell Sinn whether he had passed or not. Sinn knew if he failed the test, he wouldn't be able to leave.

The next morning Sinn's name was called again. Again, he answered more questions. He tried hard to remember what he had answered the day before for identical questions, for example, "When is your birthday?" In prewar Cambodia, no one celebrated birthdays, only the Cambodian New Year and a few other holidays. Since it was the first time anyone had ever asked Sinn when his birthday was, he had quickly chosen 1/1, or January first. It was easy to remember. When asked how old he was, he said fifteen.

He passed the second test, and they took photos of him. He went into another room for a physical, took off his clothes and a doctor looked him over. He passed the physical and was taken to another camp where he waited with everyone else for his name to be called on the loudspeaker.

When his name was called, Sinn was taken to the Thai airport. He was afraid to board the plane as he had seen planes flying up high and dropping bombs, but nothing else. He was worried that the plane might crash.

When it was time to climb aboard, he turned everything off—didn't feel anything, didn't think anything—and just sat. He didn't talk to the boy in the seat next to him and that boy didn't talk to him.

"I hadn't really talked to anyone since I left my family," he said later, when he was describing his journey. "I didn't talk to anyone after they took me away from my parents."

He was sick during the flight. Although the journey took several days he only ate once because he felt so sick.

The plane was full of people of all colors and nationalities. Sinn didn't know a word of English and had no idea what was happening. Sometimes the pilots and flight attendants spoke in French but he didn't know French either. He didn't recognize anyone on the plane from Cambodia or the refugee camps. He felt completely alone.

The plane flew to Hong Kong, then Japan, and finally landed in California. Sinn disembarked with the others, but didn't know what country he was in, or even what part of the world.

As Sinn came off the airplane, he saw a building. It was the airport. The passengers went in the building, sat down and someone gave them dinner. They were each given a can of soda. Sinn was extremely thirsty but had never seen a can of soda before so he didn't know how to open it. He saw a drinking fountain, but didn't know if the water was safe to drink or not. He couldn't ask anyone because he didn't speak English. So he sat and waited until someone opened the can of soda for him. Then he drank it.

After a while, he was put on another plane. This one flew to Minneapolis, Minnesota. When he got off, people were hugging and greeting one another. Sinn stood there, still feeling sick from the flight. A sponsor came and gathered Sinn together with four other Cambodians that had arrived at the same time. None of them knew each other. The sponsor drove them to a house in Richfield, where they stayed with an American family.

After a few weeks Sinn went to live with the Streeds, his foster family, and begin his life as an American teenager. He was fifteen years old. Over the years he would graduate from Minnetonka High School, take classes at vocational-technical school, and attain a position as a skilled woodworker in a cabinet-making shop. His first few weeks in America were the start of a road of cultural adaptation that would culminate in his becoming a citizen of the United States at age twenty-five.

Sinn has a sense of bewilderment about the autogenocide. Because he didn't see a lot of soldiers, or guns, he didn't know what had happened until he reached the United States and began hearing the reports. When he was in Thailand, he heard a bit, but it was whispered and uncertain.

He says, "While all that was happening, we Cambodians never said anything. We just kept working and tried to keep our mouths shut. You never trusted anyone; you never said anything. If you said something to someone, that person might tell someone else, an informer, or someone who would tell an informer."

Shortly before he became an American citizen, Sinn found out—unbelievably, given the autogenocide left two million of the country's seven million people dead—that the rest of his family was still alive in Cambodia. However, by then he knew it was too late for him to go back. Too much had happened; he hadn't seen his family in twenty years.

"I don't know why something like this happened to me," he says. "Sometimes I wonder why all my family is over there in Cambodia, except me. I'm over here. What did I do different? I don't know."

"I don't feel like I have a family," he continues. "I've been separated so long from my Cambodian family, and also, I came over to America by myself."

He expresses his uncertainty and confusion to his foster family, the people he calls his family now: "I feel my life has been lonely, that I've never really known anybody. I don't feel like getting close to anyone. It's hard to trust anyone. Ever since the Khmer Rouge I haven't been able to trust anyone—Cambodian or American. I've been tricked twice—once, when the Khmer Rouge told us we were going to the party but put us in work groups instead, and the other time when they told us we were going to Phnom Penh but put us on a boat and we ended up in Siem Reap. After I was tricked the second time, I decided never to trust anyone again."

5

Crappie Fishing
on Galpin Lake

My parents live on the far shore of Galpin Lake. Galpin is a small lake of seventy acres and very shallow—fifteen feet down at the deepest part. It is diminutive compared to the other lakes in Minnesota, but seems especially so since it is adjacent—in fact, connected by a culvert—to the "big" lake of Minnetonka. Seen on a map, Lake Minnetonka sprawls voraciously in blue isles and inlets, leaving Galpin Lake a tiny blue dot all but obliterated by the capital "E" of the printed name "Excelsior." Long ago, Excelsior was a cabin community for executives fleeing Minneapolis during the hot summers; now it is the permanent community for Minnesotans who don't care one whit about executives—fleeing or not.

My parents live in a group of homes on the far shore that were originally built as cabins and have been winterized during various years and in various ways. Their house is on a hill directly across the lake from another small peak, bearing, appropriately enough, the Hilltop Restaurant. Highway 7 runs between lake and restaurant; the culvert connecting Minnetonka and Galpin runs underneath. Each morning a group of Galpin and Excelsior old-timers—including my father—gather at the Hilltop to drink coffee and exchange "news." (If it were a group of women it would be called gossip.)

The public access beach of Galpin is next to the highway. Years ago, a Minnesota Department of Natural Resources official came out and posted a weathered sign at the beach. It read, "This lake has been designated for promiscuous fishing," meaning anyone fishing in Galpin could catch anything, anytime, in any amount. Upon viewing the sign, the locals laughed uproariously because everyone knew that Galpin Lake didn't have any fish; in winter the ice gets so thick that there's no oxygen for the fish to breathe. The one time a desperate fisherman had gone out with a fish finder in January he hadn't been able to locate a single fish.

Sarah and Brian holding northerns caught in Galpin Lake. (Photograph by Jack Streed and from the personal collection of Jack and Joan Streed.)

When Sinn joined our family, my parents had already had some experience with raising Cambodian refugees. Like Noeun and Bunna, Sinn was a teenager when he arrived; like them he had spent years of his childhood surviving Pol Pot and his Khmer Rouge. But unlike Noeun and Bunna, Sinn had grown up on a rice farm in the countryside, and thus, had spent many hours fishing in prewar Cambodia. As soon as Sinn saw Galpin Lake—even though it was winter and frozen over—he was aching to fish in it. Undeterred by local talk and knowledge, he determined that when it got warm enough, he was going to go fishing in Galpin.

So one spring day when the ice had been out for about two weeks, Sinn went down the hill to my parents' ancient rotting dock and threw out his line. Three hours later he came trudging back up the hill with a bucket holding thirty fish. My parents came to look at the silvery sunfish swirling around in the white five-gallon pail. After their initial astonishment, they called the neighbors over to look in the bucket. The neighbors' reactions were uniform: a look of admiration, awe, then a short whistle followed by the words, "Who'd have thought it?"

Turns out that crappies—a kind of sunfish highly esteemed for eating—are the first fish in the lakes to leave the deep cold waters of winter and go towards the sun-warmed waters of spring. Because Galpin is so much smaller than Minnetonka, the ice there goes out a full week before the ice on Minnetonka. Thus, in those first few weeks of spring, the entire crappie population of Minnetonka comes flooding in through the culvert to bask in Galpin's shallow waters. Later on, as big Lake Minnetonka warms up, the crappies go back through the culvert; tiny Galpin could never support that many fish all year round.

Sinn's discovery became the first of an annual tradition of crappie fishing on Galpin Lake. Each spring—early to middle of May—Sinn and Noeun and four or five friends gather at my parents' house to spend a weekend fishing. Over the years, as Sinn and Noeun and their friends have married and started families, the number has grown, so that on any given fishing day in spring the driveway holds eight or more parked cars and fifteen or more people fishing down by the lake.

One year someone caught a good-sized northern pike. This set off a frenzy of fishing among Sinn and Noeun and their friends—and everyone else. Apparently, the northerns had entered through the culvert when young, then grown up in Galpin. Once someone had caught the first one, the word was out and there were out-of-towners parking their cars off the highway and fishing from the public access. Soon the northerns had all been caught. The out-of-towners no longer parked off Highway 7 and the lake was left to the faithful who came every spring.

On Crappie Fishing Day 1995 the fisherfolk begin to arrive at the house toward noon: Sinn and Phary, Noeun and Prum and their children, other friends—Tia, Bat, Pol, Bo, Hun—and their wives and children. All park in the driveway and greet the others, then grab rods and reels, tackle boxes, minnows in Styrofoam pails, buckets for the catch and go on down to the lake.

Fishing is done from the few boards of the dock that remain above water, or close to shore in the canoe, or simply off the shore. The equipment is good: Shakespeare or Diawa rods and reels. Mostly crappie jigs—a small hook with a pea head and feathers—are used with bobbers; but sometimes minnows are used, or the special crappie catcher someone came up with one year—tipping a jig with a minnow. Everything is tried, and what works and what doesn't is remembered from one year to the next.

Everybody fishes some, but it is usually the men who fish the most. The children fish with their fathers' poles that are way too big, but the reward is great; shortly after they drop a baited hook into the water, a crappie bites. After twenty minutes they can't sit still any longer and run from the dock up the hill to the house, then back down to the dock. Their lithe brown legs flash in the sun as they scamper from lake to car to house to car to lake, too impatient to sit, but excited and happy with the warm air and the festive atmosphere and the thought of the all the fish to eat.

Noeun's children come up the hill to talk to Grandma Joan, or "Nana." They tell her about the fish their dad has already caught, then ask for a treat. Nana goes inside and comes back out with Popsicles. The two children lick the neon-colored confections while walking on the stone walls, playing the unchanging game that every generation plays on stone walls as children: Trying-Not-to-Fall-Off.

After the Popsicles are finished, the children go with Nana to pick flowers. The three of them wander through the gardens while Nana cuts bouquets of the daffodils. She gives one bouquet to each child and tells them they can take the pretty flowers home. The children run to take the flowers to their mother, who is with the other women down by the lake.

After an hour or two at the lakeshore, the women gather up at the house in the screen porch. They relax and chat because they know at the end of the day they will spend hours cleaning and filleting the catch to store in freezers; everyone loves the delectable panfish, small and delicately flavored. A new mother goes out to the car to nurse her infant in quiet. The other mothers keep an eye on the rest of the children who run back and forth between the mothers and the fathers. They open bags of chips and cans of soda. The children stop and eat, lingering to try and catch their mothers' whispered comments and stifled laughs.

A Camaro glides up the driveway and comes to a halt: it is Sim arriving late with his fiancée. Resplendent with health and beauty, they get out of the car. She pats her moussed hair and tugs at her short summer skirt; he adjusts his Varnet shades and squares his shoulders under the polo shirt. Without talking, they split up. He grabs a fishing pole and tackle box and heads down to the lake; she goes to the screen porch, sits down with the women and talks about the upcoming marriage.

The afternoon wears on. The babies and toddlers fall asleep in the cool of the porch and their mothers take this chance to wander back down to the lake. The men, fishing from the dock and canoe, shift spots, and each shift brings in more and more fish. Occasionally, they grab a soda or a sandwich or a cigarette, but never stop fishing. They have spent hours in the sun, talking, laughing, smoking and all the while removing one fish after another off the hooks.

Neighbors come by and walk down to the lake. There, they stand mesmerized at the buckets, watching the small iridescent fish swim frantically against the white plastic walls, splashing silver. Even though it happens every year, anyone who is within walking distance comes to see the fish for themselves. My parents chat with the gathering crowd as the late afternoon fades away.

In the deepening twilight, the men climb back up the hill to the house, laden with paraphernalia. They make several trips, carrying the white buckets bursting with fish. As these are covered and being put into the trunks, the man from next door sees the crowd and comes over. He is on his way to the health club dressed in a Adidas warm-up outfit and Nike shoes. The covers are removed so that he can see. Looking into the buckets, he whistles in amazement—so many fish! And all from Galpin Lake? Shaking his head, he goes to his car, his workout already paling beside such a potent performance.

Mothers call to their children who obediently come to the cars; babies are strapped into car seats. The light over the garage flickers on, then off, then stays on as the automatic light sensor registers nightfall. The Camaro races its engine, and Sim, still wearing the shades, calls from the open window to his fiancée. She says goodbye to the other women and gets in on the passenger side.

All are ready to go but everyone waits as Noeun—unofficial head of the group because of his strength and position as older foster son—goes to thank my parents for the use of the driveway and dock. Sinn, quiet and steady, stands with Phary at his side. He tells the departing men that he won't be playing volleyball later that night, but instead will stay at Mom and Dad's to spend time with his foster siblings.

Noeun returns, slams down the trunk, then the cars start, one after the other, engines all tuned. The Camaro races its engine once, then backs up, unerring and fast, down the long driveway. The rest follow—five, six, seven—and they are gone, as fast as silvery fish slipping underneath the dock. The house and yard with fifteen people suddenly gone is quiet, echoing, still. After a few minutes, a loon calls from Galpin Lake.

6

Coming to
a Third Country:
The Story of Prum Nath

Before the war, Phnom Penh—the bustling metropolis of two million—was a hive of activity from sunrise until long into the night. The wide boulevards lined by tall white apartment buildings were crammed with trishaws skimming along the streets like water bugs, wide-leafed palms shading street vendors selling everything from sandals to yams, and people shopping, talking and looking. The capital city was the center for commerce of all kinds; goods arrived from the country both by truck and boat as the Tonle Sap and Bassac rivers intersect with the giant Mekong in Phnom Penh.

In 1973 severe U.S. bombing, strafing, napalming and defoliating of the countryside, along with the ongoing civil war fought between the Khmer Rouge and Lon Nol's troops, destroyed previously tranquil country lives and drove tens of thousands into the city. The Nath* family, along with thousands of other refugee families, fled to the outskirts and tried to eke out a living on the streets of Phnom Penh.

The family of eight lived in a shelter they had built of palm fronds at the side of the street. Mr. Nath lay sick in bed while Mrs. Nath operated a kiosk that supported the entire family. Under an awning, in one of the many open market stalls, Mrs. Nath displayed and sold clothing, vegetables and any other item that might attract a city dweller on his way home from work or a rice farmer coming in to buy something that couldn't be found in the countryside. Prum*, a girl, was the fourth child of six, preceded by a brother and two older sisters, and followed by two younger brothers. While Mrs. Nath was at the kiosk, Prum and her older sisters stayed at the hut caring for their sick father and younger brothers.

*pseudonym

Children at a community gathering, 1992. (Photograph by Susan Cook and from the personal collection of Susan Cook.)

Prum was six in 1974 when the Khmer Rouge attacked Phnom Penh for the first time. The soldiers invaded the outskirts of the city but couldn't penetrate further due to the defense of Lon Nol and his soldiers. The Naths, living right where the fighting was taking place, packed up some clothes and rice and fled into the center of the city where they found an empty hut—small, dirty, with a leaking roof made of palm fronds—and appropriated it for their own.

Mrs. Nath immediately began selling things at the main city market in order to make money. Mr. Nath, lying in the hut, grew worse until he began coughing up blood. Things went on like this for a year until the Khmer Rouge overcame the Lon Nol soldiers and entered the heart of the city in April 1975, ordering immediate evacuation of the inhabitants.

Fleeing for the third time, the Nath family grabbed a cow and wagon off the street, put some clothes and rice on it and ran alongside the wagon all the way back to their original hut on the outskirts. They were only able to stay there for a few days; however, until the Khmer Rouge came, put the entire family in a jeep and drove them to the faraway city of Kompong Thom.

The Khmer Rouge installed the Nath family under a shelter of palm fronds in Kompong Thom and told them to get to work, referring to this process as "the relocation." The soldiers were understanding at first and forced only the adolescents and able-bodied to go work in the fields. Prum was deemed too small and her father too sick to work so they were allowed to stay in the shelter with Mrs. Nath and the younger boys; however, Prum's older brother and sisters went out to work in the rice fields every day.

The rice harvest was small that year because the Khmer Rouge had moved the original farmers away from their fields and abolished traditional ways; no one was left who knew about planting or harvesting the crops. The Khmer Rouge grew angry at the insufficient yield and made almost everyone—no matter how old or sick—go out to the fields to work. Mr. and Mrs. Nath and Prum's oldest brother were ordered to go out to the fields; Prum and her sisters were given permission to stay in the hut with the two littlest boys.

Food became very scarce and the Khmer Rouge stopped giving out even small portions of rice. People were starving. Mr. Nath became very ill, partly because of starvation and overwork, partly because he could no longer obtain the medicine he needed. Five months after relocating to Kompong Thom, Prum's father died in his bed.

Prum's two little brothers grew very sick. The youngest was a baby and there was no milk to be found anywhere. Mrs. Nath was starving so her milk dried up; when she tried to breast-feed, nothing came out. After a few days the baby died.

Prum was still strong enough to go out and look for food so she walked around and picked up every kernel of corn she saw by hand. She brought the food she found to her family but it was never enough—one ear of corn, a tiny bit of rice—for all of them. Sometimes when Prum brought back rice and gave it to her mother, her mother didn't eat it but instead gave it to Prum's sisters and younger brother.

Even with Prum going out to search for food, there still wasn't anywhere near enough to eat. Soon Prum's younger brother—a toddler—died of starvation. The sister next to Prum lay in the dirt all day long with edema, a direct consequence of starvation; her hands and feet swelled up like balloons so that when Prum poked her skin with a finger, liquid came out. She died shortly.

In an effort to replace dying workers, the Khmer Rouge made a sweep of the country, taking away all the older boys and girls to form labor gangs. They took Prum's oldest brother away to a lake and told him to fish. After a few months he obtained permission papers to return and visit the family. During the visit, the Naths' palm frond shelter burned down—along with the permission papers—so the brother had to try and return to work without his papers. The Khmer Rouge caught him and threw him in jail.

After a period in jail, he came to see the family but was so changed—old and shrivelled like a grandpa—that Prum hardly recognized him. He told Prum and his mother that he had received hardly anything to eat, whether working or in jail, just watery rice soup. He returned to the lake work site and Prum neither saw nor heard from him again.

Mrs. Nath, Prum and the oldest sister were left. They clung to each other and stayed in the shelter, just trying to stay alive. Prum and her sister went out daily to bring back any food they could find. This went on for a year.

One morning Prum woke up sick. Mrs. Nath took her to the Khmer Rouge hospital—a makeshift wood and bamboo structure without any medical staff or medicine—and left her there. After a couple of nights Prum felt better and Mrs. Nath returned and brought her back to their hut. On Prum's first night home from the hospital, Mrs. Nath, Prum and her sister slept on the same mat together, as was their custom. In the morning, Mrs. Nath didn't wake up; she had died during the night.

Neighbors heard the girls' cries and came and told the older sister to take Prum away. Prum's sister took her hand and led her away to hunt for food. While they were gone, the neighbors buried Mrs. Nath. Prum and her sister were orphans.

When the Khmer Rouge saw that all the family was dead except for the two girls, they arrived in a jeep and drove Prum and her sister to an orphanage far away in the country. The sisters were put to work planting fields of corn and potatoes, working hard every day.

After five months the Khmer Rouge came and took the older children in the orphanage away to work in the rice fields. Prum's older sister was taken and Prum was left planting vegetables. Prum neither saw nor heard from her sister again. Prum Nath was now alone in the world.

Prum became friendly with a girl named Sheng, who was her own age at the orphanage. Sheng said that although she was in the orphanage, she had a mother still living. The two girls became very close and watched out for each other.

In 1979 the Vietnamese invaded Cambodia, overthrew Pol Pot and his government and installed the Communist puppet regime of Heng

Samrin. Although Prum and Sheng didn't understand the politics, they understood they had a chance to escape and slipped away one night and ran twenty miles to Sheng's mother.

Sheng's mother seemed glad to see them, but was agitated, telling the girls that everyone was saying it was safer to be in Phnom Penh instead of the countryside. The three of them packed up everything in the house and ran to the city, where they found an empty hut and moved in.

The Vietnamese soldiers were raping the older girls; people said the soldiers liked Cambodian women. Fortunately Prum and Sheng were still little girls without breasts and feminine curves—although nine, they looked about six because of malnutrition. The soldiers weren't interested and passed them by in favor of the pretty teenagers. Sheng's mother was too old for the soldiers' taste, so the three were left alone in safety.

Sheng's mother had saved some gold from before the war and had carefully transported it with her during each move. At this time she took the gold and gave it to a rickshaw driver in exchange for a ride to the border for the three of them.

The rickshaw man kept his part of the deal and left them exactly at the border, still in Cambodia but right next to Thailand. The three built a small hut and moved in.

A couple months later, the two girls and Sheng's mother made a dash for the border. They crossed over safely and were running toward Khao-I-Dang refugee camp when Sheng's mother physically broke down. She lay on the ground in excruciating pain and couldn't move. Sheng and Prum sat down next to the sick woman. After several hours a doctor drove up in a car and took the three of them to Khao-I-Dang. Prum always considered this to be a stroke of luck since most refugees never had a chance to ride in a car or get into Khao-I-Dang.

The doctor put Sheng's mother into the Red Cross hospital and the two girls stayed by her side. The staff gave Sheng's mother rice to eat which she shared with Sheng and Prum, so they were all eating enough again. Sheng's mother slept in the hospital bed and the two girls slept on a cot next to her. Prum observed that white people ran the hospital; she assumed they were French because she didn't know any other kind of white people.

Slowly, Sheng's mother's condition improved. After a year, she was able to get up from her bed and move around. From then on, she would walk around every day, getting stronger and stronger.

One day Sheng's mother called Prum and Sheng over.

"I can't afford to support you," she said to Prum, "I don't have any rice and besides, I'm just a newcomer to the Khao-I-Dang camp."

She left the hospital, taking Sheng with her, leaving Prum forsaken and forlorn. Prum didn't know what else to do so she stayed where she was, sleeping in the cot at night. The staff kept giving her rice and didn't seem to mind.

As Sheng and her mother abandoned Prum, another patient in the bed across the way was watching. She was also a mother—her husband, three older children and a younger girl named Chea were staying in the hospital with her. She approached Prum and spoke to her; gradually they got to know each other. Prum found out that Chea had been "unofficially adopted" by the family. When the mother was discharged four months later, she approached Prum.

"Do you want to come and live with us?" she asked Prum. Prum said yes and the mother "unofficially adopted" Prum also.

Once Prum had joined the family and the family was back in their shelter in Khao-I-Dang, the father began making Prum work. He forced her to carry big buckets of water all over the camp to sell to other refugees. Prum said she wanted to go to the school that had just opened in Khao-I-Dang but the father said she must work instead. He began to hit her and call her lazy.

Sometimes when Prum finished carrying water to sell, she ran off to play with the other children. Each of these times, the father searched her out, dragged her home and beat her with a bamboo stick on the back. The beatings increased; he began to beat her for no reason. Prum was very unhappy and cried constantly.

One day Prum couldn't stand it any longer. She ran away to the school and stayed there all day. When the school closed for the day, she went to the market and walked around and around. When it grew late and the market closed, she went back to her neighborhood but slept in another backyard. The next morning she made sure she was gone by 6 a.m. before any of the family woke up and saw her. She did this every day and night for a week and during that entire week, she didn't eat anything.

A friend from school—Hia—saw her on the eighth day and asked why she wasn't going home to her family. Prum replied that she had run away. Hia said Prum could come and live with her; she had a father and one younger brother but her mother had died.

Prum moved in with Hia's family and they all treated her very well, including the father. It was a good situation and Prum felt very content.

One day Hia's father took Prum aside and spoke to her very gently.

"Prum," he said, "I can't support you any longer. If you go into the orphanage here at Khao-I-Dang you would have plenty of food and maybe even a chance to go to another country."

He spoke kindly and was very considerate of her feelings but Prum didn't want to listen because she liked living with the family. So she pushed aside the father's words and continued on as before.

A couple of days later, Prum saw Chea, the girl that the family with the abusive father had "unofficially adopted" before Prum. Chea had run away and was searching for Prum.

Prum asked, "What are you doing here?"

Chea said, "I ran away from home."

Chea joined Prum in staying with Hia's family. One night Prum realized that she and Chea had to leave; Hia's father simply couldn't support the both of them. Prum understood this and knew what she had to do.

"Do you want to go with me to the orphanage?" she asked Chea. Chea said she did.

"If we're in the orphanage," Prum went on, "we'll have a chance to go to a third country."

(No one talked about going to America, they said "going to a third country." Cambodia was the first country, Thailand was the second country and any other country was the third country.)

Without saying goodbye, Prum and Chea ran to the orphanage in Khao-I-Dang. In the orphanage they were given plenty of food, new clothes, and best of all, they were told they would start school the next day.

"I'm going to school again!" Prum told Chea excitedly.

Every month the orphanage officials walked around and interviewed various children, asking them all sorts of questions: What is your background? Are you healthy? and so on.

A year later Prum was transferred to Chon Buri Orphanage in Thailand on the Gulf of Siam. Chea stayed behind.

For three months Prum stayed in Chon Buri and underwent a battery of tests. She was seen by doctors who asked about her health, gave her shots and asked about her background: what did her mother and father do? They even checked to see if she was going mad. She was taken into a room with a doctor and some officials and told to take off her clothes and spin around to see if she had any diseases. She didn't. She was asked what her last name was but couldn't remember, so she chose the name "Nath" out of thin air and said that on the spot.

While undergoing the tests, Prum remembered that Hia's father had said that in the orphanage she'd have a chance to go to a third country. With each test, Prum grew more and more certain that she was going to go to a third country. Toward the end of the tests, when they told her she was going to America, she was ecstatic: America! America was freedom! America was heaven!

They told her that she was going to the state of Minnesota and added, "That state is very cold."

Prum didn't have any idea about real cold, so they said, "There's a lot of snow there."

Prum asked, "What is snow?"

They answered, "Snow is ice falling."

They told Prum that a family was waiting for her in America. Prum assumed they were talking about her Cambodian birth family because she thought her brother and sister were still living.

The orphanage officials took her to the airport and helped her board the plane. It was her first plane ride. She couldn't eat and vomited as they crossed the Pacific Ocean. The plane stopped in Taiwan, Hong Kong, France, Seattle, and finally: Minneapolis, Minnesota.

As Prum disembarked and walked out into the waiting area of the Minneapolis airport, the first person she saw was the Cambodian social worker. Because she was expecting her Cambodian birth family to be there, she thought this man was her brother and went forward eagerly, only to be brought up short when she saw that he was a stranger.

The social worker greeted her in Khmer and told her that he was going to take her to live with her American sponsor family. Instantly Prum realized this was the "family" that the orphanage officials had spoken of and that she wasn't going to see her brother and sister. She was devastated but didn't show it to the social worker.

The social worker drove her to the Skipstead home in Richfield, Minnesota, where there was another girl named Terry who spoke Khmer. Prum began to feel slightly better. Mrs. Skipstead introduced Prum to other Cambodian refugees and enrolled her in ninth grade at the local high school.

When three months had passed, Prum was moved to her permanent home with the Larson* family in Excelsior, Minnesota. The Larsons had a girl named Jennifer* who was Prum's age and a boy named John*. The family seemed nice enough to Prum; however, she had been in so many families that this was just one more. She and Jennifer seemed to get along well; the two girls shared a room and talked at night while lying in their twin beds. Prum began tenth grade at Minnetonka High School.

A boy named Bunna called Prum on the telephone. He said that he

*pseudonym

had heard that a new girl from Cambodia had arrived and since he also attended Minnetonka High School, he would introduce her to his friends.

The next day Bunna came up to Prum at school, wearing a huge smile. He introduced Prum to a group of boys: Bo, Bat, and lastly, his cousin-brother, Noeun Nor. Prum liked all the boys except for Noeun who seemed cool and unfriendly. He didn't seem to like Prum either. (Later, he was to tell her that he had been intimidated because she was so pretty.)

Prum was having a hard time learning English so Bunna began tutoring her; Bunna was an excellent student. They became very close like a brother and sister; in fact, he informally adopted her as his sister. When he called her on the phone, he said, "This is your brother, Bunna."

On the occasion of Prum's sixteenth birthday, Mrs. Larson gave a big party and invited all of her friends. Noeun came but was still cool toward her.

Suddenly it seemed that everywhere Prum went in a group, Noeun was also there. They kept seeing each other in group situations and after a long time, Noeun began to like Prum more and more. Prum, on her part, grew to know Noeun better and see that the gruff, angry facade was not the real Noeun. They began dating.

Prum graduated from Minnetonka High School. She and Noeun talked about Prum getting her own apartment. Prum was a bit fearful of the idea but said she would talk to Mrs. Larson about it.

Mrs. Larson said, "I don't know. People might think you are a loose girl and spread rumors around."

Prum grew angry. She didn't like the idea of people talking about her and judging her by whether or not she had her own apartment. She didn't like the sound of the whole thing.

So the next time Noeun came to pick her up for a date, she put all her stuff in his car and he drove her to Mathy's house. Mathy* was a Cambodian girl who lived with her sponsor in Minneapolis. Prum knocked on their door and said she needed a place to stay. They asked her inside, gave her a room in the house and she moved in.

While living at Mathy's, Prum learned how to drive. She also got a job at Delta Dental in Bloomington, Minnesota, doing data entries. Things were going well: she had a job and was making some money. She and Noeun were dating but not yet talking about marriage.

Noeun located his birth mother in Boston. He went to Boston on a

*pseudonym

visit and to consider the possibility of a future move to that city. Prum wanted to visit Boston and—even though they weren't yet talking about marriage—she wanted to be near Noeun, so she went along.

Prum and Noeun stayed with Noeun's mother, brother and sister as well as Bunna's mother and some other relatives, in a house in Boston. The situation was tolerable for Prum but not pleasant. Mrs. Nor didn't like her and made that very clear.

As Prum and Noeun became more serious, Mrs. Nor took Noeun aside and said, "I want a different type of girl for you. I want someone that I pick, a traditional Cambodian girl—not an orphan from the war."

Noeun and Prum went ahead and set a date for the wedding despite the objections of Mrs. Nor. They returned to Minneapolis and then came back to Boston in 1989 to be married in a traditional Cambodian wedding over the course of several days. All the relatives, as well as Prum's foster parents, Mr. and Mrs. Larson, celebrated in Cambodian style with sumptuous feasts, exquisite costumes and elaborate ceremonies. As she knelt in a silk gown at the side of her strong and handsome husband in front of the Cambodian monk, Prum felt very happy.

Prum and Noeun returned to Minneapolis after the wedding and rented a small apartment. After their return, Bunna—Noeun's cousin-brother and the boy that called himself Prum's adopted brother—died in his sleep in Boston. Prum had lost yet another brother.

Prum applied for a job at Norwest Bank. When she went in to apply, they gave her various tests—a typing test and other tests that involved asking her lots of questions on how to execute different procedures. While she was answering these questions, she noticed that a Caucasian girl came in to apply for the same job and no one gave her tests nor asked her questions.

Both Prum and the Caucasian girl were hired. Prum was glad to have the job but resented having had to take all the tests. Then, after they both began working, Prum found out the Caucasian girl didn't even know how to type! Prum got very angry and felt she had been unfairly treated but didn't know what to do. Mrs. Larson said she should report the incident to the Department of Labor because they secretly sent in people of various nationalities to apply for jobs to see if they were discriminated against during the application process.

"I don't think Americans like Asians," Prum said to Mrs. Larson, "American people have it 100 percent easier. They have the right background, the right education. I'm not like Americans. I'm not Cambodian; I'm not American. I don't know what I am now." At last she concluded simply, "I'm Prum."

Prum continued to work for Norwest Bank until she was ready to deliver her first child a year later, then quit. Seventeen months later she had another baby. She and Noeun were now the parents of a daughter and a son and she thought no more about working at Norwest.

The first years after the children were born were difficult, a situation exacerbated by Noeun's mother, Mrs. Nor, who didn't visit, even to see her new grandchildren. Prum felt Mrs. Nor was not acting like a proper grandmother and knew why: Mrs. Nor had made it clear that she didn't want her son marrying Prum Nath.

She said Prum wasn't a traditional Cambodian woman. For example, Prum doesn't *sampeah*. In America, a woman can say "hello" and leave it at that, but in Cambodia, it is correct for a woman to *sampeah* or bow in the traditional way as a sign of respect. Many Cambodian girls learned traditional behavior from their mothers but Prum never had the chance.

When the children were one and two, Prum went back to work as a data analyst. After several years—shortly before their daughter was to start kindergarten and their son was four—they had saved enough money to put a down payment on a new house in Chaska, Minnesota.

Prum doesn't like to think about the Pol Pot years but they are always there in the background.

"I think about my family that died, how my brother was beat up, how my father died, and I cry," she says. "It's hard. At times I feel really sad because there was no one there for me. When that one 'adopted' father at the camp beat me, I was so sad because I knew my own, real, father would never beat me."

"I can't explain why I lived," she continues. "I'm strong. Also, I'm healthy—I never got really sick. I was able to go out and find food."

Then she grows downcast. "Also, my mom didn't eat her rice, instead, she gave it to us kids. That's also a reason for how I was able to live. But for that, my mom had to die."

Prum occasionally grows depressed when she thinks about her life, how there has been no one there for her, no one to take care of her and protect her. She calls Mrs. Larson "Mom" but recognizes that's not entirely accurate. She feels like she doesn't have a mother.

When Prum was living with the Larsons, she felt Mrs. Larson liked her own daughter, Jennifer, better than Prum.

She once said to Jennifer, "Why don't you think Mom loves me?"

Jennifer said, "She loves you—but in a different way."

To Prum, this wasn't an answer. The way she perceived it, Mrs. Larson either loved her like a daughter or she didn't. Prum knew that Mrs. Larson "liked" her, but not in the same way that she "loved" Jennifer.

Once again, Prum felt abandoned. Life in America, in the land of plenty, mirrored life in Cambodia during the war for Prum: she didn't have a mother or a father or any family. She was still an orphan.

7

Why Do Some Survive?

Upon spending time with survivors—hearing the stories of torture, starvation and narrow escapes—the listener asks the question: "Why did this survivor survive and not others?" I know I certainly asked it; throughout my recording of each survivor's story that question nagged at the back of my mind. Why this person? What did this person do that separated him or her from all the others who died? It was as if I could answer that question, the world would still make sense; otherwise, the Cambodian autogenocide would have forever turned the norms of our world upside down.

The survivors themselves are mystified by the question.

"I just don't know how to answer that question," Sinn says. "Sometimes I think that I was able to work harder on less food, and that's how I was able to survive. But still, I don't know. After all, why me? Another thing was, you had to listen to the Khmer Rouge and do what they wanted and not talk back. But everyone did that—no one ever talked back to the Khmer Rouge—everyone was too scared, so that doesn't explain why they didn't kill me."

Noeun says, "There were many times I should have died. A lot of people just like me were killed. It's like someone has taken care of me— God, Buddha, whatever."

However, he also did whatever his potential killers told him to do. "Some soldiers were nice and others were just mean—like if you didn't walk fast enough they kicked you in the back. Or if they told you something and you looked at them, they took the end of the gun and hit you across the face. No one did that to me—but I never looked at them. Whatever they said, I did it. That's why I'm alive. You cannot fight them; you cannot win."

Noeun also made it possible for Bunna to survive. It seems unlikely that Bunna could have survived without Noeun's help—there were too many obstacles that he would not have surmounted on his own. He would not have escaped the camp because he could barely walk; Noeun had to physically drag him to the Thai border. Bunna would not have survived in the jungle because he wasn't strong enough to kill animals for food; every day Noeun laid Bunna on a towel and then went out to kill animals that they could eat. "Bunna could not run," Noeun states. "So I had to grab him and pull him all the way. ... We killed animals that we could eat. I had to do all the killing because Bunna was too weak. He just laid on the ground."

Buddhist monks Mouth Ouk (on right) and cousin in 1951 standing in front of an altar marking the beginning of the construction of a pagoda in Kompong Chhang province. There were 2,800 pagodas and 82,000 monks in Cambodia before the Pol Pot regime. The agents of Pol Pot destroyed pagodas and articles of worship (including two bronze statues from the Angkor period), burned Buddhist books and killed monks. No pagodas and only a small number of monks survived the auto-genocide. (Photograph from the personal collection of Sophea Mouth.)

Bunna was taken to the refugee camp—and from there to America—because of Noeun. The doctor found Nouen, wounded, by the border and so took him to the hospital in his car—and Bunna came along.

There is no one answer to the question: Why me? For each survivor, the answer is as varied and complex as the story behind it; however, there are, I believe, certain similarities in the lives and unfolding of events for survivors that offer general explanations.

First, there is the matter of luck. When I interviewed the survivors, they consistently spoke of having "luck" and "being lucky." Or of some-one or something looking out for them—which could mean the same thing.

"Before the war, I was a Buddhist," Noeun says, "I went to the pagoda with my grandmother, my mom, my dad, and prayed to Buddha. I think he has protected me. But here in America I believe in God. I believe in all religions—anything that keeps you safe, keeps you from being wild. It's more like I believe in myself. If I do good, no one can hurt me; if I do bad, I'm going to get hurt from somebody else."

So, due to being lucky or experiencing the luck of the gods, some survived. All day long in the work camps people fell down from exhaus-tion, were kicked out of the way to die in the heat or bludgeoned to death on the spot by a guard, but then suddenly, inexplicably, a guard asked one boy who had fallen down if he felt all right and helped him to his feet. Luck. It's the only word to describe the turn of events that allows some-one to live when killing is the norm.

But there must be more than luck. Or perhaps, a better way to put it is: Why then, are some lucky when others aren't? I myself noticed a certain personality trait in the survivors whom I interviewed. They were aware of the environment around them and were able to adapt quickly and respond to changes. They seemed to sense particular "saving" truths and were then able to act quickly upon these. I came to label this the "sur-vival instinct."

This meant that when everyone around was starving on the daily ration of one cup of watery rice-gruel per day, and the Khmer Rouge killed anyone caught with food from another source, the survivors found a way to get more food. Sokhary You managed to hide and tend a veg-etable garden right under Khmer Rouge noses; Sam You ate raw rice while transporting it but never stole because the punishment was imme-diate execution.

Moxie is perhaps too frivolous a word to use when referring to such dire circumstances, but it certainly took that, or a more noble form of it—courage—to respond immediately and correctly in such an adverse envi-ronment. Again and again, it was the survivors' ability to read the environment and then respond to the new realities that led to them liv-ing when others died. Moments of choice leading to enormous conse-quences—either for good or bad—came suddenly and the survivor was one who could intuitively read the situation and make the right choice.

Also, moral courage: the morally right action in the face of adver-sity, which then led to life, rather than expected death. I think of the boy who told the Khmer Rouge that he would not go kill his parents even after being ordered to do so—and they let it go. He did what he knew was right and was not killed. One could say that perhaps this was simply luck; or perhaps the showing of such courage made the guard pause and alter his usual reaction, thereby changing the outcome.

But of course none of these—luck, adapting to the environment, moral courage and strength of character—were possible without physical strength and prowess. During the first few years of Pol Pot's rule, the first segment of the population to die were the sick, the elderly, the very young, and the infirm. The death march of April 17, 1975, immediately eliminated the very weakest from the population.

Only sheer physical strength made it possible to survive years with hardly any food or water, constant physical labor and little rest. Pol Pot, in reforming Cambodian society backwards into a rural, agrarian society, turned the country into a giant forced-labor camp, where the rules of civilization protected no one, and certainly not the weak. The only law was one of survival.

There was an amendment to this law of survival, and that was help from one's fellow humans. Yes, one survived if one physically could, but also, time after time, one survived because another—in time of crisis or need—reached out a hand to save. I think of the mother who slowly starved herself to death by giving her grains of rice to her daughters day after day. Or the nurse who somehow found real medicine to give a sick child, when the Khmer Rouge had forbidden all real medicine and were using grass.

Or the father whose story was recounted by his son, Mr. Kim Sokha, in the genocide trial of Pol Pot and Ieng Sary in Cambodia in 1979. Here is the son's account as published in *Genocide in Cambodia: Documents from the Trial of Pol Pot and Ieng Sary* (De Nike, Quigley, and Robinson, eds.):

> On the night of June 2, 1975, at midnight, in the moonlight, my younger brother, my father, and I were sleeping in the same bed, in front of our cottage. I heard a man call to me, "Brother, brother." I got up quickly and saw a man named Sok, the head of our village, and a soldier carrying a rifle on his shoulder.
>
> I asked him, "Whom are you looking for?" Sok replied, "Angkar is looking for your father." I awoke my father by shaking his legs. He got up quickly, quite frightened. The soldier told my father, "Brother, get your luggage ready and come with me. The organization orders you to go to the political school for two weeks. Don't bring much with you because you will be back soon."
>
> Thinking back on my conversation the other day with the

soldier, I asked, "Are you asking for my father or for me?" My father interrupted, "He is calling me, not you." Then my father went into the cottage to say goodbye to my mother, who was shaking in fear. He came out and joined the two men with his luggage and left. They headed south. But at a distance of about fifty meters, I saw seven or eight men, all armed, coming out of the bamboo woods to take my father south of the woods. My mother, my grandmother, and I watched until they were out of sight. ...

The next day we wanted to do everything we could to find out where they had taken my father. I went to make inquiries, but that morning there was a meeting. The following day, at noon, I asked my uncle to go with me south of the woods that was about five hundred meters from my village, under the pretext that we were looking for wood to build our shelter.

When we got to the middle of the woods, near a kdol tree I saw an old scarf stuck on a thorny plant. It was my father's scarf. I jumped back. Five meters to the south I saw a new grave. There was blood on the ground and on the plants near the grave. There was also a bamboo stick all bloody near the grave. That is how my father was killed!

Like golden threads through the dark fabric of the survivors' stories run the examples of people who gave of themselves in order that others might live. I see this as the single hope for a world that can descend into such violence and brutality. Some are known, some will never be known. In the time of Pol Pot and his bloody Khmer Rouge, these few retained what it meant to be human. Pol Pot was attempting to rid the world of humanity; he wanted a society where moral fiber was irrelevant, where one worked and obeyed orders and that was all.

François Ponchaud, a French missionary in Cambodia at the time when the autogenocide was beginning, writes of his own emotions when witnessing the revolution and its lack of consideration for human factors: "Refusing shelter to the sick and injured makes one feel one has lost one's last shred of human dignity."

Ponchaud also quotes a Khmer Rouge soldier interviewed by the Thai journal *Prachachat* in the June 10, 1976, issue, during the second year of the autogenocide. The Khmer Rouge voices this loss of humanity in the interview, but, chillingly, appears not to recognize it as such:

The Khmer methods do not require a large amount of personnel; there are no heavy charges to bear because everyone is simply thrown out of town. If we may take the liberty of making a comparison, the Khmers have adopted the method which consists in overturning the basket with all the fruit inside; then, choosing only the articles that satisfy them completely, they put them back in the basket. The Vietnamese did not tip over the basket, they picked out the rotten fruit. The latter method involves a much greater loss of time than that employed by the Khmers.

Clearly, when one is talking about humans rather than fruit, tipping over the basket involves some loss of the human soul. The few who retained their humanity by refusing to go along with the collective were the few who carried along and insured the survival of human civilization.

There is a cost for surviving when others do not. The symptoms of Post-Traumatic Stress Disorder include: Recurring and distressing dreams of the event, flashback episodes, feelings of detachment or estrangement from others, limited range of feelings, difficulty falling or staying asleep, irritability or outbursts of anger, and difficulty concentrating. Nearly all survivors of the Cambodian autogenocide—and all the survivors I interviewed for this book—exhibited some of the symptoms of Post-Traumatic Stress Disorder. Many are incapacitated to the point where they have difficulty living a functioning, normal life in America due to these symptoms.

In 1984 a team of professors from Oregon Health Sciences University began observing a group of Cambodian youths in order to study Cambodian refugee trauma. Massive trauma occurred to these youths when they were between six and twelve years old; all were attending a local high school when first interviewed in 1984. Half of the 40 adolescents who had gone through the Pol Pot regime qualified for a diagnosis of PTSD.

In 1987 the team reinterviewed 30 of the survivors. They found that PTSD among Khmer refugees persisted but that it fluctuated over time. They also found a slight decrease in depression; depression disappeared with time and adaptation to the new culture. In summary, the symptoms of PTSD became less frequent and intense over time.

In 2000 another group of Cambodian refugees in Utah were interviewed concerning their mental health. This study found that PTSD and depression were still rampant among Cambodian refugees. The greater the number of war traumas, the greater the risk of both PTSD and major depression. The refugees who experienced stress due to resettlement increased their risk of both PTSD and major depression.

The stresses of resettlement were: lack of adequate English language skills (77 percent); thoughts about family members who had been left behind (63 percent); transportation problems (62 percent); and thoughts about people they had known who had been killed during the Pol Pot years (60 percent). In the year preceding the interview, the participants rated as "very stressful" the following: worries about the future in the United States (27 percent); health worries (26 percent); worries about family left behind in Cambodia (24 percent); and worries about not having enough money (23 percent).

Those who were able to survive the Pol Pot regime will always bear scars from their experience. These scars are the cost of survival.

So yes, there is a price to survival, and it's never fully paid. In a sense, even those who survived Pol Pot and his Khmer Rouge are still condemned. They'll live out their lives bearing the effects, never to forget, always suffering. But the strength that made them survivors can also carry them through to a new life in America, to living in the now despite the awareness of what happened then, to holding onto hope in the face of a world which has once gone terribly awry.

8

A Land of Opportunity: The Story of Sam and Sokhary You

Sam and Sokhary You grew up in rural villages in Cambodia. Sam was born in the village of Prapaing Peap in Kompong Speu Province, where his family—although not wealthy by any means—was regarded as the most prominent in the village. While still in lower school, Sam decided that he was not going to be a farmer like his father and grandfather before him. His parents supported him in this unusual decision, even to the point of giving him a motorbike so he could attend school in a neighboring village.

Sokhary was born to a family with eight children in the small village of Samrong Yong. Her parents were also farmers. Sokhary met Sam when she went to help her sister—who had married a man in Prapaing Peap—with a new baby. Sam and Sokhary bumped into each other on a village path and stopped to talk. From then on whenever they ran into each other they exchanged greetings.

In 1970 the Khmer Rouge were battling Lon Nol's forces for the countryside; however, the Khmer Rouge called themselves "revolutionaries" and hid their Communist roots because, on the whole, Cambodians distrusted Communism. Many Cambodians had emigrated from China and told dire stories of life under Communist rule.

The Khmer Rouge were guerrilla soldiers; they hid in the jungle and woods during the day, then crept into the villages at night to "explain about the situation," or forcibly recruit young men for their cause. Fortunately, Sam, who had by this time decided to become a schoolteacher, had moved to Phnom Penh to attend *lycée*, or high school, and had thus avoided being drafted, or abducted, by the Khmer Rouge.

In an effort to counter the nighttime visits, the Lon Nol govern-

ment—backed by American advisors, planes and bombs— began bombarding the countryside. The nightly bombings brought irrevocable changes to prewar Cambodia's peaceful rural villages. A plane dumped gasoline on Prapaing Peap and then bombed it. Although the You family survived, the entire village of 100 houses burned to the ground, including their house, so they had to move to Phnom Penh.

After the village of Samrong Yong was bombed one night, Sokhary's family also prepared to move to Phnom Penh. At the last minute, Sokhary's mother and father refused to go, so Sokhary stayed behind with them. They dug a hole behind the house to use as a bomb shelter and

Sam and Sokhary You with their newborn son in front of their shelter at the Khao-I-Dang refugee camp, 1981. (Photograph by Catholic Relief Services worker and from the personal collection of Sam and Sokhary You.)

continued to farm. Six months later Sokhary was out in a field with their cow when she spotted a B-52 flying low in the distance. She left the cow, ran home, grabbed her parents and they ran to the shelter. They huddled there for hours as bombs landed all around them, the ground shook, and fire flashed. The noise was deafening.

When it was over, they came out. The village lay in ruins; whatever hadn't been hit directly had caught fire and burned to the ground.

Sokhary's mother surveyed the damage, then turned to her daughter and said, "All right, let's move."

Within days they were living in Phnom Penh. Sokhary went to stay with a married sister and her three children while her parents went to live with another daughter. Sokhary and Sam discovered that they were living next door to each other. Sam told Sokhary that he was working as an elementary school teacher in Phnom Penh; despite the turmoil he had finished his studies and been certified as an elementary school teacher.

Sam and Sokhary met more and more often. In time they disclosed their mutual attraction. They were married in 1972, when Sam was twenty-one and Sokhary was eighteen.

Although the government of Lon Nol nominally controlled Cambodia, the Khmer Rouge kept moving closer and closer to their goal of the capital city. Sam accepted a government teaching position in Siemreap Oddar Mean Chey Province adjacent to Thailand, even though—due to the war's effect on the country's economy—the salary of an elementary school teacher was not enough to live on. Sam and Sokhary decided that Sam would first go by himself and Sokhary would follow a month later. They were together in Siemreap Oddar Mean Chey Province when their first child Elida, a daughter, was born in 1973.

By 1974 inflation had risen so rapidly and the fighting in the countryside had become so severe that Sam and Sokhary moved back to Phnom Penh. However, in Phnom Penh, things had gone from bad to worse. Before the war, the government-controlled teacher's salary had been the equivalent of $200 a month, now it was the equivalent of $10 a month. Before the war, one dollar had equaled 56 *riel*, now one dollar was worth 2,500 *riel*. These conditions prompted a general month-long, nationwide teacher's strike of twenty thousand teachers which was finally resolved by teachers agreeing to teach for two months, then take ten months off to work at another job in order to make up the salary lack.

Following this strike settlement, Sam went off for a two month teaching stint in Kompong Speu Province, leaving Sokhary and Elida with his family. But the fighting was so close to Kompong Speu that after one month he frantically searched for a way back. Cars couldn't get through any longer, but he was able to buy a ride back to the city on a military helicopter. He rejoined his family in Phnom Penh in January when all the newspapers and radio broadcasts were saying that the U.S. had cut off all aid to Cambodia. When the Cambodian people heard this, they knew it was only a matter of time until the Lon Nol government—and Phnom Penh—fell. The Lon Nol soldiers stopped fighting and dragged their guns behind them as they returned to Phnom Penh to wait for the end.

On Cambodian New Year, April 13, 1975, Sokhary and Sam left Elida with Sam's parents and rode bikes to a suburb to visit Sokhary's mother. The fighting grew so fierce along the way that Sokhary wondered whether she would ever see her daughter again. She and Sam arrived at Sokhary's mother's house, handed over the food Sokhary had brought, stayed for a half an hour, then Sokhary's mother sent the couple back home.

Four days later, on the morning of April 17, 1975, Sam and Sokhary awoke to the sound of gunfire. They got up, went outside and met the Khmer Rouge invading the city—children and teenagers dressed in black, carrying AK-47s.

A Khmer Rouge soldier came up to Sam and Sokhary standing with their neighbors and said, "OK, you can go anywhere you want now—go back to your own villages."

Another soldier came along, pointed, and said, "No, go this way."

Then some others said, "Oh, don't worry. Just stay here."

For about two hours everyone was hopeful: Peace at last! End of the war! Sam thought of how he could begin a new life with his family and return to teaching.

Then some other Khmer Rouge soldiers came along and flatly said, "Get out."

When people demurred, they gave out easy reassurances: "You won't have to leave your homes for long, so don't take a lot of things. You just have to leave for a few days because the new government of the Revolution is worried that the U.S. is going to bomb the city. Don't take too much; we'll take care of everything."

A man asked if he could go get his wife and the soldier said, "Don't worry about it. She'll meet you there. Go this way."

Everyone began putting things in carts and leaving. The You family decided to stay one more night because the streets were so crowded. The next morning, the extended You family, consisting of Sam, Sokhary, Elida, Sam's sister, Sam's brother and his family, Sam's parents—fourteen people in all—left the city. All they had for transportation was one bike. Sokhary carried a bag of clothes on her head and walked beside Elida, who at two was still nursing; it soon became clear that Elida couldn't keep up so Sokhary carried her on her hip. Mrs. You was so weak that the brothers took turns pushing her on the bike.

The roads were a seething mass of people. The family saw corpses lying alongside the road. They passed houses burning with people still inside. They saw some Khmer Rouge ordering a man and wife out of their house; the couple resisted and the soldiers shot them on the spot. Sokhary was shocked and very frightened, carrying Elida in a daze. There were so many people leaving the city that the You family covered only two miles the entire day. They slept on the road that night.

The next day they covered a few more miles. After several days of walking, they reached the outskirts of the city.

At the edge of the city, a female soldier swept her eyes over the mass of people, pointed at Sam and said, "Come here."

Sam had four ID's. During the walk, he had torn all of them up except for the one that identified him as a teacher because he thought the Khmer Rouge liked teachers as teachers had a history of supporting the revolution.

Sam went forward and the soldier asked, "What do you do?"

Sam said, "I am a teacher."

Sokhary's heart stopped. She didn't know what the new government liked or didn't like, but they had seen dead people, bodies lying in the road, houses burning with people inside. She was sure her husband was going to be taken away.

But Sam was lucky. The Khmer Rouge soldier, who was probably trying to ferret out Lon Nol soldiers, said, "Are you sure that you're a teacher?" giving Sam a chance to change his answer.

At this, Sam's father went forward and assured her that Sam really was a teacher. Sokhary, standing at the back, was dumbstruck at the stupidity of the men. The soldier shrugged and let Sam go back to his family.

When Sam reached the group, his cousin said to him, "Don't say that you're a teacher again. Don't say that anymore. You might not get a second chance."

Upon hearing his cousin's words, Sam began to think what a lucky escape he had had. Sam also thought of how the Cambodian people had been duped into believing that the new government would be fair, good and full of justice.

The You family finally reached their home village of Prapaing Peap. Though they had once been villagers, or old people, since they had moved into Phnom Penh, they were now considered slaves, or new people, and their old neighbors, farmers of the countryside, were the rulers, or old people. The Yous were now shunned by their old friends and neighbors.

Some old friends took Mrs. You aside and whispered, "We can't be seen talking to you. We have to follow the rules because we're afraid too."

The Yous settled in at Prapaing Peap. There was little food for the new people to begin with and it got to be less and less. Sam felt *Angkar* was trying to kill the new people by starvation, overwork and other indirect means—but as long as the Yous stayed in Prapaing Peap it was difficult. Distant relatives would put food inside their shirts so the guards wouldn't see and then slip it to the family. Or the Yous would go visit people and would be given food while they visited. Also, it turned out that Sokhary was an expert at producing food out of nowhere. The You family began to rely on her indomitable strength—whatever it took to stay alive she would do.

After three months of this the Khmer Rouge seemed to realize how hard it was going to be to starve out the new people while they were living in the midst of old friends and relatives.

One day the Khmer Rouge came and said, "You are moving to Battambang where you will get new houses. Don't worry, everything will be fine."

They loaded the new people into the backs of forty-eight trucks—Sokhary counted them—and drove to Battambang Province in the north, about 350 kilometers from Phnom Penh.

When the Yous got off the truck, they were issued a large ration of rice—approximately enough to last three days—and the Khmer Rouge left. There were no houses or anything else for them. That night they slept under a tree.

The following morning Sokhary went to work. She organized the family and helped them cut down bamboo saplings and tie them together into walls and cut the tall *shov* grass to make a thatch roof. Sam didn't know how to do any of this because he had always been a student.

Ten days later, the rice rations were cut in half. They were also told the rules:

> No one can walk without permission.
> No one can go from one place to another to find food.
> One must only eat the food that the Khmer Rouge gives out.
> No one can own food privately; all food is collective.
> No one can own their hut.
> No one can go out and forage for food.
> Breaking any of these rules is punishable by beating or worse.

At this point the new people were working for part of the morning and had the rest of the day free, so the Yous started to bend the rules and look for small crabs on the way to and from work. They were careful not to get caught because the punishment—if caught breaking the rules—was to be beaten with a big stick. People were slowly starting to starve. Sokhary was still nursing Elida but could tell she was losing her milk because of lack of food.

After three months of this, the Yous decided to move. They had heard that a neighboring village might have more food so they picked up and ran three miles farther to another place. Mrs. You was so weak and sick that her sons had to carry her in a hammock.

It was the same pattern as before: In the beginning they received a large ration of rice, but then the ration was cut and cut until they were starving again. Only this time Sokhary was prepared and had planted a little garden of corn and potatoes away from the soldiers' prying eyes. All the family ate of the produce from this garden and that helped a little.

But then the garden crops were gone. Mrs. You was starving and on the brink of death.

She called Sokhary to her and whispered, "Fix me anything to eat, anything you can find."

So Sokhary went to the Khmer Rouge leader of the village and begged him for a tiny bit of rice.

He said, "No, you can't have any. It's private."

On her way back to the hut, Sokhary looked for anything edible, but saw only bare dirt. Finally, in desperation, she surreptitiously gathered some weeds from around their hut, put them in water and added salt. She set this stew to cook for quite a while so it wouldn't be tough, but before it was done, Mrs. You died.

The Khmer Rouge wouldn't let Sam and his brother go to find wood to make a coffin, so the family had to wrap Mrs. You up in a sleeping mat that was torn and full of holes and bury her that way.

Sam was never to recover from his mother's death. The woman who had borne and nursed him, who had always supported him in his studies; he had let her die from lack of food. He was always to blame himself in some way for not having done more, even though at the time of her death he was so weak himself that he was crawling like a baby.

Shortly after, Mr. You also died of starvation. The older people died first. One of Sam's sisters died of starvation, his nephew, his brother-in-law; nine out of the twenty-one in Sam's extended family died at this time. People fell down and died as they were walking to work in the rice fields. Sokhary saw so many bodies that she stopped caring. Sokhary nursed Elida until one day her milk was completely gone—not even a drop.

Twenty years later Sokhary was to find out what happened to her family during the evacuation and afterwards. Her brother, who was a Lon Nol soldier, was sent back with his wife to his wife's old village; since everyone knew he was a soldier, he was taken out and killed right away. His wife had been a nurse and after finding a blood pressure cuff in her bag, the Khmer Rouge took her away and killed her. Only their children were left. An aunt—who was with the Khmer Rouge—asked if she could save the baby and the Khmer Rouge said no, so the children were killed. Sokhary's father and brother both died of starvation in 1976. Her mother told Sokhary that her father got so hungry at the end, he asked his daughter if she wanted to go fishing. The daughter went and came back with a little sunfish. The father said he would take a tiny nap before eating, and died in his sleep. Many nieces, nephews and brothers-in-law also died during this time.

The Khmer Rouge separated the couples. Sam and Sokhary were put in different huts a mile apart from each other. Sam was too weak to walk the distance and Sokhary was only granted permission to visit once or twice a month so they hardly saw each other. They decided Elida would stay with Sam because Sokhary still had to go out and work in the fields every day. Sam was so weak he couldn't walk, so they let him stay in the hut.

Rations were cut until finally everyone was given only one cup of rice-water with a few grains of rice floating in it per day. Sokhary tried to go out and find food for Elida, but her leg swelled up so that she couldn't walk. She limped out to a dam where she could get water, fell down and had to crawl back. Elida grew so weak that she would walk to Sokhary and fall down on the way and say her head hurt. Sokhary just looked at her. There wasn't much feeling for others; she thought, "Today I die; tomorrow, she does." It didn't seem to make much difference.

Sam grew so weak that he lay on the floor of his hut day and night.

The Khmer Rouge leader came, looked around, then counted on his fingers and said, "OK, we're going to bury thirteen people this week. They aren't dead yet, but by the end of the week they'll be dead."

He named Sam's name first because he was the weakest.

He looked straight at Sam and said, "We're going to bury you this week."

Two mornings later, Elida, who was staying with Sam, got up and walked out of the hut because she missed her mother. Sam didn't go after her because he couldn't get up, but also because it didn't matter to him. With the terrible conditions came a different kind of attitude. It was only a matter of time; they were all waiting for their time to die.

Sokhary was working in a field a mile away when she saw her daughter standing at the edge of the field. It was the rainy season and yet somehow she had crossed the flooded road that lay between them.

"Someone helped me," Elida said to her mother. Someone must have not only helped her to cross the road, but also helped her to walk, because she couldn't really walk herself. (She was three but with the size and strength of a one year old because of malnutrition.)

Sokhary took Elida back to Sam, who was lying immobile on the floor of his hut and left the both of them to go back to work in the field.

It was 1976 and Sam knew he was close to death. Using all his remaining strength, he wrote a note in French. In a kind of literary disguise, he wrote about the "barbarians" and how they were so cruel and killed their own people.

"The barbarians' hands are bloodied by Cambodian blood," he wrote. "Pol Pot's hand has killed Khieu Samphan's hand."

Sam knew that when people died, the Khmer Rouge took the clothing for other people to use. So he put the note inside his shirt so that someone would find the note and read it.

Sam knew when the day of his death had arrived. He knew because he did not even feel hungry, or open his eyes. Lying in a woozy, semi-conscious state, he was faintly aware of his brother coming into the hut, opening his mouth and putting some rice in it.

Sam didn't die that day; he was pulled back from death by the mouthful of rice his brother had given him. Sam's brother was still working out in the fields and thus got more rice than others. Every day he continued to sneak in a few mouthfuls of rice for Sam to eat.

When the Khmer Rouge leader returned at the end of the week, all the other twelve he had named were dead. Only Sam wasn't—because of his brother's grains of rice.

At the harvest season that year, the Khmer Rouge increased the ration of rice from one spoonful of rice per day to one bowl of rice per day. After Sam ate an entire bowl of rice one afternoon he could move his leg a little bit. The next day the Khmer Rouge said, "No more rice" and he couldn't move his leg anymore. Thus Sam knew he had to keep getting more and more food so that he could get stronger. He decided to get more food no matter what.

He began crawling out to the fields each day and working from a seated position so that the Khmer Rouge would give him a worker's rations. He grew stronger and began to walk with a cane.

Sokhary was given permission to move back with Sam and Elida. She was always on the lookout for food. On her way to the full rice fields ready for harvest, she picked up rice grains and put them in her pocket. At the hut she ground them into powder and put the powder in a pan and cooked it over the fire. Sokhary knew that to survive she had to do anything she could to help herself. Occasionally, she stole rice for Sam and Elida, but not all the time, because they were separated and living apart.

Sokhary disobeyed the rule about not owning anything privately and secretly planted all sorts of things. She grew vegetables around the huts and made stews. Another rule was that no one could go out to find their own food. Sokhary also disobeyed this rule and gathered fruit off the trees. The penalty for stealing food was to be killed on the spot, but Sokhary figured that whether she died by stealing or by starving, it was all the same. She was never caught stealing.

The Khmer Rouge were clever. For example, at one point they issued the order that everyone could have their own garden. Then after all the gardens had grown to fruition, the edict came down that the gardens belonged to the Khmer Rouge. Sokhary went ahead and took her own produce anyway.

Sokhary thought Sam was very honorable because he never stole food. Sam knew that he was too afraid to steal; he would rather die by honesty. Sam was half envious of the way Sokhary let nothing get between her and survival—not ethics, not principles, not orders, not fear. Sokhary knew if she had relied on Sam, she would probably have died.

In April 1976 Pol Pot announced that he was in control of the new government of Democratic Kampuchea (the Khmer Rouge name for Cambodia) and put Khieu Samphan under house arrest. Up until then, a specific person in charge had not been named; orders had come down from the ubiquitous *"Angkar."* After April 1976, when the Khmer Rouge turned on the radio to let the people listen, Pol Pot's name was heard frequently. The radio announcer would say, "Pol Pot, Secretary of the Party, today met with ...."

The political fall-out from this change trickled down to the New People. Pol Pot promoted his own type of person to the higher ranks—ruthless and without human emotion, the type that could kill easily. These new Khmer Rouge leaders killed outright, not waiting for starvation to kill people.

The previous Khmer Rouge had been more flexible. They had followed the rules, but only to a minimum. For example, when the order came down to give ten people one can of rice, some of the previous leaders had given ten people two cans. In 1977, when the new Khmer Rouge leaders came in and replaced the previous leaders, the old Khmer Rouge leaders began to starve also. They were as equal as they had parodied at being all along. But they had had no practice in surviving, they didn't know enough to plant food on the sly or to secretly steal small amounts of food throughout the day. The former assistant leader—a Khmer Rouge soldier—began to approach Sokhary and ask for food. Sometimes Sokhary gave him some because he had bent the rules a little bit for them in the past and was now starving like the rest of them.

Sokhary was getting more and more angry at the Khmer Rouge and with her anger she became more bold. When she went to get food for the community pig, she took some for herself instead of giving it all to the pig. She went to the machine where the rice was ground, gathered the rice husks, shook them in a basket and collected parts of the kernels which she cooked and ate with the family.

The harvest season of 1977 arrived and Sokhary, Sam and Elida were moved to the new village of Prey Svay, in Battambang Province, once again able to live together as a family. There was a tile factory in Prey Svay and Sokhary was given the job of putting rice husks into bags to load onto carts—the husks were burned in a kiln to fire the tile. Sam was given a bullock-cart and the job of carrier, carting rice from one place to another. He was given this rather exalted position because the Khmer Rouge knew he did not steal.

Although Sam couldn't bring any rice home, he could eat all he wanted while he was transporting it. For her part, Sokhary was able to plant an entire hidden field of potatoes and sugar cane. She harvested two large crops of both of these. She also planted a small crop of tobacco which she harvested and traded for fish and other things. Some people wanted tobacco so badly that when Sokhary held it out in front of them, they gave her anything she wanted.

At this time the Khmer Rouge began trying to kill all the educated people. Many people were "disappearing." Often, the soldiers didn't even question the person, just investigated what a certain person had been before the war, then came and took that person away.

The new Khmer Rouge leader and the former assistant leader came to Sam and Sokhary's hut in order to question Sam.

The new leader asked, "What were you doing before the war?"

Sam was caught in a quandary because the former assistant leader was present and knew that he had been a teacher.

"I was a student," he replied.

Sokhary became very angry when she heard this—once again her honorable husband who seemed impervious to consequences was talking too much—so she quickly broke in, "Oh no, he was a student when he was very, very young."

The men left without taking Sam and nothing happened afterwards. Sam and Sokhary thought that maybe the former assistant leader had dropped a compliment about Sam to the new leader. Or else, Sam had been spared because he was a model worker. The new leader seemed to like Sam; however, he was very cruel and the type that didn't hesitate to put anyone to death whether he liked them or not.

By the end of 1978 Sokhary was eating more and her body was getting stronger. For several years she hadn't had a period because her body was so malnourished. She never did get a period; instead, she got pregnant.

She had no idea at first. She was feeling sick and had fierce cravings, but didn't want to eat. Then one day the baby moved inside of her and she knew. It was not the time to be pregnant but there was nothing she could do.

Sokhary hid the pregnancy for as long as she could, but at seven months along, she began to show. Because of the increased food and being able to live together as married couples, five women out of the work group became pregnant at this time, including the former assistant leader's wife. They were all due approximately at the same time. When the Khmer Rouge found out, they took the five women twenty miles away to a mountainous jungle area and left them with another group of 50 people; the group was told to cut *sbov* grass for thatch roofs.

Sokhary and the other four pregnant women stayed with this group, living at the foot of the mountain range comprised of three mountains: Phnom Leap, Phnom Trayon, and Phnom Tralach. Sam, back in Prey Svay and distraught with worry, repeatedly asked for permission to visit. After two months, he was finally granted permission for a night's visit and set off.

Incredibly, when Sam arrived in the jungle towards midnight, Sokhary was in labor and had been taken to the crude building that served as the Khmer Rouge hospital. There wasn't water anywhere. There were no medicines and all the doctors or nurses had been killed or had concealed their pasts. There was only a peasant woman who was one of the Khmer Rouge "barefoot doctors"—people who had no medical knowledge or training but had been given the role of doctors. For example, previously when Sokhary had had a pain in her heel, this woman had injected coconut milk into her foot.

"Go find some water," the peasant woman told Sam.

"Be back before the baby is born," Sokhary gasped out between labor pains.

Since Sam transported rice for the Khmer Rouge, he had his bullock-cart so he jumped in and tried to make the oxen go fast—an impossible task—and went looking for water. Left in searing pain, Sokhary wondered what was going to happen. Would she die? Would the baby die? Both of them?

Sam drove the bullock-cart to a hut with a well and pleaded with the family, "Please, my wife is having a baby. Give me water."

The family finally gave him a half bucket of water. He returned to Sokhary and the peasant woman.

Toward the dawn of April 6, 1979, their son Elicasith was born, perfectly healthy. The barefoot doctor cut the umbilical cord with a pair of rusty scissors.

Sam had to return to work as he had received permission to visit only for one night. After looking over his newborn son, he returned to Prey Svay.

The other four pregnant women in the jungle had their babies around the same time. One had delivered her baby ten days before Sokhary, the others a few days after. Sokhary and Elicasith were part of a group of fifty people, young and old. After the births, the other fathers came to join their wives in the jungle. Sokhary waited for Sam to come and join her, but he never came.

The babies had all been delivered by the barefoot doctor who had cut the umbilical cords with the same pair of rusty scissors. One by one, the babies became sick with tetanus. All the newborns—including Elicasith—had temperatures, some high that got higher, some low-grade and climbing. The mothers tried to find water to bathe the babies in order to lower their temperatures; there was nothing else to do.

The former assistant leader's wife had delivered her baby ten days before when the former assistant leader came to join the group. The others didn't like a Khmer Rouge in their group, and neither did Sokhary, but she felt she had to help out the wife. Sokhary and this woman had gone to get water together, gone to find bamboo together, and Sokhary felt the bond of motherhood must be stronger than political distinctions.

When Elicasith was four days old, the group in the jungle heard guns and saw tanks approaching, so Sokhary and the others knew the rumors they had heard about the Vietnamese invading were true. They decided they had to leave. Some of the group spoke in secret and decided that instead of going forward up and over the hilly jungle, they would go backwards towards the Vietnamese and their guns. Sokhary agreed to go with this group because she wanted to go back toward Sam.

The group waited till the next evening and gathered all that they had: an ox but no cart, some rice and clothing, and four newborn baby boys. They ignored the former assistant leader, his wife and newborn son and started off. The former assistant leader and his family followed them.

The group walked that night and stayed hidden the following day. The next night they began walking again. Sokhary carried six-day-old Elicasith wrapped in her *krama* scarf. Elicasith got so hot that he wouldn't nurse. Sokhary told this to an old woman in the group and the woman told Sokhary to stop and rest underneath a tree. When Sokhary unrolled the *krama*, the baby laid there and didn't move. The old woman went and got her *krama* wet in a well and brought it back. They laid the *krama* on Elicasith and when he was completely wet, he began to move.

Sokhary asked the group if the ox could carry her sack of rice. They said yes, so she put the sack on the ox, put the baby in the *krama* on her back and tied up her few clothes and dishes into a bundle that she carried on her head. She continued to walk in this manner throughout the succeeding nights.

The former assistant leader's baby died; it was their first baby. They had to bury him secretly at night. The mother cried and cried, seeming to lose her mind with grief. Sokhary couldn't be of much help to her because she was so worried about Elicasith. Another baby died, then two days later two more babies died until finally only Elicasith was left and he was very, very sick.

Whenever they ran into other people fleeing the Vietnamese, Sokhary asked if they had seen Sam.

One person said, "Oh yes, I saw Sam walking with his brother."

Another said, "Oh, Sam went down that road."

Sokhary didn't know it at the time, but she was getting closer and closer to Sam.

When Sam returned to Prey Svay after Elicasith's birth, the village was in turmoil because the Vietnamese were coming. The Vietnamese had invaded the main cities of Cambodia on January 8, and were just reaching the villages in the countryside in April.

The Vietnamese came so close that Sam could hear their guns while he was working on the kiln. The new people knew the Vietnamese were approaching and were excited that they were going to be freed from the Khmer Rouge. Sam was drafted by the Khmer Rouge leaders to transport ammunition in his bullock-cart from a train to the soldiers.

Sam was desperate to find Sokhary and Elicasith. He and two other men went in search of the group in the jungle. They walked ten miles— about halfway—but didn't see any sign of the group so they turned around. On the way back, Sam was walking along a canal when he saw red nylon cords sticking out of freshly dug dirt. Already knowing what they were, Sam pulled at one, but not hard. The other men stopped and looked around. They were in a killing field. The victims' hands had been tied behind their backs with red parachute cord; after the executions the bodies had been hastily dumped and covered over with the dirt of the field so that the cords were still sticking out of the ground.

The day that Elicasith turned four days old in the jungle, Sam began planning on how he and his brother and Elida would escape. The other men with wives and babies in the jungle left to join them. Sam was distraught with worry and indecision. He didn't want to leave Elida behind and furthermore, rumors were circulating that the people in the jungle had already been evacuated or bombed.

Sam's brother said to him, "We don't know what's true. But I do know that I don't want to lose you. I want you to stay with me. If we are lucky and Buddha helps us, we will meet up with Sokhary."

Sam's brother usually didn't talk about Buddha in this way so his words carried some weight. This was also the brother that had put rice in Sam's mouth the day he was dying and pulled him back from death, so Sam felt he owed this brother his life in the first place.

Sam loaded two huge jars with juice made from the sap of bristly sugar palms. He loaded 400 pounds of palm juice on his bullock-cart, his brother took Elida by the hand and they left. No one tried to stop them because the Khmer Rouge were also running. On the road out of Prey Svay the trio merged with streams of people fleeing the Vietnamese.

Upon reaching Battambang, Sam and his brother found their sister. Happy to be reunited, the three siblings decided to stick together from then on. Leaving Elida in his sister's care, Sam went off with his brother to look for rice.

While they were gone, Sokhary met up with her sister-in-law and Elida. She immediately concentrated on Elida; it was so good to see her again. She also talked with the sister-in-law about all that had happened. They waited together but Sam and his brother didn't return that night. Sokhary and the baby slept on the ground.

The next morning Sam and his brother returned. Sokhary cried with relief and joy at seeing Sam again but at the same time, she was furious.

She asked, "Why didn't you come and try to find me?"

Sam told her everything that his brother had said—that if they had luck and Buddha was willing they would meet up with Sokhary again.

This seemed rather feeble to Sokhary; after all, she had been searching continuously and asking strangers for help in order to find Sam. He should have done the same.

But Sam had no time for past recriminations. He immediately realized that his newborn son was very sick. Elicasith lay absolutely still as if in a coma, with a high fever. If Sam picked him up to try and play with him, he had a seizure. Sokhary and Elida sat looking at the baby, crying. Sokhary told Sam about all the other babies dying and Sam thought back to the barefoot doctor cutting the cord with the rusty scissors at birth and guessed tetanus. He knew enough about medicine to know that the baby needed antibiotics.

The whole family sat waiting for the baby to die and Sam knew he had to try something—anything. He took his palm juice and went to the Vietnamese and traded it for some Streptomycin in powder form. Sam brought back the powder and he and Sokhary frantically puzzled over how to give it to the baby; the directions said to mix with water and inject with a syringe, which they didn't have. Finally, Sam boiled some water in a pan and collected the steam from the underside of the lid and mixed enough of this with the powder to make about 500 ml. of medicine. He gave this to Elicasith to drink. Both he and Sokhary regarded the baby with bated breath and almost immediately the baby's condition improved. They repeated this many times for a month until Elicasith had fully recovered.

The You family tried to decide upon the best course of action. The Vietnamese seemed to be letting people move from one place to another. Should they return to their family village? They had just decided to do this when Sam happened to meet an old friend on the road.

"There's going to be another war," the friend said. "Another faction is going to fight the Vietnamese."

This seemed likely to Sam so the family decided to stay close to the border between Cambodia and Thailand, where, in case of another war, it would be a good place to be.

After six months at the border, Sam began to hear reports that the new government was researching the backgrounds of people to see what their occupations had been before the war. He knew what this meant; they had already been through this with the Khmer Rouge. Sam decided to get his family out of Cambodia. First he spoke to his brother who agreed to travel to the actual border line to gather information—a treacherous trip because of the landmines along the way.

Sam's brother returned safely from the journey and said there were plans to create a refugee camp in Thailand. The family group gathered together and came to the conclusion that things might be better if they went to the camp: more food, safety, maybe even free rice.

Sam, Sokhary, the children, Sam's brother, Sam's sister and her son gathered all their possessions and got ready for the trip. They had two oxen, a cart, a bicycle, a motorcycle pulling another cart; they were in such good shape that they wouldn't have left except Sam was nervous about the new government.

Halfway to the border they had to leave the motorcycle, oxen, cart and bike behind because the road was so full of landmines and soldiers, and to proceed the rest of the way on foot. They walked very carefully and hid from any soldiers. Elicasith was six months old and still nursing. Sokhary and Sam took turns carrying him in a *krama* and pushing Elida on a bike.

They walked through mud in the jungle at night, afraid that a soldier might jump out from behind each tree. Sokhary was continually worried that the baby would cry. Whenever he made a whimper, she stuffed her breast into his mouth; she was nursing him constantly as they walked along.

They had made it past the Vietnamese checkpoints and were beginning to breathe easier when they bumped into some Khmer Rouge who had caught five Vietnamese students trying to escape. The Khmer Rouge asked if anyone could speak Vietnamese. Sam spoke up and said that he could speak English. Sokhary was beside herself: Why did her husband have to say things like this? She was rarely truly angry with Sam—they had been through a lot together—but at this moment she was livid.

Sam realized he shouldn't have spoken up but it was too late. He went over to translate for the Khmer Rouge guards. The five Vietnamese students said that they were from Saigon and were escaping to Thailand through Cambodia. After hearing this, the guards took the five students away, leaving Sam and his family on the road feeling bewildered and shaken.

After the soldiers had gone, Sokhary turned to Sam and shouted, "Why do you have to speak English again?"

They approached the border crossing, close enough that Sokhary noticed that the United Nations drove trucks onto the Cambodian side of the border every morning, loaded up anyone that wanted to get to Thailand, then drove back across. The family group had a discussion. Everyone decided to cross into Thailand except for Sam's sister and her son, who decided to stay on the Cambodian side of the border. The next morning, they said goodbye to the sister and nephew, got in the back of a truck and rode across the border into Thailand.

The truck took them to Khao-I-Dang refugee camp, where there was plenty of food to eat. Almost immediately Sam got a job as a teacher for the children in the camp. The United Nations gave him two cans of tuna fish for each day that he taught.

Sam left Sokhary with the children in the hut each day and went off to teach but Sokhary didn't mind. Before, she'd had to go out and look for food and leave the children alone. Now, she knew there would be enough food, so she could stay and watch over her children.

After they had been in the camp a little over a year, Elicasith seemed sickly, so Sokhary took him to the camp doctor. The doctor asked if she was pregnant. Sokhary said that she didn't know. The doctor tested her urine and the results were positive. Again, she had never had a period.

The doctor told Sokhary that she should stop nursing because possibly that was making Elicasith sick. Sokhary stopped and it was extremely hard on both her and Elicasith. He cried all the time and it made Sokhary feel terrible. After some days of this, Sokhary took Elicasith to the CARE center in the camp, where they gave him baby food. Baby food made all the difference; he grew so strong that he started to walk.

The lack of freedom in the camp began to bother Sam. The entire camp was surrounded by barbed wire and if someone walked outside the wire, they were shot. Sam began writing letters to all the embassies—United States, Canada, France, and so on—to ask for refuge.

As the pregnancy advanced, Sokhary felt very positive because the conditions in the camp were so good. She saw a doctor each week and was given vitamins.

Sokhary's third labor and delivery went right on schedule. A doctor was present and their third child, a son—Elikreutya—weighed in at over eight pounds! He was the biggest baby Sokhary had ever had. Sokhary felt the birth in the camp was the best birth of all. After the birth, Sokhary and the newborn got to stay in the hospital for nine days; Sokhary felt she was in heaven. The two boys were one month short of being two years apart.

When Elikreutya was nine days old, one of Sam's letters to the embassies got a result. A list arrived with the names of people going to the United States and the You family was on it.

Sokhary sighed. "Every time I have a baby, we have to move," she said to Sam.

The family spent the next few months going from one camp to another, undergoing physicals, interviews, and a series of shots. In the last camp they received the news that they were being sponsored by the Trinity Episcopal church of Excelsior, Minnesota, and the church wanted them to come right away.

The You family first touched American soil on November 5, 1981. In Oakland they were put up in the Hampton Hotel and served a meal of beef. Beef! Sokhary was euphoric—they hadn't tasted beef in years.

They flew on to Minneapolis. Sokhary was airsick the whole way and the baby had an ear infection. When they landed, one of the first things that Sokhary noticed was the cold. She was wearing slippers—not even socks—and her feet were freezing. One of the sponsors was waiting in the airport with a sign reading: "Welcome to the United States Sam You."

The church had arranged for the family to rent half of a house that had been made into a duplex on Lake Street in Excelsior. It was a big old white house across the street from Lake Minnetonka. The children immediately loved it.

The house was owned by a white-haired lady named Maude Johnson who lived in the other half. She was very nice to the family and the children quickly learned to call her "Grandma" in English.

The family moved into the duplex on November 18. On November 19 Sam began his job of setting up banquet tables at the IDS Tower in Minneapolis; he took the city bus to and from work. Later, he switched to washing dishes in a big restaurant because he could work more hours.

The church paid the $400-a-month rent for the Yous' half of the duplex for two months, then said it was the family's responsibility; however, the church still kept an eye on them to make sure they were doing all right. The family received food stamps, so they only had to earn enough for rent and a few other items.

Elikreutya, the baby, was eleven months old and learning to walk in January of that year. One morning Sokhary turned on the electric tea kettle to make a cup of tea. After the water was boiling, she fixed her cup, carried Elikreutya into the family room, put him down and walked back into the kitchen. Without her knowing it, the baby followed her right back into the kitchen. She didn't hear him because he was so quiet, and because she wasn't expecting him to be able to walk. As she went to the sink, he reached up and pulled the cord of the electric teapot that was hanging over the counter. Boiling water poured all over his body—his front, his arms and one leg.

He screamed in pain. Sokhary leapt to him and when she removed his sleeper, a layer of skin came off with it. Sokhary began screaming too. "Grandma" Maude heard the screaming from the other side of the duplex and came running over.

Sokhary sat sobbing, holding her burnt baby and saying one of the few words she knew in English, "Help, help."

She was able to gasp out the phone number of one of their sponsors from church to Maude. Maude called and she and some others came over immediately. They took Sokhary and Elikreutya to the Methodist Hospital Emergency Room where the baby received emergency medical treatment and was sent on to the Hennipen County Burn Unit.

After Elikreutya was settled into a bed at the Burn Unit, Sokhary had to call Sam at work and tell him what had happened. Sam was angry at Sokhary and said she should have been watching. Sokhary sobbed as she tried to tell Sam that she didn't understand how it had happened: the baby had never taken that many steps before; she didn't hear him right behind her. To this day she still can't understand how it happened.

The doctors said Elikreutya had second degree burns over much of his body. Sokhary stayed with him in the Burn Unit for three weeks. She was nursing the baby in the hospital but then the doctors and nurses said that Elikreutya's skin wasn't getting enough vitamins so she started Elikreutya on the bottle and he loved it. He was the only one of her three children to have a bottle.

After three weeks, Sokhary and Elikreutya returned home. The baby had to wear a special suit for a year in order to prevent severe scarring. A nurse came out periodically to help Sokhary change his dressings. (Today, a tiny scar on his leg is the only sign of the burn.)

Sam and Sokhary were worried about paying the doctor and hospital bills, but then found out they qualified for Medical Assistance because of their lack of income. Medical Assistance said everything was covered. This was a great solace to them.

Elikreutya's burn was the beginning of a difficult three year period for the You family. Money was very tight. The duplex was old and didn't have good insulation—heat alone during the winter months was $200. Rent was $400 every month. One month Sam had $200 in the bank and couldn't pay the rent. He called their sponsor who collected money from various people in the church and came over with $200 so that Sam could pay the full amount.

Sokhary began working as a dishwasher in the local restaurant where Sam and his brother already worked. The three adults tried to divide up the child care, which wasn't always successful. They didn't know any other Cambodians for support or social connections. All three had to walk to their jobs because they didn't have a car.

Sokhary got a job at a factory that made contact lenses. It was an increase in pay and she took overtime that other people didn't want—for example, Saturdays—and made good money that way. Sam's brother had a nighttime job so he helped Sokhary with the children during the day. Sokhary also kept her weekend job as a busgirl at a big restaurant.

Sam got a job helping Cambodian refugees at Minnetonka High School. He liked this job because it used his skills as a teacher, but it was only part time—thirty hours a week—so he kept his dishwasher job. His schedule was frantic. One night he worked at the restaurant until four in the morning, walked home in the sunrise and arrived home just in time to walk to his job at the school.

With money being such a worry, both Sokhary and Sam were fearful of another pregnancy. They didn't have good jobs and they didn't have insurance. Sokhary went to their sponsor and told him that they didn't want any more babies.

He asked, "Are you sure?"

When Sokhary said they were, the sponsor made an appointment with one of the church members who was a physician.

Their sponsor drove them to the appointment. Both Sam and Sokhary signed a lot of papers, then the doctor performed a tubal ligation on Sokhary. He wouldn't accept any money and said that he wanted to help; Sokhary has always been grateful for this act of generosity.

The family kept desperately trying to save money and after a long time it seemed as if they might be succeeding. In 1983 Sam, Sokhary and Sam's brother put all their money together and bought a car; now they could drive to their jobs.

Bit by bit, things became easier. In 1984 Sam's nephew came from Cambodia to live with them. With the money he added to the family's savings, they were able to afford a down payment on a house in Excelsior, behind the Country Kitchen Restaurant.

The Yous were happy to own instead of rent, but there were thirteen people living in the house and it was clear that it was too crowded. There were the Yous, Sam's sister, his niece and her husband and their three children, Sam's brother and a nephew. However, since the Yous paid only half of the rent, they were able to save yet more money. In two years they had saved enough to purchase a big rambler in Minnetonka, close to Minnetonka High School and Sam's job.

They met other Cambodian refugees and the children made friends through school. They bought another car. They sent money back to Cambodia, money to build a temple where young students can go and study and—with other refugees—money to build a small medical clinic.

With the easing of financial pressure, both Sam and Sokhary began to regret their decision not to have any more children.

"Maybe it would have been nice to have one more child," Sam said to Sokhary.

"Families in Cambodia have more than three children," agreed Sokhary. "But here in America people have only one or two, sometimes three."

"Think of how much money it will cost for our children to go to college," said Sam. "That's it—we made the right decision."

As Sam and Sokhary's children entered the teenage years, Sam and Sokhary became more aware of the perils facing children in America, something they discussed with other refugee parents from Cambodia.

"The schools in America offer a lot of classes and equipment," Sam says, "but the children themselves are careless. They have the attitude: Who cares? Instead of listening to the teacher, they sleep."

"I see a real difference between Cambodian children and American children," one parent says. "The ones raised in Cambodia have a respect toward the parents, the teacher, older people."

"And there is discipline in the class," says another. "You cannot put your leg on the table, you have to listen very good."

"It's hard to raise the children because of drugs," says Sokhary. "I'm so worried. You don't know—some day they might get into that. In Cambodia people worried about food. But here in the U.S., it's a rich country, people have so much money that they don't know what to do. So they think only about having fun."

"We're having a hard time with discipline with our kids now," says Sokhary. "They're Americanized. They don't act like Cambodian children. I'll give you an example. My son says, 'I want to go to a movie.' I say, 'no.' He says, 'What's the matter, Ma? We're having fun. What's the matter with having fun?' He argues with us. When I grew up, if my dad said no, I just shut up and walked away."

"Another thing, here in the U.S. they talk about having freedom," says Sam. "Well, freedom is good, but I think it should be limited. Someone should be able to say, 'You can only go this far.' The parents, and the law, should be able to say this."

But at the end of the discussion, the parents agree, "Our children belong here in the United States. This is their country."

Today the You family is fully settled into life in the United States. Everyone is healthy and living full and productive lives. Sam enjoys his work at Minnetonka High School; Sokhary is involved in the lives of Cambodian refugees in the area, especially the orphans. All three children are doing well. Elida, born in Phnom Penh, came to the United States at eight years old, and was graduated from St. Cloud State University in Minnesota in 1997. Elicasith, born in the jungle during the Pol Pot and Khmer Rouge years, came to the United States at two years old and is now a senior at the University of Wisconsin in Eau Claire. (He is following in his father's footsteps and going into education.) Elikreutya was born in the Khao-I-Dang refugee camp in Thailand, came to the United States at eight months old and is now a sophomore at St. Thomas University in St. Paul, Minnesota.

For people like Sam and Sokhary, America is the land of opportunity. They came with empty hands and now they have a house, two cars, two television sets, a phone in every corner and a bedroom with attached bath. Their children attend good schools, have received excellent educations and have everything they could ever need or want.

Sam and Sokhary feel good about having all this but at the same time, they know that they have had to work very hard to pay for it. If they were living in Cambodia, they wouldn't have all the possessions, but then again, they wouldn't need as much money to live on. But it is a moot comparison because right now Cambodia is not a safe place to live.

A few years ago, Sokhary went back to Cambodia to visit. She went back to her own village. She walked upon the same road that they had walked when she had been forcibly driven out of Phnom Penh. It was like a dream; she could not believe it.

"We had an experience under the Khmer Rouge," she told Sam upon her return. "It was not a good experience, but it was still our experience and part of our lives. We can't discount it."

She and Sam have been through some very bad times. They came here with nothing. Sokhary wore slippers on her feet and didn't speak a word of English. The United States was the land of opportunity for them—and they made the most of it.

Looking back, Sokhary says, "I think if you want to, you can do it."

9

That Ordinary Monster, Pol Pot

Pol Pot: The name is synonymous with the Cambodian autogenocide. It is the name of the man who is responsible for the deaths of 1.5 million of his own people and who attempted to eradicate his country's culture and society. Did he purposely set out to wreak such long-term havoc and destruction? It is hard to say.

When Pol Pot died on April 15, 1998, he was without remorse for the ruin and devastation he had brought upon his country and people, declaring, during the last year of his life, "My conscience is clear."

The man later known as Pol Pot, or Brother Number One, was born to a peasant family under the given name of Saloth Sar. After some basic schooling, he went to Paris to study radio electronics in 1949, became a Communist and—after failing three sets of exams—returned to Cambodia in 1952. Upon his return he led a double life of teaching at a private college and working for the Cambodian Marxists. He abandoned his job, and the double life, in 1963, when he fled to the Vietnamese border to join the guerrillas. By then he had become deputy general secretary for the underground Communist Party.

American journalist Nate Thayer was granted what was a last interview with Pol Pot in 1997, the year before his death in 1998. Thayer pressed Pol Pot for an answer to the question: Did he admit guilt for his murderous 1975–79 rule—and thus, for the two million more or less who died during that time? Pol Pot was slippery as an eel, alternately insisting upon his innocence and blaming the Vietnamese.

"Our movement made mistakes like every other movement in the world," he said. "But there was another aspect that was outside our control—the enemy's activities against us."

When Thayer persisted, asking directly about the millions of people who suffered during that time, Pol Pot responded, "That question has been raised time and again. I would like to say first that my conscience is clear. Everything I have done and contributed is first for the nation and the people and the race of Cambodia."

Thayer then tried yet again, asking, "Do you feel that you were indeed responsible for crimes against humanity, against your own people?"

Pol Pot answered, "I am going to reply. I want to tell you clearly. First, I would like to tell you that I came to carry out the struggle, not to kill people. Even now, and you can look at me, am I a savage person? My conscience is clear. ... As I told you before, they [the Vietnamese] fought against us, so we had to take measures to defend ourselves. ... To say that millions died is too much. Another aspect you have to know is that Vietnamese agents, they were there. There was rice but they didn't give rice to the population."

Pol Pot continued in this vein: "... There are two sides to it, as I told you: There's what we did wrong, and what we did right. The mistake is that we did some things against the people—by us and also by the enemy—but the other side, as I told you, is that without our struggle there would be no Cambodia right now."

He then said flatly, "I'm tired of talking about it."

If his evasions and semantic posturings weren't the whitewash for such horrendous crimes, they would be almost laughable; the monster speaks in such ordinary banalities and trite phrases.

The national anthem of Democratic Kampuchea—Cambodia's name during Pol Pot time—seems to tell a different story. Entitled "Glorious April 17"—after the date of the death march when the Khmer Rouge emptied the cities—it makes no apology for all the blood that was spilled, but revels in it:

> Bright red Blood which covers towns and plains
> Of Kampuchea, our Motherland,
> Sublime Blood of workers and peasants,
> Sublime Blood of revolutionary men and women fighters!
> The Blood changing into unrelenting hatred
> And resolute struggle,
> On April 17th, under the Flag of the Revolution,
> Frees from Slavery!
>
> Long live, long live Glorious April 17th!
> Glorious Victory with greater signification
> Than the times of Angkor!
>
> We are uniting to edify
> Splendid and democratic new Kampuchea and new society

With equality and justice,
Firmly applying the line of independence, sovereignty and
    self-reliance.
Let us resolutely defend
Our Motherland, our sacred Soil
And our Glorious Revolution!

Long live, long live, long live,
Democratic and prosperous new Kampuchea!
Let us resolutely raise high
The red Flag of the Revolution!
Let us edify our Motherland!
Let us make her advance with great leaps,
So that She will be more glorious and more marvelous than ever!

In 1979 the People's Revolutionary Tribunal was formed in Cambodia in order to put Pol Pot and Ieng Sary on trial for genocide. The evidence from that trial is damning—and horrifying. The killing methods were inhumane, rudimentary and cruel. The most common way was to line up a large number of people next to newly dug mass graves and hit their skulls with bamboo sticks, axes, picks, or hoes— much as one would kill animals. The agents of Pol Pot and Ieng Sary dubbed this particular method "the top method" because the victim did not immediately die but turned around in place under the feet of the executioner like a top before it spins itself out. Consider these following statements from Pol Pot's former agents (all published in De Nike *et al.*, eds.):

Statement 2.2.01 of Mr. Men Khoeun:

The killing of the two thousand and five soldiers was carried out upon an order of Pol Pot and Ieng Sary to celebrate the April 17, 1975, victory. After April 17, 1975, the head of Toek Phos district, who is named Meak Vy, got together fifty agents of all the subdistricts of the district. He declared that it was Pol Pot's order that all the Lon Nol soldiers are our enemies, and that we must kill them all to celebrate the victory of April 17, 1975. Those failing to comply with this order would be tried themselves. After hearing that, we had no choice but to obey. If we failed to kill, we would be killed. But I did not see Pol Pot's directive, which was issued ten days after April 17, 1975. ... The two thousand and five persons were killed in ten groups, one group each day for ten successive days. We killed them during daylight hours. Our commanders said that these soldiers were being taken away for a few days of reeducation. When we got one kilometer away from the camp, we tied them up and led them to the place of the killing, which was five kilometers from the camp. We began each session of killing at 7 a.m., and at 9 a.m. we stopped to eat. On the first day we killed fifty persons, and later on sometimes five hundred, sometimes one hundred persons per day.

After ten days, we had killed two thousand and five soldiers and the last day we killed one hundred fifty soldiers. We led them to the ditches we had prepared to bury them in the Ko Prich wood.

We killed each one with blows of a bamboo stick. After killing them, we pushed them into the ditches. We avoided killing them with guns to save bullets. Before doing the killing we determined the method to use: We would strike them three times on the neck.

… After I married, the high command let me live as a civilian. Now I think a great deal about the offense that I committed by order of Pol Pot, who thereby forced me to commit genocide [p. 219].

Statement 2.2.06 of Mr. Sao Soeun:

At first, I lived in Bos village and was then transferred, by Pol Pot, to Thmey village. … I, and four other killers, worked under the direction of Prak Sambo, head of security for the district. I was an agent in the district. I was working in the rice fields when I was called to the site of the killing. The four others and I were ordered by Prak Sambo to tie the victims before killing them. Prak Sambo threatened us, saying: "If you do not kill them, I will kill you." We had to obey.

The slaughter took place in a concentration camp which held 100 people. Nearby, ditches had been dug to bury the bodies. There stood a group of guards and it was they who led out the prisoners for us to kill. The place of the massacre was 100 meters from the camp. There was a rumor that the killing would not be done with firearms, because we must not make a lot of noise. The massacre was a secret.

The one hundred victims were all men from the ages of 20 to 50 years old. They were all soldiers and students. Before killing them, we tied their arms behind their backs. They were killed at 3 o'clock in the afternoon [p. 225].

And finally Statement 2.2.05, where Mr. Siv Samon speaks of killing babies for the reason that they were K.G.B. or C.I.A. agents:

... In February 1978, I was named security chief of Meanchey district. I served in this position until the end of the Pol Pot regime. On August 12 and 13, 1978, by order of the district chief, my seven comrades, the district chief himself, and I beat 250 persons, among whom I recognized 110 women, 80 old and young people, and 60 small children about one year old, and two other children. These people were accused of being agents of the K.G.B. or the Vietnamese, or were family members of soldiers of Lon Nol or the C.I.A. These persons were beaten to death with iron pipes and bars, after having their hands tied and their eyes blindfolded [p.224].

Tuol Sleng is the former high school in Phnom Penh in which the Khmer Rouge incarcerated, tortured and then killed some 14,000 Cambodians during Pol Pot's regime. Known only by the code-name of S-21, the prison was a secret facility of the Khmer Rouge; S-21 stands for security police or special branch. In just less than the four years it was functioning, only seven of the approximately 14,000 who entered S-21 ever emerged alive.

David Chandler, world-renowned historian of Cambodia, wrote a book on S-21, titled *Voices from S-21: Terror and History in Pol Pot's Secret Prison*. In this book, he recounts the story of the grisly discovery made in 1979 when two Vietnamese photojournalists first approached the building because of the smell of decomposing bodies. After making their way through classrooms converted into cells, they found the bodies of fourteen recently murdered people, their blood still wet on the floor. In other classrooms they found heaps of shackles, handcuffs, whips and lengths of chain; in some cells they found ammunition boxes containing human feces.

Over the next few days, in nearby houses, Vietnamese and Cambodian assistants found thousands of documents in Khmer, thousands of mug-shot photos and undeveloped negatives, hundreds of full notebooks and stacks of Khmer Rouge publications.

They also found typed and handwritten confessions, like the one from Siet Chhe, a former student and loyal comrade of Pol Pot for many years. He was told, after much torture, that he had to write out a confession of incest with his daughter. He replied with a lengthy written memorandum, saying at the end:

Organization, I love my daughter a little more than I love my three sons. Because she is the only girl in the family and was more responsible than her brothers. ... She was put in prison by the enemy when she was twelve ... This all causes me to pity her and love her the most. When I saw her during my travels, I touched her on the head or shoulders with the love and pity of a father for his child. In the matter of sexual morality, I am certain that she is a proper child who can be trusted. From then until now, I am certain she is a virgin with no moral blemishes with me or any other man. The accusations that I took advantage of my own child are ridiculous.

From a captured document we know that the prisoners of S-21 were deliberately prevented from dying during torture so that they could be tortured again and again. An excerpt from Document 2.5.27 from the Conference of "S-21" on Conduct of Interrogations of July 23, 1977, states, "As for the methods of torture, lessons must be drawn to avoid means of torture that cause death" (De Nike *et al.*, eds., p. 410).

Men San or "Comrade Ya" as he was called, was another of the 14,000 tortured to death in S-21. In a handwritten note, the prison commandant wrote of Ya: "The Organization decided that if this guy continues stubbornly to hide his traitorous linkages and activities, that he should be executed and not allowed to play games any more ... Therefore, with this Ya you can forcefully use the hot method and for prolonged periods, even if you slip and it kills him." Then the chief scrawls a chilling addendum across the bottom: "Ya to read so that he can think it over."

And yet, when Thayer brings up Tuol Sleng prison in his interview with Pol Pot, Pol Pot replies that a journalist made it up. As proof that it is a hoax by the Vietnamese to discredit him, Pol Pot says that someone researched the skulls stacked on the site and they are smaller than those of the Khmer people.

Thayer, facing this incredible lack of logic, asks, "Are you saying that you never heard of Tuol Sleng before 1979?"

"No," says Pol Pot, "I never heard of it."

Thayer, understandably frustrated, responds, "Sir, let me say that there is overwhelming scientific evidence, overwhelming proof that thousands of people, Cambodians, were executed at Tuol Sleng while you were in control of Phnom Penh. There is no dispute among anybody else in the world ... that it is true."

And how did Pol Pot, the man who has been referred to as the Asian Hitler, respond to this? He gave no response.

Pol Pot was never tried for his crimes in person. Nate Thayer's interview was the closest Pol Pot ever came to enduring some sort of public

Pol Pot speaking in Phnom Penh in 1975 after the Khmer Rouge victory. (Photograph from the personal collection of Professor Ben Kiernan, Director of Genocide Studies Program, Yale University.)

examination. In April 1998 President Bill Clinton ordered plans for a military capture of Pol Pot and trial by an international tribunal. This was the equivalent of a death warrant for Pol Pot who, during a public trial, would surely place blame on his cohorts: Nuon Chea (known as Brother Number Two); Khieu Samphan (official head of Khmer Rouge); Ta Mok (the strongman of the Khmer Rouge); General Khem Nuon (Ta Mok's chief of staff) and others.

Sure enough, within a week, it was announced that Pol Pot had died of a heart attack. Although his body was shown to journalists, it was unclear as to whether he died a natural death or was killed—either by his fellow Khmer Rouge or by his own hand.

Ta Mok delivered the only epitaph, saying: "Pol Pot has died like a ripe papaya. No one killed him, no one poisoned him. Now he's finished, he has no power, he has no rights, he is no more than cow shit. Cow shit is more important than him. We can use it for fertilizer."

Without wife or young daughter present, his body was set aflame atop a stack of used tires. Although ignominious, this ending was no comfort to the thousands of Cambodians all over the world who wanted some sort of justice *for*—or at least acknowledgment *of*—what they and their families had suffered.

I first heard of Tuol Sleng prison—without it being identified as such—from my foster brother, Sinn Lok. When he told me of his time in the children's labor camps under Pol Pot and the Khmer Rouge, he mentioned a building that everyone knew about but had no name, a building the children referred to as a house of death.

"People go in there but never come out," he said, "The Khmer Rouge say it is a hospital but everyone knows that if you go in, you don't get better, you die."

"The people who were very sick, the most sick, they put in a certain house," he told me with a look of disgust and horror. "When they put someone in that house, no one can survive. ... Another kid, he got sick and he was sick for only one day and people came to take him and put him in that house. He screamed and screamed that he didn't want to go, that he didn't want to die, but they picked him up and put him in the house and the next day, he died. I don't know if they were killing people in that house, but somehow, that house was like a ghost house."

From those words came the title of this book. Years later, when I was doing research, I read a similar story in *Voices from S-21*:

> A factory worker in a nearby compound, interviewed in 1989, referred to S-21 as "the place where people went in but never came out." The factory workers were uncertain about what went on inside its walls but were ready to think the worst. Party leaders never referred to S-21 by name.

In a flash of intuition, I realized that "the ghost house" Sinn was telling me about was the same place that the factory worker spoke of in Chandler's book. I was puzzled however, because S-21, or Tuol Sleng prison, was in Phnom Penh and Sinn had been working in the north, near Siem Reap, when he encountered the terrible house. How to explain this geographical impossibility?

The answer was revealed to me in *Genocide in Cambodia: Documents from the Trial of Pol Pot and Ieng Sary*. Wilfred Burchett said, in document number 2.6.06:

> It is hard to find words to describe the nightmare that lasted nearly four years of life, torture and death in the Kampuchea of Pol Pot. Are there any remotely possible comparisons, or precedents? Tied with irons hand and foot, their eyes and hair pulled out from blows of iron bars, bamboo sticks thrust under their nails, suffering atrocious torture before being finished off with axes, hammers, or knives, the victims of the former school Tuol Sleng in Phnom

Penh converted into a house of detention and execution, they number as many as those who perished at Hiroshima.

In every provincial capital there were similar torture and death chambers [De Nike *et al.*, eds., p. 416].

Thus, the "kid" that Sinn saw taken away kicking and screaming was put into a local death house, or ghost house.

The survivors now living in America were never put in S-21, or they most likely wouldn't have survived; however, they seem to be just as effectively in a house of ghosts here and now—a prison of torture and suffering from which they cannot escape. Tuol Sleng is now a museum in Phnom Penh, visited by thousands of foreigners and Cambodians yearly, but its living exhibits are all over the world: survivors who are quietly, desperately trying to escape from the house of ghosts and go on with their lives.

10

Boat People:
The Story of Sokkhom Ngep

Buddhist New Year is an exciting and important holiday for Cambodians. Somewhere around April 13, 14, or 15, young and old alike stop working and celebrate the holiday by playing traditional games, eating special treats and making offerings with incense and candles in the Buddhist temple. It's a joyous and happy time, especially for children and teenagers who have free run of the village and are able to play games—even in the pagoda.

Sokkhom Ngep distinctly remembers New Year's Day 1975 when he was nine years old. He was running around with his friends in the pagoda of their village of Phum Sre in the province of Kompong Thom. The children and adults were celebrating with much noise and merriment when suddenly a man ran into the pagoda.

"The Khmer Rouge have captured Phnom Penh," he shouted. "I just heard the news on the radio."

This news was not a complete surprise to the people of Phum Sre as the Communist guerrillas from the countryside had been fighting the American-supported military of Lon Nol for some time. But everyone knew that the Khmer Rouge capture of the capital was obviously a turning point in the war and Cambodia's future.

The Khmer Rouge reached Phum Sre that very day, coming through on a victory march to the next village which held the local headquarters for Lon Nol. The villagers stood by and observed the black-clad soldiers—mostly adolescent boys—in interested silence. They were not afraid nor were they fully supportive. Most were waiting to see which way the wind would blow.

It was quiet for a few days after that. Then the Khmer Rouge returned and inexplicably took everything away from the villagers: food, clothes, kitchen utensils, tables, motorbikes, bicycles.

Sokkhom Ngep in front of wooden house on stilts in Kompong Thom, 1986. (Photograph from the personal collection of Sokkhom Ngep.)

When questioned, they said, "If you need anything, just ask the Khmer Rouge."

The Khmer Rouge appointed a village leader. They were clever about it and didn't pick someone from the village but brought in someone from the other side of the country who would have no attachments and be able to follow orders—including those to kill—quickly and without compunction. Since Phum Sre was close to the Lon Nol headquarters in the next village, this leader was appointed chief of the entire area and given the title of district commander.

As the Khmer Rouge had taken away everything needed to prepare food, it was necessary for everybody to eat together in one main building. After meals, the villagers went back to their separate houses to sleep. The Ngep household was large enough that their house had a kitchen housed separately nearby.

The Khmer Rouge destroyed this kitchen, saying, "You won't need this now."

One month later trucks loaded with people—mostly women and children—drove into the village; these were the new people from Pnom Penh. They told the villagers that they had been loaded onto the trucks to go live in the country, that the Khmer Rouge didn't want anyone living in the city anymore. They said the Khmer Rouge wanted everyone to become farmers and work in the rice fields. The women quietly said that most of the men had been killed or had been taken somewhere else.

The old people—the Ngeps and the other villagers—didn't know what to do with all the new people. The new people were very hungry and the villagers didn't have anything for them to eat.

The thatched village houses were built on stilts in typical Cambodian style, both to keep out flooding water as well as snakes during the wet season and for ventilation—to "get enough air," people said. The district commander arbitrarily assigned new people to live underneath the houses and when these spaces ran out, he placed new people right in houses with families. Some new people tried to build makeshift houses from wood in order to have their own space to live in. The Khmer Rouge divided the village into groups—ten to twenty houses per group—and told each group that they would eat together in one building.

A new person—a lady—was assigned to live with the Ngep family. She was a single woman whose husband had been killed. She was a very good person and she and the Ngeps grew fond of each other. In fact, after a while Mrs. Ngep tried to protect her just like one of her own children. At various times the Khmer Rouge would try to take her away but Mrs. Ngep always stopped them.

The Ngep family originally consisted of father, mother and ten children. Sokkhom was third from last. Mr. and Mrs. Ngep had a little stall in the village and sold things that the villagers needed. After the Khmer Rouge came, the stall was torn down and Mr. Ngep was put to work driving a bullock-cart, carrying rice from one place to another for the Khmer Rouge.

The villagers were told to grow rice, a long and arduous task; it took months to get one rice field growing. First, the trees had to be cut down and the stumps burned out, then the ground plowed and the rice planted. The children carried water and human waste to the fields to nourish the young shoots.

One day the Khmer Rouge took everyone twelve years and older away, saying they were needed to build a dam. Being only ten, Sokkhom was too young to go, but all his older brothers and sisters were taken away. The Ngep family now consisted of Mr. and Mrs. Ngep, Sokkhom, little brother Sokheng and a sister Phary, a baby at two years old.

Every day Mrs. Ngep, Sokkhom, Sokheng and Phary went to work in the rice fields with the other villagers. Mr. Ngep was rarely home because he was away driving the bullock-cart.

Meals were at 12 o'clock and 6 o'clock. The entire village of 200 people was fed with one kilo of rice per day which meant that each person received a bowl of watery gruel in which the rice had been cooked with just a few grains of rice. People tried to find wild potatoes and cassavas to supplement this starvation diet, but most people were starving at this time.

Mrs. Ngep gave birth to a baby girl. She continued to go to the rice fields every day after the birth. She carried the baby; Sokkhom carried some water. When they reached the fields, Mrs. Ngep handed the baby to Sokkhom, then took Phary and went off. Sokkhom tenderly watched over his new sister all day long, taking care of her. He wasn't alone in doing this; there was a group of ten- and eleven-year-old children who hadn't been taken away by the Khmer Rouge, watching their younger siblings.

Since there wasn't enough food and Mrs. Ngep was putting full days in at the fields, her breast milk wasn't sufficient and the baby got sick. There was no food to give her and no medicine. When it became clear that the baby was very sick, Mrs. Ngep took her to the hospital in Kompong Thom. Hospitals under the Khmer Rouge were a sham; after taking over Phnom Penh the Khmer Rouge had killed most of the professional class, including doctors and nurses. There were no medical supplies, or medicine; the Khmer Rouge often used grass. There were stories of how if someone went to the hospital with an infection, the barefoot doctors cleaned it up and put ground tree root on the wound, or how if a delivery didn't progress the Khmer Rouge nurses physically pushed on the pregnant stomach to get the baby out.

Mrs. Ngep came home a few days later without the baby, looking desolate. Sokkhom knew that his new baby sister had died. He was very sad at the loss of the baby, after all, he had been the one to take care of her all day long while his mother was working in the fields. (Even at age thirty-four he can still picture her tiny face.)

Sokkhom no longer had a job to do in the rice fields because the baby had died, so the Khmer Rouge sent him to school where the children were taught such things as: to hate former city dwellers; to find and exterminate enemies within; and *Angkar* is the benefactor of children. The school was taught by one of Sokkhom's cousins who was sickly and couldn't do any physical labor. This man had a disorder whereby he fell down with a seizure at least once a day, twitching and frothing at the mouth, so that the children ran away in fright.

School was held for an hour or two every day, then the children went into the rice fields to work; the classes were mostly an excuse for the children to work afterwards. The children were responsible for finding fertilizer for the rice fields. They located ant hills and dug them under; they also collected water buffalo manure. The Khmer Rouge told the children that if they carried many loads of manure, they could rest.

But for most children, it took all day to get one load, so the rest never came.

After two years the schoolteacher died. With his seizures and sickliness, his death wasn't a surprise. Since there wasn't a teacher anymore, the children worked all day long. It was 1977, and Sokkhom was eleven, approaching twelve—the age where he would be expected to work apart from the village.

The Khmer Rouge came to Sokkhom and told him to look after the water buffalo. The other men looking after the cattle were fifty or sixty years old and couldn't do anything else. Secluded from the others with the cattle, they spoke of what was happening: how the Khmer Rouge came at night and took away the men from the new people. They told of how the men were tied up, driven four kilometers away and beaten to death in the rice fields. Sokkhom listened very carefully to these conversations.

Later, after killing most of the new people, the Khmer Rouge began killing the old people. However, they didn't kill Mr. Ngep because he was transporting rice in the bullock-cart.

At the end of 1978, things began to change—slowly at first, then with gathering speed. There were only a few new people left. The ones who were still alive went around pretending to be feeble-minded, not knowing or saying anything, so that they wouldn't be killed. There were only a few old people left too, for that matter, and they also did whatever they were told, just to stay alive.

Some people were put to work logging trees in the forest. They had access to radio broadcasts and told the villagers that Cambodia was at war with Vietnam. It became clear that the Khmer Rouge were losing the war. The bulk of the Khmer Rouge went off to fight the Vietnamese, leaving the district commander and a few others in charge of Phum Sre.

Two of Sokkhom's older brothers and sisters came home, along with family members of other villagers. Sokkhom's brother Sokkha was so thin and weak that he couldn't walk; he had been carried home in a bullock-cart after someone took pity on him. He was only able to walk a few yards and then had to sit down and rest. Since the entrance to the Ngep house on stilts was a stairway of fifteen steps he went up a step, sat and rested, went up another step. Finally someone from the family heard him and went to carry him in.

The Khmer Rouge told the villagers to dig a huge trench, saying, "The Vietnamese are going to kill everyone—even the children. You can go in this shelter to be safe."

The villagers could hear guns in the distance and see burning tanks down the road. Soldiers passed by the village all day long.

When the Vietnamese troops approached the village, the district commander and a few Khmer Rouge guards forced the villagers into the jungle, saying that the Vietnamese were going to kill everyone. The people from the village next to Phum Sre ran towards the Vietnamese—not away from—because they had been listening to the radio and knew that the Vietnamese weren't going to kill them.

A group of 300 villagers from Phum Sre, including the Ngep family, were driven into the jungle by the district commander and the guards. The commander and the guards killed several pigs, roasted them and held a party, which the villagers thought very strange.

The guards were on their way back to the village to check if anybody had been left behind when they were captured by the Vietnamese army. Because the guards had thrown away their guns, the Vietnamese didn't know they were Khmer Rouge and confiscated the remaining bullets and questioned them with the help of a translator.

"There are a lot of people in the jungle over there," the guards said, pointing the way, "living under the Khmer Rouge. If you let us go, we'll tell them to come out so they can escape the Khmer Rouge."

Meanwhile, the district commander had gone to another village and rounded up 100 Khmer Rouge soldiers to kill the villagers, whom he was then planning to bury in the trench he had had them dig earlier.

Upon being released, the guards ran back to the jungle and found the group of villagers.

"The district commander is planning to kill you all," they said, "Quick, escape. Run towards the Vietnamese."

Even though these Khmer Rouge guards had killed with their own hands—otherwise they couldn't have held the position of guards—the villagers didn't consider them to be killers like other Khmer Rouge. These guards had killed because they would have been killed if they didn't; it was kill or be killed. So the villagers believed the guards and both villagers and guards together rushed back to the village to join the Vietnamese troops. Incredibly, on the way they met the district commander, lagging behind his killing troops that had passed down the road earlier.

"What's going on?" the district commander asked, seeing the villagers very much alive.

Cleverly, the guards said, "The Vietnamese are coming. If you don't run away, you'll be killed by the Vietnamese."

The commander immediately let them go and left to save his own skin. The villagers estimated they had missed being killed by three hours!

The Ngep family and the other villagers returned to Phum Sre where the war continued for months as resistance forces fought the Vietnamese. People looted the market stalls and the stores of rice but still didn't have enough food, and began to starve. Mr. Ngep attempted to exchange clothes and jewelry for food but there wasn't any food to be had. Somehow, the family managed to stay alive through the next season when they could plant their own rice crop.

The war ground on. Sokkhom and his older brother left the village in 1983 to attend secondary school in Kompong Thom when Sokkhom was seventeen years old. The Ngep family was attempting to build and secure better lives; the parents built a small house for the brothers to live in while going to school.

King Sihanouk joined with the Khmer Rouge to fight against the Vietnamese in 1984. Hun Sen became prime minister of the Vietnamese-backed Communist government.

Through the schools, the Hun Sen government picked certain promising students to be part of the Communist Youth Organization. These students were called the leaders of the future; Sokkhom and his brother Sokkha were both chosen. They underwent special training and attended a political school once a month titled "How to Be a Leader." In addition, Sokkhom was chosen to be the class captain, which meant he had to guard the school one weekend a month.

In order to fill these roles, the chosen students had to act like the Khmer Rouge. For example, Sokkhom had to look after all the students in his class and decide who was good and who was bad, then select particular ones to be members of the Communist Youth. He had to act like a Khmer Rouge leader, giving orders and forcing others to follow them. In his exalted position as class captain, Sokkhom felt quite proud of himself.

Sokkhom called himself a Hun Sen supporter. There wasn't any other choice when one compared Hun Sen to the Khmer Rouge. Sokkhom felt Sihanouk wasn't a choice because he was working with the Khmer Rouge. Sokkhom became known for his high rank in the Hun Sen Student Government Organization, which was referred to as "the right hand of the Communist government."

Sokkhom and his friends were approaching the age of eighteen, when, if you left school, it was a citizen's duty to serve in the army. One of Sokkhom's close friends—someone with whom he had spent many vacations— left school to join the army. Six months later he was dead. While at the funeral, Sokkhom determined that he was not going to join the army.

Some of the young men in Sokkhom's village got married at age eighteen in order to escape the army but found they still had to join up. Thus, five or six joined at the same time; they were in the same battle and all died. Sokkhom began to lower his age by a few years on various papers so that he could stay in school.

The idea of selecting out his fellow students and thus deciding their fates began to weigh upon Sokkhom and he fell behind in his studies. In previous years, he had gotten the certificate for being the best student; now he dropped to number three. His teachers weren't worried; they said that he had a lot of responsibility and that's why his standing had dropped.

During 1988 and 1989 the three parties tried to negotiate: those of Hun Sen, King Sihanouk and the Khmer Rouge. Each party was trying to force the other parties to give as much as possible without giving anything themselves, so negotiations came to a standstill. Many Cambodians ran away to fight for Sihanouk at this time.

By 1990, Sokkhom had to stop visiting his home village of Phum Sre because of his high rank in the Hun Sen party. The Khmer Rouge still controlled much of the countryside and if Sokkhom were caught, he would be killed. Once the Khmer Rouge came into Phum Sre and burned the Ngeps' house; fortunately Mr. and Mrs. Ngep were visiting Sokkhom at the time. The parents visited Sokkhom and his brother at school even though the road between the school and the village was often in the midst of the fighting.

In April 1990, Sokkhom was given a short break from his duties for the Cambodian New Year. Being class captain, he had a lot on his mind and wanted to get completely away, so he went to stay with a friend in the Baray Province. They threw a party and relaxed.

When Sokkhom returned from his vacation he saw that his school had been burned to the ground by the Khmer Rouge. All the records in the administration building were gone. The only thing left was the student card he was carrying. Sokkhom realized that if he hadn't been away, he could very well have been on duty inside the building and burned along with it.

Sokkhom went to stay at another friend's house. There he heard that the Khmer Rouge had captured Stung Treng Province in the north, adjacent to Kompong Thom, forcing the inhabitants to flee to Phnom Penh for safety. The Khmer Rouge were saying they were going to take over Kompong Thom Province in the New Year—which was fast approaching. Sokkhom wondered if his only choice was to give himself up to the Khmer Rouge.

His parents were staying with him and he told them, "I give up. My school has burned down, the Khmer Rouge are going to capture Kompong Thom, so if I stay I might have to join the army. I'm going someplace else."

Sokkhom's older sister had fled to the U.S. with her husband and children in 1975, just as the Khmer Rouge were taking over. She had been able to escape because she and her family had been living close to the Thai border at the time. Although she had written them several letters since then, the Ngeps had burned them immediately and hadn't answered, because if anyone saw they had received a letter from America they could turn Sokkhom in to the Hun Sen government or the Khmer Rouge.

Sokkhom was still young and idealistic enough to think that perhaps he should join the army and die for his country. He wondered which side he would fight on—both seemed repugnant to him. He had secretly been listening to "Voice of America" radio broadcasts and learning more about the outside world, and it occurred to him that perhaps it would be better to live in another country entirely.

His younger brother Sokheng said that he also felt this way. The Ngeps had a clandestine family discussion about the matter. Secrecy was of the essence; if someone found out the Ngep boys were trying to escape, this piece of information would be a prime tidbit to turn in to the authorities and their lives would be in danger.

Mrs. Ngep asked her sons, "Are you sure you want to leave Cambodia?"

"Yes," they both replied.

"If you are set on going," Mrs. Ngep said, "I can quietly look around and see if someone is leaving the country."

Sokkhom turned to his brother Sokkha, four years older, "You're in the know and have a lot of friends. What do you think?"

"I've heard that a friend of mine goes back and forth over the Thai border," he said. "But it's dangerous. Especially for you two because you are well known to be part of Hun Sen's government. If you are captured by the Khmer Rouge or the Thai government, you'll be killed. There are also landmines along the border."

"It's too risky," said Mrs. Ngep hastily.

"I'll check into it," Sokkha said.

"My friend is going to another country by boat," Mrs. Ngep said, "I'll ask if you two can go along."

Mrs. Ngep secretly went to see her friend and was told the brothers could come along if they paid the fares in gold. She went home and talked with her sons who decided that leaving Cambodia on a boat was safer than being caught by the Khmer Rouge or fighting for the Vietnamese—both of which would happen if they stayed or tried to cross the Thai border.

The friend had told Mrs. Ngep the fare was the equivalent of $1,500 per person; they were to pay him in gold and he would give money to the captain. The family gathered together their gold jewelry—mostly Mrs. Ngep's—but it wasn't quite enough, so they borrowed the little bit needed from relatives and came up with the equivalent of $3,000 in gold for the two brothers to go on the boat.

On the arranged date, Sokkhom, Sokheng and Mrs. Ngep's friend left Kompong Thom by army truck in broad daylight. Army trucks were driving all over the country and were inconspicuous. They drove south towards Sihanoukville. On the way they stopped in Phnom Penh for a night and slept on the flat roof of a friend's house. Things were tense and they didn't really get to eat, because whenever a policeman approached the house, they quickly left the meal and hid.

The next day they continued in the army truck to Sihanoukville on the Gulf of Thailand in the South China Sea, where five boats waited to smuggle people to Australia. All five boats were old fishing trawlers with ragged nets and a scattering of equipment.

The five trawlers moved out to sea during the night of May 4, 1990. Four hours later, the passengers were transferred to the holds of native Indonesian fishing boats going to Australia. The boat Sokkhom and Sokheng boarded was built to hold a maximum of twenty people, but the two brothers plus seventy-seven others were crammed in the hold. As soon as Sokkhom boarded he had become seasick, perhaps because of the overpowering smell of fish. There were so many people on the boat that they had nowhere to sleep except on each other. That first night Sokkhom tried to sleep, then awoke near death from lack of air—another man was sleeping on him. He worked himself loose from the bodies and tried to sleep on the man.

The fishing boat chugged for days—past Thailand, past Malaysia, past Singapore. In Singapore—known for its strict maritime laws—the Singapore Coast Guard escorted them to Indonesian waters. Because they were an international ship, albeit small and battered, the Coast Guard gave them some oil, food and water.

Near Indonesia the boat began leaking, so the captain stopped in Kalimantan where they stayed for a week while the captain and some others tried to fix the leak. The emigrants asked to stay on because they had heard there was a refugee camp in Indonesia; however, that turned out to be a false rumor so they had to continue with the journey. As they were leaving, the captain told the Indonesians they were headed towards Australia, so some men sketched a few directions on the captain's map—this many degrees this way, this many degrees that way.

They had been at sea several days when a ship was viewed in the distance. Their boat pulled up alongside and the other captain pointed out the way on their map. After this, the boat the Cambodians were on was continuously lost, foundering in the vicinity of Australia but never reaching a port. At one point, as the boat neared East Timor, they came across a man with his head above water, drunk and nearly frozen. They rescued him and he directed them to his home town in East Timor, where they docked and disembarked, only to find they were in the midst of a war. The drunk man took them to his house, which happened to be in the worst of the fighting; as they were walking there, gunshots erupted. (Later, when they told the Australian government about this part of the journey, they were told, "East Timor—you might as well be in Cambodia!")

The drunk man invited them to spend the night. The Cambodians were sleeping on his floor when a soldier appeared, pointing a gun. The host took the soldier out and explained everything. The soldier radically changed his manner and escorted them safely to some shops so they could buy some food. The next morning the Cambodians piled back on their decrepit boat and left, again to try for Australia.

In the middle of the Timor Sea a big storm blew up, turning the boat around. The boat didn't have an accurate compass and the captain became completely lost. The waves grew bigger than the boat. Everyone was sick, even the captain, who was so sick that he couldn't steer and gave the wheel to someone else. No one was eating because of the tossing of the small boat on the huge waves. Mutually, the Cambodian passengers and the captain decided their only hope was to turn the boat back toward Indonesia.

The boat began to fill with water. The boat pump, broken during the beginning of the journey and fixed, broke again during the storm. The captain and some others were trying to bail out water by hand but everyone was too sick and weak to have much of an effect on the building water. The boat steadily sank lower and lower. It seemed like the end.

Then they saw an Australian fishing boat out in the storm. One of the Cambodians was sent to board it and came back with the news that the Australian boat was also lost; however, the Australian boat had radioed the Australian Coast Guard.

When the Australian Coast Guard reached the two boats, the Cambodians had been lost for a day and a night. Their wreck of a boat was half full of water, hours from sinking fully under the waves. It took two hours to transfer the Cambodian refugees to the Coast Guard boat. Once they were on board, the coast guard asked the Cambodians where they wanted to go. Everyone said Australia, except for Sokkhom and Sokheng, who said America, knowing that their sister was there.

The Australian Coast Guard took them easily and safely ashore in northern Australia. Including the week's stop in Kalimantan, Sokkhom, Sokheng and the other Cambodian refugees had been at sea for a total of twenty-eight days.

Shortly after Sokkhom and Sokheng had gone on the boat, their older brother Sokkha escaped to Thailand, where he established himself on the border, farming and preparing for his parents' escape. While in Thailand he was able to reach a phone and call his sister in America. She told him the family must go to a refugee camp so that she could sponsor them from America.

Mr. and Mrs. Ngep escaped over the Thai border in 1992 and stayed in a refugee camp until they went to live with their daughter in Minnesota. From Minnesota, they promptly began filling out applications to sponsor both brothers and added these to the applications the sister had already filled out.

After landing on Australian shores in the battered craft in June 1990, the brothers were put through a medical and customs check, then transferred with the other Cambodian refugees to the Immigration Detention Center set up in an abandoned army barracks in the Australian bush near Darwin. Although Sokkhom's and Sokheng's sister in America had applied to sponsor her two brothers, now that they were safely ensconced on Australian soil the American government appeared in no hurry to relocate them.

Sokkhom spent his first year in Australia at the detention center. He met three men who would prove to be extremely helpful in what would become a long and arduous quest to live on American soil: Dennis Shoesmith, Paul Luschich and Colin McDonald. Shoesmith taught Asian Studies, Luschich was an English teacher and McDonald was a lawyer; all three men worked with refugees at the center.

After a year Sokkhom was transferred to another detention center in Port Hedland, where he was to stay for four more years. This detention center was like a jail, surrounded by a set of double fences, one topped with barbed wire. During his stay Sokkhom acquired much education as the camp held classes in English, computing, typing and so on. He used his time in the detention center to take as many classes as possible, learning the basics of computing.

Sokkhom met his wife-to-be, Thangying, in one of his classes. She was a refugee from China and had also fled her homeland by boat; she and her family had left China because of the lack of freedom. She and

Sokkhom became close but made no plans; life was too uncertain. In 1995, they decided that—uncertain futures notwithstanding—they wanted to spend their lives together and became engaged to be married.

Also in 1995, the Chinese government issued a statement that all fugitives who chose to return to China would not be punished. Thangying and her parents decided to return to China. Sokkhom said goodbye to his fiancée and promised that as soon as he was released by the Australian government, he would come and marry her. Like the rest of their relationship, their parting was uncertain.

By 1995 Shoesmith, Luschich and McDonald were working vigorously on the Ngep brothers' case, writing letters to the director of immigration to try to secure their release. Although theNgep sister in America had long since filled out the correct sponsorship forms, the Australian government kept refusing to release the two men. Finally, Shoesmith said the brothers could live with him in Darwin so that they would at least be able to leave the detention center. The brothers lived with Dennis Shoesmith from 1996 to 1997, receiving a work permit visa. Sokkhom worked in a hotel at night and studied during the day. The hotel paid for his classes and in this way he was working toward a degree in hospitality management.

In 1997 Sokheng married a Cambodian refugee who lived in Canberra; both brothers moved there whereupon Sokkhom finished his schooling, receiving a diploma in hospitality management.

Sokkhom was finally granted permanent resident refugee status in 1998; however, he still was not able to go to America. Paul Luschich, who is American, wrote to a senator he knew in the U.S., telling of Sokkhom's plight and how the Australian government had kept the brothers such an inordinate amount of time in a detention center.

At long last in 1999, papers came from the U.S. saying Sokkhom's visa had been approved. Sokkhom knew that if he and Thangying wanted to be together in the United States, they must marry first. Ironically, if they had married in Australia, they could have both gone to America at the same time, but since Thangying was in China, she would have to apply for her visa separately. So Sokkhom flew to China and they were married there. Mr. Ngep wrote saying that he had applied to sponsor both Sokkhom and Thangying.

In November 1999, Sokkhom flew to Los Angeles and then on to Minneapolis, where he was reunited with his parents and siblings. Just short of ten years after leaving Cambodia on an old fishing boat, Sokkhom Ngep had arrived in America. He happened to arrive in Minneapolis on the night of his brother's wedding, so only his two sisters and brothers-in-law were waiting for him at the airport. When they took him home to the family, it was a night of double celebration. Mr. and Mrs. Ngep were overjoyed to see their son whom they had put on a dilapidated fishing trawler ten years earlier.

Sokkhom got a job in manufacturing and began working on getting his wife a visa. In June 2000, her visa was approved and she began the several-month process of medical exams. Thangying joined her husband in America in September 2001. They now live and work in Chanhassen, Minnesota, close to the rest of the Ngep family. From Cambodia to America over a period of ten years—one man's personal odyssey.

11

The Next Generation

As the survivors of the autogenocide began to trickle into the United States during the 1980s, many people and organizations stepped forward to help. My family, along with many others, gave freely of time and money in an attempt to help Cambodian refugees adapt to life in America. I think what none of us realized at the time was the extent to which Pol Pot and his Khmer Rouge had irrevocably altered not only the lives of the survivors, but also our own.

Those of us living and working with the refugees were prepared for the damage done to that first generation out of Cambodia—especially the children—who had experienced such terrible sufferings first hand. Of course, we reasoned, a child seeing their father executed or their mother starve to death would have lifelong effects from that experience. But I don't know that we ever considered those effects over the course of a lifetime: What happens when those children grow up and have their own children, when the foster parents become foster grandparents? I think we all believed that with new lives in the land of plenty— maybe some therapy thrown in for good measure—the survivors could make it.

Now, twenty years later, the damage inflicted by Pol Pot and his Khmer Rouge has spread like a cancer, the malignancy metastasizing to all parts of the body. The psyches of many children who were five, six, and older during Pol Pot's reign have been so injured that by the time they are adults it is a struggle to raise their own children.

The survivors' physiques were also injured, sometimes irreparably. Many were so starved and malnourished that they looked like "old men," or as one survivor put it, "like a skinny old grandpa." They skipped what is usually a time of enormous physical growth—childhood and adolescence—and went directly to a condition physically similar to the end of life when the body is broken down and wasted away.

One survivor who was five when he was tricked into a Khmer Rouge work gang says, "I decided not to trust anybody again." How can one build successful relationships—at work or at home—without trust? Pol Pot and the Khmer Rouge ruined one generation; when that generation grew to adulthood and had their children, the long arm of Pol Pot and the Khmer Rouge was still reaching out for another deadly embrace.

I think of the ten-year-old daughter of two survivors, now attending elementary school in California. She looks like her parents with brown skin, white teeth that show only occasionally in a smile and dark eyes. She says she hates school but loves animals and being in the kitchen. Whenever I see this girl I think of what a different life she would have had in prewar Cambodia, working in the rice fields, preparing the family's food over the open fire and taking care of the family oxen. By contrast, her future life in the States looks uncertain; skills at housework and cooking are valued little and jobs that demand such skills are often demeaning and underpaid.

But for the long arm of Pol Pot and his Khmer Rouge she could be in Cambodia, working in the fields and hearth, making a home in her village. Now, uprooted and torn from her heritage, she finds herself out of place without knowing why. Her parents' lives were destroyed by Pol Pot and his Khmer Rouge when they were six and eight; now, despite their best intentions, their daughter's life is being damaged in a different way.

Part of the problem is that this girl learned her skills from parents who weren't able to adapt and develop culturally relevant skills themselves because of the trauma they suffered. Possibly that same trauma resulted in secondary effects—such as neglect and abuse—that have stunted their daughter's skills. In short, the main role models in this girl's short life thus far have been people who have been traumatized and are unable to adapt.

Over the years, I have had the opportunity of watching my foster brothers get married and have children. It's wonderful to rejoice in a new life, to see their pride in a son or daughter, to see a perfect baby that shares some of a parent's physical features. It's frightening to look at the new baby and think of how the baby's parent started out just like that: perfect and loved. Then their world went terribly wrong.

Noeun was six years old when the Khmer Rouge invaded Phnom Penh and his family was forced to flee their home only with what they could cram in a cart. He was still six when he was taken from his parents and put with thousands of other boys and told to dig canals. He was eight when, incredibly, he saw his father tortured and killed before his own eyes.

Noeun and Prum married a few years out of high school. Although they carried some emotional wounds from the war, signs seemed positive for the marriage to work. They were both devoted to the other and had never seriously dated anyone else. They were strong, smart and good looking. Noeun had a good job with chances for advancement. Their first child, a girl, was born a year after the wedding; they named her Sarah, after me. A year later, they had a boy who they named Brian. The children were healthy and adorable; Noeun and Prum were working hard and saving money to buy their own house.

I remember Noeun telling me about the time the Khmer Rouge attacked the Pochentong Airport in Phnom Penh. "The soldiers shot a big bomb at the Pochentong Airport and destroyed it all— it was burning about a week," he said. "Airplanes, gas, bombs, everything exploded like popcorn."

Ivison Pakaday Lok, son of Sinn and Phary Lok. (Photograph from the personal collection of Sinn and Phary Lok.)

That is what happened to his life—it exploded, like popcorn, with the kernels of his family flying out every which way.

When Alec, our first child, was a newborn and the first grandchild on my parents' side, I saw a part of Sinn that I had never seen before. He loved children! He held Alec in his arms gently—albeit a little fearfully— and smiled at him.

Sinn had worked at the cabinet shop for years and could do beautiful things with wood. One time, during a visit, he brought Alec a present: a wooden car, with wood wheels that really worked, exquisitely painted and varnished. Then when Drew was born, he made a wooden dollhouse for her. Because my parents had to bring it along on the plane to Tucson—where we were living at the time—he made it so that it could come apart and be reassembled, with wooden pegs that went into corresponding holes on the other pieces.

So we all said to each other, "Won't it be wonderful when Sinn has his own children."

When Sinn married Phary, all the family was present, at least for parts of the three-day wedding ceremony. It was moving to watch our stoic Sinn weep as he knelt with Phary in brilliantly colored wedding costumes before candles and incense. Later, after blessings and songs in Khmer, the guests tied lengths of red thread around their outstretched wrists, symbolizing good wishes for their future happiness.

I didn't know Phary well, but I was hopeful for the marriage. Not only was Phary beautiful and accomplished, and—the best of all Midwestern attributes—nice, but Phary's birth family was intact. The parents and most of the children had made it through the years of Pol Pot rule and the Khmer Rouge, so they were a strong support for the couple and would also be later on for any children. Also, Sinn was older—almost thirty—when he got married, and, thus had had time to come to terms with his past and how to integrate it with his life as an adult.

Sinn and Phary came to Christmas 1999 with Phary barely showing her pregnancy. They were both sick—Sinn with a flu and cough; Phary with morning sickness—and not getting the care they needed. Over the next few days Roger (who is a physician) and I made phone calls on their behalf, trying to access the medical care covered by their insurance; both Sinn and Phary have good jobs with excellent benefits.

After being quite aggressive, I finally succeeded in getting a doctor who called Phary at 9 o'clock on a Sunday night and was very thorough in his dialogue with her. By the next day she was feeling better. I then called her before we left to return to Wisconsin, and spent a long time with both her and Sinn on the phone. I went through—step by step—what they should do if they were ever worried about something. They had the name and number of the right clinic; they were to call and give their health card number to the receptionist. When the doctor or nurse called back, they were to explain clearly what their worry was and listen to the instructions.

"Remember," I said to them. "You have paid for this health plan. It is paid for by money taken out of your paychecks. So you can get all the care you need. If you have any worries, no matter how small, call the number, say your name and talk to the doctor or the nurse."

Once that initial connection had been made, their care improved dramatically and Phary continued to see doctors throughout the pregnancy. Had the professionals starting taking the situation seriously when they heard it explained by a family member without an accent? Or had Sinn and Phary not known how to access the system and get the help they needed?

Both families continued to be very important for the pregnancy, all the way up to the birth in late May. Throughout the long hours of labor Phary's family was there, as well as my mother. There were scary moments: the baby was born with the cord around his neck and looked blue, but the doctors and nurses took care of everything, resulting in a healthy baby.

When I saw Ivison Pakaday at two weeks old, he was beautiful. His skin was a light shade of brown, right in between Sinn and Phary's colors; he had Sinn's alert, watchful gaze and nose and Phary's mouth. A baby holds such high hopes. There is the hope that he will grow up to be healthy and happy. The hope that he will live in a safe country and will never have to experience war. The hope that his parents will be able to surmount their own ravaged childhoods in order to give him a healthy, nurturing one.

Nancy Smith-Hefner has extensively studied the Cambodian refugee community of metropolitan Boston and the results of her long-term research are illuminating, if troubling. She points out that Khmer Americans (her term for Cambodians here in the U.S.) struggle with the contrast between the American moral and cultural codes and those held by the community elders who cling to the old codes of Cambodia. As the next generation is pulled into American society faster than their parents and grandparents, a generational dissonance results, where the moral messages of Khmer households are often in direct conflict with those of mainstream American society.

The survivors of the autogenocide are clashing with the next generation of Cambodians growing up in America. The parents look at their children and see a lack of respect towards what was once the foundation of their lives in Cambodia: Buddhism, the family, honoring the elders. There is a discord between the beliefs of the parents and the new, Americanized beliefs of the children. Because of this ongoing conflict experienced by many immigrant groups, the Khmer community is having difficulty assimilating into the broader American culture.

Buddhism is an important ingredient in the Khmer makeup. Many Khmer state, "To be Khmer is to be Buddhist." In the American culture where Buddhism—certainly the Theravada Buddhism practiced by most Khmer Americans—is ignored and misunderstood, assimilation and adaptation is made all the harder. For example, Khmer parents believe that grown children should recognize their moral debt to their elders by performing acts of merit; this belief is rarely reciprocated by the grown children.

Sophea Mouth remembers how in prewar Cambodia it was common for young males to go into monkhood for one or two years in order to repay their parental debt, a practice common in Thailand and Laos as well.

Sophea recounts a Cambodian folk tale: A boy had a strong desire to become a monk. His parents said no but he kept asking because he wanted to be a monk with all his heart; his parents still refused. Finally, the boy became so discouraged that he didn't eat any food for seven days. At this, the parents relented and said yes. The boy rejoiced and went off to join the monastery. Some years later the father died and went to Hell. The gatekeeper of Hell looked in the book and said, "It's marked that you don't belong here." So the father went up to heaven and was admitted inside. He asked, "How did I get in?" and was told, "It was because your son was a monk."

This story conveys the importance Cambodians previously attached to the concept of "making merit" and "repaying the parental debt." In the tale, the father is able to enter heaven—despite the bad deeds he had committed—because his son had repaid the parental debt with his monkhood.

The basic tenets of Buddhism—good deeds, as well as evil ones, will have their effects but the Buddhist is always free to pray for guidance; to perform good actions; and to "make merit," or to gain spiritual credit by performing righteous acts—have always been the guiding precepts of Cambodians. When Cambodian refugees state, "I am Khmer, therefore I am Buddhist," they are illustrating that Buddhism is not simply a religion but at the core of the Khmer identity. Folk tales, like the one Sophea Mouth told, were a source of instruction and wisdom to residents living in Cambodia. Now, in a new country where young Cambodians are bombarded with different—and often contrary—precepts and instruction, a folk tale like this one merely seems irrelevant to the next generation.

As the next generation moves away from the family and into mainstream American society, it causes much intergenerational misunderstanding. For example, parents in the Khmer American community often lavish elaborate and costly weddings upon their children in the hope that the children will reciprocate by caring for them when they are old. This is an especially acute issue since there is not an extended family network available to care for the elderly as there was in prewar Cambodia. As the parents age, however, they realize that in American society the elderly don't live with their children.

The first generation of Cambodian refugee parents fear for, and seem bewildered by, the next generation of Khmer Americans. Sam, Sokhary and Sarith—all interviewed for this book—specifically mention this fear. They, along with other Khmer parents, feel that the tried-and-true methods of child rearing and instilling values simply haven't worked in the United States. They want their children to learn and preserve the cultural and moral traditions from Cambodia but find it difficult to achieve this transmission in a foreign country after an autogenicide.

There is also a distinct gap emerging among the next generation between the "haves" and a much larger group of "have-nots." There are the survivors who have assimilated into and succeeded in American culture—this is usually indicated by financial success. Then there are the survivors who are unable to shake the demons and exorcise the ghosts of the past and thus, are unable to succeed. This gap is clearly illustrated by the stories of the survivors in this book. The divide seems to be growing and Smith-Hefner, based upon her observations, thinks it will only continue to widen.

What is the answer? It is crucial that the Cambodian refugee community re-creates its culture here in America and decide what is essential to the new Khmer identity and what it can forsake. This is the only resolution for what Smith-Hefner calls "... a small diasporic community attempting to reconstitute itself after a holocaust." The future of the next generation depends upon the ability of Khmer Americans to undertake this task.

12

The Price of Success:
The Story of Samantha Samreth

Samantha Samreth was just four years old when she was entrusted to bring food to her father, Mong Samreth, who lay ill in a Khmer Rouge makeshift hospital. Mong's wife—and Samantha's mother—Narouen Kum had been assigned to work in a labor camp some distance away and couldn't return to Battambang more than once every few days. Mong's mother took care of Samantha and her one-year-old brother Pay, but was too old to make the trip twice a day. So it was up to Samantha to bring rice and any other food to her father as in the Khmer Rouge hospital huts there were no medicines, doctors, nor food. Samantha was proud that she had been chosen for such an important task and she loved the chance to see and talk to her beloved father.

Mong Samreth had been a sergeant in the Lon Nol army and had been taken prisoner with the other officers when the Khmer Rouge had conquered Battambang on April 1975; however, Khmer Rouge chief of state Khieu Samphan had ordered that instead of being immediately executed, a certain number of officers were to be released and sent back to their villages to work. So instead of facing death, Mong had joyfully rejoined his family near Battambang.

He and his wife, Narouen Kum, were sent to work in different Khmer Rouge labor camps. Their only choice was to leave their children, Samantha and Pay, with Mong's mother. After some months of doing back-breaking work building dams and dikes, Mong became ill and was sent to the hut designated as a hospital by the Khmer Rouge, where he languished for several weeks and Samantha came with food twice a day.

While Mong was lying in his cot, a Khmer Rouge soldier came several days in a row and stared at him. Soon Mong received word that *Angkar* was going to "relocate" him and send him to work somewhere else. Mong knew this meant that he was going to be killed. He had been a

Lon Nol soldier—most of whom had already been executed—and now he was ailing and couldn't work for the Khmer Rouge. He knew they weren't going to relocate him—that was merely a euphemism so that they could take him away and kill him in secret.

Mong's main concern was to somehow leave word for his wife, Narouen. The Khmer Rouge had destroyed all remnants of education when they took over, so there wasn't pencil or paper to write a letter. There were however, pieces of cloth lying around the makeshift hospital—used for bandages and so on—so Mong cut his gum until it bled profusely and then wrote a message with his finger dipped in his own blood on a piece of cloth. After he was done, he folded up the cloth and placed it under his cot. He didn't say anything to Samantha when she visited as she was just under five years old and he didn't want her to worry; however, Samantha could feel her father's preoccupation and knew something was troubling him.

When Samantha entered the hospital with a bowl of rice the next morning her father wasn't there. Usually the curtain was drawn around his bed but now it was pulled back and his bed was empty, with a folded blanket and bedpan lying on top. Samantha searched frantically and found the cloth with the message written in blood folded under the bed.

The lady in the next cot looked at Samantha with tears in her eyes and said, "Give that to your mother to read and you'll find out what happened."

Samantha was extremely curious about the contents of the letter but had to run home and wait for her mother to visit from the labor camp. When Naroeun came in, Samantha gave her the piece of cloth. Naroeun read the piece of cloth, then began crying uncontrollably. At first, she couldn't say anything. Then she haltingly read to Mong's mother and Samantha from the cloth:

"They killed your father. He said to take care of Samantha and Pay. He's sorry he's gone. He knew this was coming because he's seen the same soldier come and look at him each day. He knew he was going to be killed but couldn't escape because he had only one leg that worked."

"At the end, he writes: 'So if you don't see me that means I'm gone and I'm dead. They've killed me.'"

(Samantha held onto the hope that her father was still alive until twenty-five years later when she met with two of Mong's army friends in Madison, Wisconsin. They told her that they had seen her father killed with their own eyes. He had been tied up by the Khmer Rouge and shot.)

During the next few weeks, whenever she was able to visit, Naroeun

Emigration photograph of Samantha Samreth (holding sign) and her mother, Narouen Kum (holding Veasna), 1980. They are standing in front of the refugee camp. The photograph is stamped by the United Nations High Commissioner for Refugees on the back. (Photograph from the personal collection of Samantha Samreth.)

told Samantha stories of herself and Mong. It was as if she wanted to impress Mong's memory upon Samantha's brain and heart.

"Ours was an arranged marriage as most are in Cambodia," she said. "I was told that I was going to marry Mong Samreth, a man I had never seen. When he came to visit on a bicycle, it was the first time I laid eyes on him. I was eighteen when we got married and nineteen when you were born."

"Before our marriage," Naroeun continued, "I was a good volleyball player. Once I played before Prince Sihanouk in the Olympic stadium. My mother saw to it that I was educated and this was in a time when girls weren't thought worth educating. I knew French and went to secondary school."

"We had a good marriage," Naroeun told Samantha. "After you were born we had a baby boy who got sick and died at three months. When you were three, Pay was born and by then, your father had a very important position in Lon Nol's army."

A few months after Mong's death, his mother—Samantha's grandmother—also died, seemingly of a broken heart, or, more probably, from the lack of food and the worsening conditions under the Khmer Rouge. Samantha and Pay were left alone in the house while Naroeun was at the labor camp. Naroeun arranged for the neighbors to check on the children occasionally and tried to sneak back for a short visit every other night but, for the most part, Samantha and Pay were left alone. At five years old, Samantha had a mother's responsibility for her younger brother Pay.

Sometimes they went swimming in the river to cool off. Once they were playing on a dock and when Samantha looked around, she couldn't see Pay. She dove under the water again and again but couldn't find him. On the fourth dive she saw him and brought him up to the surface and placed him on the dock. He was fine. Samantha was so scared that she could hardly breathe.

Pay became sick. No one knew exactly what illness, but he grew sicker by the day. Naroeun began sneaking back every night because she knew how sick her son was. She was there the night Pay lay in a stupor with white foam dribbling from his mouth. He breathed his last breath. Naroeun's cries and screams brought the neighbors who tried to comfort her, but to no avail.

Samantha also was inconsolable. Pay had been more than a brother to her; she had taken care of him like a mother. Samantha felt a part of herself was gone with his death. She was so full of sorrow that she thought she would never recover.

Pay's death caused Naroeun to realize that there was nothing to keep her and Samantha in Cambodia. So when the Vietnamese liberated the abject and starving Cambodians from Pol Pot and the Khmer Rouge in 1978, Naroeun grabbed Samantha's hand and they fled. The streets of Battambang held a sea of people trying to leave the country. The crowd had to slow down past the city, but more and more people kept joining in, running for their lives.

Narouen and Samantha ran together for a full day. Towards dusk, the panicked crowd ran right through mother and daughter's linked hands and separated them. Samantha stood crying until an American soldier came along, said something in English that she couldn't understand, scooped her up and took her to a refugee camp on the Cambodian side of the Thai/Cambodian border.

Naroeun ended up in another camp and spent the night looking for Samantha, whom she finally located the next morning. Mother and daughter stood locked in an embrace, reunited.

After several months in the refugee camp, Narouen and Samantha went on to a second "new" camp, still inside Cambodia. Although Samantha was six—and turned seven—while living at the camp, she didn't go to school but ran and played with the other children. Naroeun made various things—food, pillow covers and so forth—to sell on the black market. In this way she made enough money for the two of them to live.

Two years later they crossed the border when they were transferred to the Chon Buri refugee camp in Thailand. To their surprise, Mong's sister, her husband and their five children had escaped Cambodia and were living in the Chon Buri camp. Life was definitely easier and more peaceful in Chon Buri; there were no bombs or war.

At twenty-five, Naroeun was still a young woman who wanted and needed companionship. She met a Cambodian-Chinese man in the camp who said his wife had died in the war. He and Naroeun became man and wife according to camp custom by moving into the same hut and soon Narouen was pregnant.

One of Mong's cousins had been a pilot during the war and, having seen what was coming, left Cambodia in 1975, just before the Khmer Rouge took control of the country. In 1978, this cousin was living in the small town of Stoughton, Wisconsin, married to another Cambodian refugee and the father of two children. News reports on the Vietnamese invasion and the refugees pouring into Thailand aired on the nightly news and he began to try to locate his relatives in order to help them obtain sponsorship and come to the United States.

Finally, in 1980, he located Naroeun, Samantha, Mong's sister, her husband and their five children in Chon Buri and sent them a letter saying they should apply for sponsorship to the United States. Naroeun's new "husband" was told he couldn't apply because he wasn't part of the family. In the ensuing years Naroeun had found out that this man had been deceiving her as he had a wife and children in the village outside the camp. Narouen stated emphatically that she felt fine about going to the U.S. without him.

Naroeun had a healthy baby boy in the Chon Buri refugee camp that she named Veasna. Samantha was very excited about her new brother and helped her mother care for him. Shortly after Veasna's birth, the family of three—as well as Mong's brother and his family—were told they had been approved for sponsorship by a coalition of churches in Stoughton, Wisconsin. Just before they were to leave, Naroeun's medical exam X-rays showed spots on her lungs: tuberculosis. Both families were sent to an interim camp in the Philippines for one year in order for Naroeun to benefit from the change in climate and medication.

The camp in the Philippines held lessons in cultural adaptation for the emigrating refugees. Some classes talked about what to do and not to do in the United States.

"It's very clean," the relief workers said. "You can't spit on the streets like you do in Cambodia."

Samantha was impressed by this; it must be very clean in the United States!

By 1981 Naroeun's lung X-rays were free of spots and the two families were cleared for going to the United States. They flew to San Francisco and from there to Madison, Wisconsin. The plane rides seemed very long to ten-year-old Samantha.

Naroeun, Samantha and Veasna arrived with their relatives in the Madison airport on September 9, 1981, where Dr. David Nelson and Kent and Judy Schroeder—all from Stoughton—were waiting in the airport. The Schroeders were holding shoes and coats for everyone, including the children. As the recent arrivals were attired in tank tops and plastic sandals, they put on the new clothes and shoes. They didn't fit but they were grateful for the warmth. Upon exiting the airport, Samantha was struck by how clean everything was in the United States—the relief workers had been right!

Dr. Nelson and the Schroeders put the Cambodians in two cars and drove to the picturesque white two-story house they would share on Main Street in Stoughton. Naroeun, Samantha and Veasna lived on the top floor while Mong's sister and her family lived on the main floor.

Samantha began fourth grade at Kegonsa Elementary School. For the first week the Schroeders drove her there for half days, feeling this was the best way for her to adjust to the new school. After the first week they continued to drive her to and from school for several weeks—but for full days—and after that, they let her take the bus.

Samantha's teacher, Mrs. Barb Beckwith, was an enormous source of help and support for a new and shy Cambodian girl. She worked out a buddy system for Samantha whereby each month a different girl from the class was her "buddy." By the end of that fourth-grade year, Samantha had become "best friends" with three of the girls in the class, two of whom would still be her friends twenty years later.

Samantha was determined to learn everything she could. She practiced the alphabet and English all the time; math came easily to her without much practice. She tried to watch "Sesame Street" on television because that helped her with English, but it was difficult because everyone in the house fought over which shows to watch.

She was determined to learn and do well at school; her English got better and better and her studies greatly improved. She went to summer school, the start of a lifelong habit. In the sixth grade she was given an assignment to write an essay on her hero. She chose Mong Samreth—her father—and her teacher entered her essay in a Stoughton-wide writing contest. Samantha was shocked and proud when she won first place and received the renowned "Golden Pen" award.

Narouen married another Cambodian refugee also living in Stoughton when Samantha was in the seventh grade. Samantha felt fine about her stepfather but knew that she would never think of him as her father. Mong Samreth would forever hold that place in his daughter's heart. Samantha's half sister Rosemary was born when Samantha was twelve.

In high school Samantha wasn't part of the popular crowd but had a close group of friends. And, although very focused and academic, she still had time to relax, be social and have fun. She started working at the local A&W for $2.30 an hour and continued to do so throughout her high school years, spending most of her paycheck on clothes and the other little extras that are so important in high school. Naroeun couldn't afford to buy them for her and Samantha wanted them, so she worked and bought them for herself.

Samantha's half brother Michael was born when she was sixteen. After Michael's birth, Samantha began saving some of her money from her job at the A&W and helping out Narouen with various emergencies or unexpected costs that came up. Sometimes Samantha went out and bought her mother gifts, like nice jewelry, just because her mother enjoyed them so much. Samantha also began saving to go to college. No one else in the family had ever gone to college. Samantha decided that she would be the first one in the family to go.

While tutoring the Alternative Learning Program students at Stoughton High School in math, Samantha talked to the director of the program, Mrs. Sue Slinde, about college. Samantha felt more comfortable talking to Mrs. Slinde rather than her mother because Narouen had never been to college.

"UW-Whitewater has an excellent business school," Mrs. Slinde told her and took her along on a tour of the University of Wisconsin campus in Whitewater.

Samantha liked the campus and was impressed with the school; it was neither too big nor too small. While on the tour, she picked up an application. She went home and filled it out that very day. Soon she received a letter saying that she had been accepted.

Cambodian custom dictates that teenage girls aren't supposed to talk to, much less date, boys. Also, the parents choose a match for their offspring. Naroeun had a Cambodian friend in Chicago with a young son so she and the other mother arranged for their children to meet.

The young man, Buna Sun, came to visit. Samantha liked him and enjoyed the afternoon. Buna was very interested in music; he played bass guitar and sang. The only way Samantha and Buna could get to know each other more or date was to become engaged, so during Samantha's junior year of high school they formally became engaged.

Samantha was able to graduate early—after her junior year—because she had taken so many credits during summer school. Later on, as an adult, she would regret this haste, feeling she should have stayed in high school and graduated with the rest of her class. But at the time she wanted to move on with her life. Because she wasn't with her friends, she felt out of place during the ceremony and didn't know many of her fellow graduates.

She began UW-Whitewater in the fall of 1989 with a rocky start. She wasn't sure what her goals were or what she wanted. She had second thoughts about her engagement. When she saw other young men on campus that she was attracted to, she felt guilty because she was engaged to Buna. She also felt that he was coming too frequently to visit her when she should be spending the time studying. Eventually, she broke up with Buna so that she wouldn't be sneaking around if she did see somebody she liked and wanted to date.

After she broke off the engagement, a graduate student at UW-Whitewater liked her and they became friends. He was much older than she was, and after a while, she thought: What am I doing? He took a job in Arkansas shortly after and when he left, she had no regrets.

Naroeun began calling and asking Samantha to drive her to various doctor appointments during Samantha's sophomore year. When Samantha was two weeks into spring semester, Naroeun was told she had cervical cancer.

When Samantha first heard the news, she resolved to keep her spirits up for her mother's sake, but as the semester wore on and her mother became more ill—and then as finals approached—she became quite depressed. She worried about her siblings, Veasna, Rosemary and Michael, back in Stoughton.

Samantha managed to get through her finals and do fairly well, then went home for the summer. Her mother was very sick, and lay swollen and immobile on the bed. Cervical cancer spreads in sheets and Naroeun's case had accelerated so fast that nothing could stop it. The doctor told

Samantha that there was no cure and Naroeun would not live past six months.

Naroeun went into the University hospital. Samantha stayed by her side day and night, sleeping on the chair next to the bed. (When Samantha looks at the photographs she took of her mother at the hospital, she cries; her mother looks like a skeleton.)

After a month the doctors told Samantha that her mother could go home to die because there was nothing more that they could do. Samantha understood but knew that she and her mother needed to talk about her brother, Veasna, before her mother left the hospital.

So she approached her mother and told her that she understood that Rosemary and Michael would continue to live with their father after Narouen was gone, but didn't feel comfortable with Veasna continuing to live with his stepfather. Naroeun agreed that it would be best for Veasna to live with Samantha after Narouen's death. Samantha hired a lawyer who came to the hospital and had Narouen sign the papers there giving Samantha legal guardianship of Veasna. It was awkward with the lawyer in the hospital room but Samantha felt that it was necessary to take care of it in order to avoid legal problems after Narouen died.

Samantha took fall semester off to care for her dying mother. Her mother's husband—Samantha's stepfather—was present and involved but couldn't do it all himself; he had the other children to look after and his job to go to every day.

Naroeun died at 1:30 a.m. on Christmas Day in 1991. Samantha felt so lost and alone in the world, overwhelmed by grief. She had lost her father, then her brother, Pay—who had been more like her own child than a brother—and now her mother.

During the weeks following Narouen's death, Samantha felt adrift, without moorings. For the first time in her life she had no idea of the next step. She didn't want to return to school for spring semester. Her uncle invited her to leave college and live with them but she didn't feel that was the answer. She grew more depressed and downcast. Finally she got ahold of herself enough to sit down and try to think clearly about her situation.

She told herself, "You can't get the past back. Things happen and you have to go on. What good will it do to stay at home and mope about things?"

So she found an apartment for herself and Veasna to rent in White-water and returned to college that spring. She made sure to schedule her college courses during the school day so that she could take Veasna to and from his fifth grade class and be there when he was home. She was a junior in college and, for the second time in her young life, raising a younger brother. Because she had no parents living, she received financial aid which paid for most of the rent of their apartment. She also applied for—and received—public assistance money. Because of this help, she and Veasna were able to make it.

Samantha met Freda Briscoe at this time, a counselor for the Minority Business Program, and they developed a very close relationship; Freda was the kind of person Samantha could talk to easily. Samantha told her about her life, her mother's death, and how she was raising her younger brother. Freda was supportive and it felt good to Samantha to be able to talk to a friend about her unique situation.

Old habits die hard; Samantha went to summer school to make up for the semester she had missed. Buna came back into her life. By this time he had his own band in Chicago—"Motion"—and they were booked months ahead. As they renewed their relationship, Samantha could see that she felt secure in Buna's love and affection. She also knew that after going through her mother's death and raising Veasna she had grown up from the time when they had previously dated. She could see now that he was what she wanted in a life partner.

Samantha graduated from UW-Whitewater in 1993 with a major in economics and a minor in home and resource management. Veasna had just finished seventh grade in Whitewater and was doing well—an honor student, in the talented and gifted program, with many friends. Samantha could see that he had adjusted well after his mother's death and the move.

She and Buna were married right after her graduation in June 1993. Following the custom of Asian women, Samantha kept her maiden name. The newly wed couple took Veasna with them to California, then left him with some cousins while they went on a three-week honeymoon cruise to Mexico.

Upon their return to Wisconsin, Samantha and Veasna moved into Buna's apartment in Stoughton where he had a job with Ortega. Buna understood that Veasna was going to live with them and had no problem with it; he liked Veasna and they got along well.

Samantha got her first real job—in retail, at J.C. Penney's in Madison. Buna continued working for Ortega in Stoughton, which later changed the name to Nabisco, but stayed the same company. Veasna began eighth grade in Stoughton and had a hard time detaching from his friends in Whitewater and making new friends in Stoughton.

The three began their new life together. Samantha and Buna went to work; Veasna went to school. Samantha and Buna were saving money to buy a house. Veasna seemed to be adjusting to a new school and friends. Life was busy and full, but the three were content. Then, unexpectedly, near the end of 1994, Samantha became pregnant.

The pregnancy was unplanned and Samantha wasn't ready. She and Buna had only been married one year; she still had debts from school. She considered having an abortion but Buna and some other friends told her to think about it first. Her spirits grew low and she felt discouragement pressing her down; she was sinking into a depression.

As she had done after mother's death, Samantha sat down and thought clearly about the situation. She believed things happened for a reason. Her life had worked out thus far and she had faith that it would continue to do so. She decided against the abortion and to continue the pregnancy.

She realized that it was important to her that their child grow up in a house, not an apartment. She began searching for a home to buy and finally found one that was perfect: two story, nice floor plan, a big back yard where Buna could put in a garden, and what's more—the house was in Stoughton where Buna worked. They began the process of buying the house.

Samantha gave birth to their daughter, Savanna, on April 24, 1995. She was twenty-three years old. Three days later they signed the papers for the house, making it officially theirs. Buna, Samantha, Savanna and Veasna moved into the house just days later, on May 1.

The newly enlarged family had just moved and was happily living in the bigger space when Buna was suddenly laid off from his job. He told Samantha that he would receive unemployment compensation which would be the equivalent of 80 percent of what he had been making and they were grateful for this much.

But Samantha was very scared. They had a new baby, the bills kept coming and they had just purchased a house. They had hardly any furnishings: no curtains, no furniture other than one bed. She felt discouraged but could see that there were some good things about the situation; for example, she had maternity leave for seven weeks and Buna would be around to help. True, they would have less money, but he also would be home for the first few months of Savanna's life—a very important time.

The months of Samantha's maternity leave passed quickly. The baby, Savanna, was a joy—everyone in the house was drawn to her delighted grin and chubby cheeks. But despite being able to see the silver lining, Samantha grew dejected and low. Then, just as her maternity leave was drawing to a close, Samantha decided to try and pick herself up. She thought about the situation and gave herself another pep talk: What am I moaning about? Why am I depressed? Things happen for a reason. Buna will find another job.

And he did. Just as Samantha was about to resume work at Penney's after finishing her maternity leave, Buna was hired by Oscar Mayer Foods in Madison. After working for some time and getting the feel for the new job, Buna volunteered to work the weekend shift—working ten hours each on Friday, Saturday and Sunday—realizing that this was a way he could work thirty-six hours per week but get paid for forty.

When the baby Savanna was just approaching her first birthday, Samantha again became pregnant—and again, it was unplanned. But this time, she didn't consider an abortion; she knew she would have the baby.

Their son Brandon, a beautiful boy with dark hair and eyes, was born on December 22, 1996. He and his big sister Savanna were only twenty months apart.

However, Samantha knew that although their family had worked out perfectly and she and Buna were very happy, she needed to use another form of birth control. Both she and Buna knew that two children were enough.

Samantha sat down and considered her options: The pill hadn't worked for her; Buna felt he was still too young to have a vasectomy and she respected this; her doctor had advised her against a tubal ligation because he felt that she was too young at twenty-four. She decided upon getting shots—one every three months—and this method proved to be effective.

During the following years Samantha and Buna successfully juggled their work schedules to fit their family's needs. Samantha worked the regular Monday through Friday weekday schedule while Buna watched the children, then on the weekends Samantha stayed home and Buna worked. This way, Savanna and Brandon were in childcare only one day a week, on Friday. Everyone was happy with this arrangement. Samantha figured out the finances; childcare was somewhere in the area of $200 for both children. Either she or Buna would make $280–$300 after taxes and paying the childcare expenses would nearly use it up. The numbers didn't support them both working during the work week.

"Plus," Samantha pointed out to Buna, "if we're both working during the day, nobody is there to pick up the kids, nobody is there to make food to eat and the stress increases. So we end up hungry and mad at each other. It's not worth it."

Buna enjoyed being at home during the week; he loved to garden and soon they had an enormous vegetable garden in back of their house. The children helped him in the garden as they grew and he showed them how to care for the plants. Every summer he gave the neighbors piles of vegetables. Samantha, on the other hand, never had to help with the yard or garden; she never had to cut the grass.

In 1998, Buna said to Samantha, "You should go back to school and get your MBA. You have a brain to study; I don't. Don't worry about anything else—I'll take care of the house, food, kids. You just have to study."

So Samantha went back to UW-Whitewater to get her master's in business administration degree. While she was there, her old friend Freda Briscoe approached her and told her there was a position open in the College of Business. Samantha applied, interviewed and got the job of academic counselor. She would work and go to school, each full time.

Veasna graduated from high school and decided he also wanted to go into business. Since UW-Whitewater was known for its business school and Samantha would be there to guide him, it seemed the perfect place for him. Veasna also became a student at Whitewater with Samantha; however, he lived in a dorm and only came home to visit the family on weekends.

For two years, from 1998 to 2000, Samantha hardly slept. She went to school full time, had a full time job and two toddler children at home. She finished her MBA in two years while the children were small and she was working full time. Their schedule was excruciating but it worked: She arose at 4 a.m. in order to be at her job by 5 a.m. and read her textbooks in the stillness and quiet of the empty office between 5 a.m. and 8 a.m. when no one else was there. Buna continued to care for the children during the week and work weekends at Oscar Mayer. True to his word, he did all the cooking and cleaning. For two years the only thing Samantha did around the house was the laundry.

Buna still played his guitar but only when Samantha was not at home. When she was home she needed peace and quiet and Buna accepted this, just as she accepted that he would always have music in his life.

Once a friend said to Samantha, "You have so much education and Buna only graduated from high school. Why did you marry him?"

Samantha replied, "Maybe he doesn't have a college degree but he has something more valuable—a heart. Besides, he's smart in other ways.

He has fixed up the house—finished off the downstairs so we have another floor. There are a lot of things in life besides school. We balance each other out."

Other people said to Buna, "Once Samantha gets all those degrees, she's going to dump you."

"Well, I can't control that, " Buna answered, unperturbed. "But I trust my wife."

These comments didn't bother Samantha and Buna; many people didn't think their marriage was going to last past the first year because they were so different. Obviously, those people were wrong.

After six years with Oscar Mayer, Buna was fed up. The management kept changing his shift and it was difficult to get babysitters at the last minute.

Samantha said to him, "Why don't you do something where people don't tell you what to do all the time—where you could be your own boss?"

For some time she had been encouraging him to open up a grocery or clothing store, partly because she felt she could be of help in a business venture with her retail experience. Buna began seriously considering opening up a grocery store.

Various people had told Samantha that Janesville, Wisconsin—a town thirty minutes south of Stoughton—had a large Asian population but no stores for Asians. Samantha thought this was a positive lead but that she should check out the facts.

"Some people don't see Asians very often, so a lot of Asians could mean six people," she told Buna and they laughed together.

But it was exactly as people had said. The United Refugee Services in Madison listed sixty Cambodian families living in Janesville alone. Samantha went online and did an Internet search to check the labor statistics to see how many Asians were in Janesville; the labor statistics reported 2,700 Asians living in Janesville.

Samantha began searching for a good store location in Janesville. She went to a Realtor and asked about spaces zoned for business. The Realtor gave her a list of sites and she asked the Realtor to give her the statistics on how many Asians lived one mile from each site, five miles, ten miles and so forth. The Realtor got back to her with the numbers and Samantha picked the spot that was in the center of the most condensed area of Asians. The research took six months to complete.

Buna's sister and her husband—Nary and Peter—had also wanted to open up a store, so the two couples decided to open a grocery store together. Nary and Peter lived in Chicago but were willing to open the store in Janesville. Buna and Samantha took out a home equity loan to cover start-up costs; Peter and Nary also put in start-up money. The four of them put in countless hours getting ready to open the doors; even Samantha, who worked the least of the four, spent every free moment getting ready for opening day.

Asian Grocery, LLC, opened on March 1, 2001 in Janesville, Wisconsin. Business was great right from the start. While doing the numbers, Samantha had estimated making a certain amount in order to break even, but business was even better than anticipated. However, the four were aware that business would slow down with the arrival of hot weather because other grocery store owners had warned them of this phenomenon. So these calculations were taken into account.

Business at the store continued apace and the couples worked hard. Buna was very happy owning a grocery store and loved being his own boss. The hours were long and hard—he and Peter were there every day—but he thrived on the new business. Nary purchased merchandise from wholesalers in Chicago. Samantha did the bookwork and also went in on weekends so the other three could take some time off. Every Thursday Peter drove into Chicago to buy fresh produce that would be on the Asian Grocery store shelves by Friday morning. He also went to O'Hare Airport to pick up produce, ethnic vegetables and so on, shipped from Florida. The store carries rice, noodles, soy sauce, peppers, canned fruit, frozen shrimp, frozen squids, mussels—to name just a few.

Samantha is going to continue helping out at the grocery store for another year and then begin work on her Ph.D., which she plans to get in four years, by the time she is forty. She wants to teach at the university level.

"I'm happy," Samantha acknowledges simply. "I have a good job and a stable life. I love my husband, and I think it's wonderful to have our children."

Samantha and Buna don't have much time for a social life these days. Samantha doesn't spend time with her friends any more because she's very focused on her family. Even if the friends also have children, they do things that Samantha wouldn't consider, like leaving their children alone or with a babysitter so that they can go out drinking. Samantha doesn't want to do that and doesn't think it's the right thing to do as a parent. Sometimes these friends complain that she's no fun anymore.

Samantha doesn't understand it. She grew up without very much and knows what it's like not to have what other people have. Thus, she's motivated to do something better with her life and be successful.

When people bother her about this, saying, "Why don't you come to parties anymore? Come on, don't work all the time, you're no fun ..."

She says back, "Come on yourself! You don't want to live in a slum all your life, get up and do something!"

They say, "I don't have the ability you do."

She says, "Everybody has abilities. You have to try harder."

She doesn't have time to sit around and talk. Samantha works full time, goes to school at night, studies and spends time with the children on weekends. On top of all that, there's the house to clean. She knows that the best time to work hard is now while she's young; when she's old she can be lazy.

People say, "You have your MBA already, why do you need to go on? Be with your relatives, have fun, relax. Hang out for a little bit."

"I can't stand that," she says to them. "I like to read books; I want to know more."

She and Buna have sacrificed a great deal in order to achieve higher things. They have sacrificed time with friends and relatives, relaxation, fun, a social life. But it has been a sacrifice they feel has been worth it.

13

Housewarming

Noeun was throwing a party to celebrate the purchase of his new house—a housewarming. The family members had passed around the news in amazement and admiration. Isn't that something? we said to each other. Coming to the U.S. with nothing—absolutely nothing—and now he owns a house. The many hours of work he had put in—weekends, overtime and holidays at the Plastics Injection Molding Factory—had paid off. From the killing fields of Cambodia to the green fields of Minnesota, he had worked hard enough and long enough to achieve the American dream.

Noeun had scheduled the party for a summer night in 1996 when all the siblings were in town: Roger and I and the kids were coming through on our way to buy a house in Wisconsin; Ellyn was visiting my parents with her family from Illinois; Steve had driven in for the weekend from his job in the southern part of the state. Erik lived with his wife in Minneapolis and Sinn still lived with my parents, so they could both easily attend. My parents, of course, would be there as they had been involved in the process from the beginning, helping Noeun with the logistics of purchasing a house and obtaining a mortgage.

The day of the housewarming was hot and stifling; when the sun set it would bring a welcome coolness with it. We left my parents' house and drove out toward what I had always thought of as the country—but things had changed. The suburb of Minnetonka once was the outer ring of a circle around the twin cities of Minneapolis and St. Paul—past Minnetonka there had been only farm towns with post offices and cowboy bars. Now the farmland had been incorporated into an unbroken sprawl of upscale suburbs engulfing the prairie.

Our car entered this stretch of development and passed multiple family homes, new schools and strip malls—each with a drycleaners, video store and Chinese takeout. We turned off the highway and drove down a side street, entering Noeun's neighborhood, then turned onto a cul-desac where the lots were radiating out from the new asphalt. Noeun's house was a white two story with fresh sod at the end.

Noeun and Sinn were bending over a grill as we drove up. They straightened and smiled in greeting as we parked. Noeun took the lawn chairs Roger got out from the trunk and began setting them up on the sod. I noticed his face was slightly drawn and his eyes were puffy and bloodshot, the many extra night shifts showing their effects.

Piling out of the cars, the younger children spotted a pile of yellow sand next door in the neighbors' driveway scattered with Tonka trucks and plastic spades, and ran off. The older children began throwing a football on the empty street.

I asked Noeun where Prum and his kids were. He waved his hand. "The kids are inside," he said, "and"—his face darkened—"Prum went in the car to buy more sticks." He motioned to a few bamboo skewers lying next to a pan of marinated meat. "She went a long time ago and hasn't come back."

He looked very irritated and I distracted him by saying his house looked beautiful.

"Go and look inside," he said. "It's very nice, very big."

The adults went inside and wandered around. The living room had a cathedral ceiling, giving a feeling of expansiveness. There was a couch and stereo equipment but no other furniture in sight. All the walls were white. When we walked into the kitchen I could see signs of the meal in progress: rice in a rice cooker, meat chunks marinating in sauce. From the kitchen were stairs leading to a landing, with three bedrooms and a bath radiating off like spokes in a wheel.

I peeked into the open bedrooms. One held kids' toys strewn around and some sleeping bags. In the other bedroom were the children, ages three and two, dark haired, adorable, but a bit unkempt, sitting passively in front of the television. Other than the TV there wasn't much else in the room, some dirty paper plates, a Power Ranger blanket and many toys. I smiled at the children and asked if they wanted to come outside and play with the others. Sarah looked at me blankly, then turned back to the television; her younger brother Brian didn't bother to look.

We went back outside where the next-door neighbors had joined the group. Noeun, in the process of handing out Cokes, introduced us. Dave looked a typical Midwesterner, blondish heading toward bald, handsome in a wholesome way. He owned a local liquor store; the family had moved in when it opened the year before. His wife, Laurie, was pretty and sweet: brown hair, sharp eyes, friendly and involved with her children. They had two, a boy and a girl much the same ages as Noeun and Prum's kids;

Laurie commented that the children had already begun running back and forth between the houses.

I moved over to Noeun, next to the cooler.

"Nouen, your house is great," I said.

"You like it?" He said, grinning at me. "Here, Sarah, have a pop."

We began talking about houses, the one Roger and I were seriously looking at in Wisconsin, the others Noeun had looked at but not bought. It was one of the more involved conversations I had had with Noeun in a long time and I was enjoying it, one houseowner to another.

Sarah and Brian came out and stood on the front stoop, then, seeing all the kids on the sandpile, they ran and jumped in. Soon all the children were playing king-of-the-hill, trying to push each other off and happily falling down in the golden sand.

Nouen and I had been absorbed into the larger group of adults while watching the kids play. Erik and Ellyn had discovered that they knew Dave and Laurie: One of Erik's best friends in high school, Joe, who had also dated Ellyn for a short time, was Dave's good friend, so Erik had been at parties with Dave and Laurie in the past and Ellyn had once been on a double-date with them. My mother began talking to Laurie about the children. As I listened to them, I remembered that my mother had mentioned Nouen and Prum's new neighbors to me previously—how nice they were, how lucky for Noeun and Prum to have such good neighbors in their first house.

An hour later, Prum still hadn't returned. Sinn went inside the house, muttering something about the rice. I could tell that my parents, and some of the other guests, were worried; Laurie asked Noeun if Prum had gone to the corner store or the big supermarket for the skewers. Nouen seemed to be worried only inasmuch as Prum was holding up the party. My father offered to go and find her, which irritated Nouen further, the patriarch was supposed to preside at the party, not go searching for a lost wife.

Sinn came outside and told Noeun that Prum was on the phone.

The guests continued chatting for a few minutes. Noeun came striding out of the house looking very upset.

"I have to go get Prum," he called, "She ran out of gas."

He asked my father to take him and they went off together. After twenty minutes, the three returned in two cars. While my father was parking by the road, Noeun brusquely got out of his car with the bag of bamboo sticks and went over to the grill. Prum got out behind him with her face averted from the guests and went inside the house.

After a while, I left the group and went inside where I found Prum standing by the rice cooker in the kitchen. Very pretty and very shy, Prum had always been a bit of an enigma to me. Even though she was essentially my sister-in-law, it was hard for us to have a conversation. Noeun and Prum had been together since they met at the ESL class in Minnetonka High School, but our family hadn't been invited to their wedding. Prum's foster parents had been at the three-day affair with a Buddhist monk presiding over the various ceremonies which, although not legal because there are no papers signed by an American religious or legal authority, is, for all intents and purposes, a wedding—and our family had not been a part of it.

So, standing at the rice cooker with Prum who was obviously upset and in need, the gaps in our history loomed large and dangerous.

"It's a nice house, Prum," I said.

She nodded.

Noeun came inside holding a plate of grilled kebobs which he placed on the counter.

"People can get food and eat," he said.

"I'm not eating," Prum quickly said.

Noeun looked at her for a minute. "OK, you stay here and eat with Sarah," he finally said.

Prum and I put kebobs and rice on paper plates and sat across from each other at the kitchen table while the other guests drifted in and out.

I ate. Across from me, Prum picked at her food.

When the last of the guests had gone, I said, "This is really good. How do you get the rice like this, all sticky and soft?"

"Oh, I didn't make the rice," she said. "Sinn made rice. I can't make rice right. I never learned. Noeun says I should learn from Sinn, but I never can. I do the same thing as Sinn but doesn't turn out, not good Cambodian rice."

I protested, "I bet your rice is fine. I'm sure it's as good as this."

"No, I can't do rice right," she said.

Prum and I finished our meals. I said I was going back outside to check on the kids; Prum said she was going upstairs. Outside, the party was in full swing. People were eating, talking and laughing while Noeun went back and forth with kebobs from grill to plates.

I went over and lowered myself down on the lawn next to Erik and Steve.

"Here's the American dream," Steve was saying, indicating the new house, yard and street with a sweep of his hand.

"We're just talking," Erik ruefully said. "How does a guy who spent his childhood in refugee camps manage to achieve all this so quickly when us Minnetonka boys are not even close?"

"Yeah, about that?" Steve said. "Here we are, drinking Nouen's Cokes—more power to him, is all I can say."

Erik and Steve were then doing fine, although, as they had pointed out, they did not own brand-new houses in suburban developments. Erik held down a business job and owned a modest house in inner-city Minneapolis while Steve was just about to start with a small law firm in northern Minnesota.

It grew dark. We told Noeun to stop worrying about drinks and food and relax, and for the first time during the evening, he did. Everyone sat back in the lawn chairs, resting, as the summer evening softly fell. We could hear the kids' voices, happy and shrill, from the other side of the sandpile. It was one of those perfect moments, encapsulated in an evening. As Ellyn said years later: "It was a happy time."

The kids were the first victims of the onslaught of mosquitoes because their thin skin was easier to puncture. They left the sandpile and came running over to the circle of lawn chairs. Soon the adults were itching and slapping, the signal that it was time to go. Everyone got up, stretched, collected children. Noeun's kids ran into the house.

We chatted with Dave and Laurie for a few minutes on how we'd probably see each other again now that Noeun and Prum lived next door. Their family left. We thanked Noeun for the party, congratulated him on his new house. He stayed outside, standing in the driveway, as the cars backed out. My last sight was of Noeun, strong and determined—albeit shortened from working under the Khmer Rouge during the crucial growing time of adolescence—waving goodbye in front of his new house.

The story of Lon Nol, Sihanouk's loyal prime minister and chief of staff who became president general of Cambodia in a coup in 1970, is similar to Noeun's story. Both men had an enormous amount of faith in the American dream. Both men trusted that America, the superpower, could take care of them and resolve their problems. And for both, that faith—and the dream—would be shattered.

Lon Nol was a loyal official to Prince Sihanouk for many years—up until the very moment that he overthrew him. Although Prince Sihanouk had steered the small craft of Cambodia wisely and well through the treacherous and stormy seas of the Indochinese wars, by the late 1960s he was spending most of his time and effort making movies instead of running the country. Unfortunately, this was at a time when Cambodia desperately needed a strong leader: the Vietnamese Communists had installed bases on the Cambodian side of the border and both American and South Vietnamese troops were violating Cambodia's neutrality by fighting inside the country.

In January 1970, Sihanouk left Cambodia for his annual vacation (some used the word "flight"). This left an opening for disgruntled officials who had been plotting against him, including Sihanouk's cousin, pro-Western Sirik Matak, who was struggling to hold Cambodia together during the prince's absence. Many speculate that, with the U.S. thoroughly embroiled in the Vietnam War and Sihanouk's troops under fire from Communist guerrillas, the disgruntled officials received encouragement and support from the newly reopened U.S. Embassy.

On the night of March 17, 1970, Sirik Matak and three army officers went to Lon Nol's house and—after threatening him with a pistol—forced him to sign a paper declaring a vote against Sihanouk the next day in the National Assembly. Reportedly, Lon Nol signed, then burst into tears. (New York Times correspondent Henry Kamm noted that at the first press conference after the coup, Lon Nol was asked, "When did you stop being a faithful servant of Sihanouk?" to which he unhesitatingly replied, "On the eighteenth of March at one o'clock"—the exact hour when parliament removed Sihanouk from the throne.)

Lon Nol was a loyal servant of Sihanouk, a devout Buddhist and a master of military detail; however, he was not a leader. His five-year rule of Cambodia was marked by inefficacy and corruption, both of which were encouraged by a steady flow of American-made goods and money. Lon Nol spent most of his reign trying to keep the roads, waterways and airports open for the flow of American goods and military assistance. Military details were his only competence and strong suit—and that was not enough.

In May 1970 the U.S. invaded Cambodia, stating as it did so that it would only invade thirty kilometers inside the country for two months. What it did not limit was the bombing that accompanied the invasion. Basically, the U.S. was committed to a brief invasion but long-term bombing; this policy fit in perfectly with the U.S. lack of regard toward Cambodia—a country it considered to be tiny, unimportant, and filled with expendable people. (Although Lon Nol believed that the giant superpower had his tiny country's best interests at heart, he was never once asked to meet with Nixon during the four years they were partners in war, an indication of his and Cambodia's value to the United States.)

The invasion protected the U.S. withdrawal from Vietnam but brought Cambodia into the Indochina War. As the countryside was steadily bombed, strafed and napalmed, perhaps as many as two million villagers fled to Phnom Penh looking for safety and a place to live. Sokhary You remembers American planes bombing her small village, not once, but twice, until, with the second bombing, her family's house was burned to the ground along with everything else, and they moved to Phnom Penh.

The refugees from the country settled in slums of huts along the main roads and on the city's outskirts. Entire families moved in from the countryside and lived on the street. Prum Nath can't remember the time her family lived in their rural village before they fled to the outskirts of Phnom Penh where Mrs. Nath supported the family of eight—including an ailing husband—by selling food and clothing to passersby. The huge influx of refugees brought reports of young men and women from the villages joining the Khmer Rouge, or Communist guerrillas. The millions of refugees into Phnom Penh also brought a dawning realization to all Cambodians that what had begun as a foreign invasion was turning into an all-out civil war.

Lon Nol did attempt to rule the country but was unsuccessful. He mounted two offensives against the Vietnamese in an effort to turn the tide of the war, both of which failed miserably. He had a stroke, was subsequently hospitalized in Hawaii for two months in the beginning of 1971 and never regained full political control. His government lasted for four more years solely due to the flow of U.S. military assistance and heavy bombing.

Mostly, his reign is remembered for the enormous amount of corruption. Sarith Ou, a member of the Lon Nol army, remembers how Lon Nol's army generals—including his uncle—would pocket the salaries of nonexistent soldiers, salaries that were provided by U.S. military aid. Instead of punishing loyal officers for the rampant corruption, Lon Nol spent most of his time writing letters to President Nixon, asking for yet more aid. Provincial governors and commanders began to raze Cambodia's great forests to the ground in order to sell the timber to dishonest officials and merchants—a practice that has continued to this day.

By the end of 1972, the Khmer Rouge controlled most of the country. What had once been a ragtag band of Communist insurgents fighting against the Lon Nol army had formed into a hardened army making inroads against the capital. Only Phnom Penh, Battambang and a few other provincial capitals remained under the control of Lon Nol.

At the end of the Paris Peace Agreement cease-fire in 1973, the United States unleashed a brutal and intense bombing campaign upon Cambodia. Over a hundred thousand tons of bombs fell on the Cambodian countryside, decimating the civilian population and the village social system. Sinn Lok recalls that the planes that bombed his village flew so low he could see the American markings. Finally, Congress forced the Nixon administration to halt the bombings, but what was now an entirely Cambodian civil war continued without abatement.

In 1973 Henry Kamm secretly interviewed Sirik Matak, who spoke openly and critically of U.S. policy.

"[I]f the United States continues to support such a regime [Lon Nol's] we will fall to the Communists," he said bluntly. "You give help to a people that wants to live freely. But when you support a regime not supported by the people you help the Communists."

Which is exactly what happened. The farce of Lon Nol's governmental leadership came to end in 1975 when the Khmer Rouge cut off the Mekong River route into Phnom Penh, thus preventing American shipments of rice and ammunition from reaching Lon Nol forces. Although the U.S. tried airlifting rice and ammunition to the capital, they were unable to bring in enough either to defend the city or feed its inhabitants. For three months, the Communists moved in closer, rocketing and shelling the city constantly, until finally in April Lon Nol flew to the United States, taking along with him a million dollars of—once again—American-provided money. His flight left the capital—and the country—open for the Khmer Rouge.

The story of Lon Nol reads like a tragedy, a story of conflict between an inferior leader and the overwhelming strength of a superpower. Lon Nol was unable to extricate Cambodia from the American conflict in Vietnam, which resulted in civil war for his country with a host of far-reaching and disastrous consequences.

Nouen's story was also a tragedy, although none of us could see it that night of the housewarming. Little could any of the family foresee how Noeun's dream would end in misfortune and disaster. Noeun and the other Cambodian refugees came to America and believed that, if they worked hard, they could achieve their goals and dreams. Some of the refugees did achieve the American dream and went on to further success, but some—like Noeun and Lon Nol—had their dreams and hopes shattered and fled to the waiting safety of oblivion and forgetfulness.

14

Born to Lead:
The Story of Sarith Ou

From 1941 to 1945, during World War II, Japan occupied Cambodia and pressed young Cambodian males into the Japanese army. Oeur Ou, a young man from a prominent family in a remote northern village, served, and, after a horrific war experience, returned to Cambodia determined to live a new life in peace. He and a comrade from the war took their wives and traveled to the northwest province of Siemreap Oddar Mean Chay next to the jungle in order to start their own village. Each man marked out a fifty acre parcel of government land and claimed it due to their veteran status. They named their new village Tasoum.

The land was lush—so near the jungle—and Oeur slowly recovered from his emotional wounds as he built a house and began to farm. Some time passed and the two men gave out pieces of their larger area of land to others in order to have company. As these few were followed by more and more people wanting to settle, Oeur and his friend sold off smaller parcels. Tasoum grew from two families to a village of 300 families, with Oeur as the undisputed leader.

Oeur and his wife had seven children. Sarith, one of the boys, was always the first to throw himself both into work in the fields and into play. Along with some of the other children, he attended school at a Buddhist monastery located in the center of thirteen villages. When school had finished for the year, the children helped out in the fields. Although some village families relied on the children to bring in the crops, Oeur always hired help so that the work was not overly hard for his children. The rich farmland provided plenty of food and if two or three families occasionally had a hard time, the other families helped them out.

The Khmer Rouge began to infiltrate Cambodian villages close to the border in the late 1960s. Young Cambodian Communists opposed to

Prince Sihanouk fled to the northern jungles, near the Thai border, and formed small groups of guerrilla fighters. They hid in the deep forests during the day and came into the nearby villages at night to forcibly recruit new members. Building up their numbers, they gradually worked their way toward central Cambodia, with the capital—and the center of government—as their goal.

The Khmer Rouge took over the three provinces closest to Tasoum, thus controlling the countryside around the village. Tasoum was located in Siemreap Oddar Mean Chay Province; sixteen kilometers west lay the small city of Pouk, the headquarters of Lon Nol's army, and between 1973 and 1975 Pouk was a pocket of intense fighting as Lon Nol forces tried to hang on. Because of Tasoum's location, there were many skirmishes in the village as the Lon Nol army tried to keep the village from falling to the Khmer Rouge. Sometimes

Sarith Ou in 1975 just after his escape; Aranyaprathet, Thailand. (Photograph from the personal collection of Sarith Ou.)

the Khmer Rouge controlled the area round the village, sometimes Lon Nol and his soldiers controlled it.

As a teenager, Sarith went to live in the Buddhist pagoda in order to become a monk. Many young Cambodian males, and most of the young men in Tasoum, spent a year or two in the monkhood for various reasons. Families felt the years of monkhood were a good opportunity to change youthful and immature behavior. It was also a way in which the children could gain merit for their parents—earn spiritual credit and possibly ensure entrance into heaven. Because Sarith was a good student, he stayed on at the monastery after finishing his training, and taught at the pagoda school for young children. When, in 1970, the influx of fighting in the area grew so fierce, three out of the four teachers left and went home to their provinces, but Sarith remained.

Sarith resigned from the monkhood in 1971 but continued to teach—until the Khmer Rouge penetrated the very grounds of the school. Because he had studied history as a student and felt that Cambodia's recent history was one of domination by Prince Sihanouk, Sarith was intrigued with the Khmer Rouge and their theories of abolishing monarchy rule. In this, he differed from his family, who had always been supporters of the monarchy. In short, he was young, idealistic and fascinated by the Communist ideology.

So when the Khmer Rouge took over the village, Sarith closed the school and went to join up, hoping, in particular, that he could study with specific Khmer Rouge leaders who had studied in China. However, he soon discovered that the Khmer Rouge's theories were quite different in reality. The guerrillas weren't organized and seemed to be controlled by somebody behind the scenes. As part of the Khmer Rouge organization, Sarith sensed an untrustworthy presence controlling the party.

After six months, he had had enough and decided to leave. His first thought was to escape to Thailand but the Thai border was completely closed off because of guerrilla warfare. He then thought of his family connections. His father and uncle had both been in World War II. Whereas his father had gone north to start a village upon his return to Cambodia, his uncle had returned and stayed in army life, serving in the royalist army where he was promoted through the ranks until in 1970 he was a four-star general in Lon Nol's army.

Sarith escaped from the Khmer Rouge and went to see his uncle at the army base in Battambang. He told his uncle what had transpired in his life and his disillusionment with the Khmer Rouge. His uncle said, "Stay here and be a soldier."

Sarith answered, "I don't want to be a soldier. I was trained as a monk and a teacher."

His uncle responded, "Well, if you don't want to become a soldier, you can stay and help me with other duties."

Thus began Sarith's life as an officer in the army of Lon Nol. His uncle quickly saw to it that he was promoted to the rank of sergeant—overseeing 600–1,000 soldiers. He was given the key to the vault where the army's money was kept and told to manage army finances. Since Lon Nol and his army were notorious for their corruption, there was a great deal of money to manage.

Although classified as an officer, Sarith never fought; he wore his uniform only when traveling and removed it as soon as he was back at the base. He didn't like the position. Lon Nol's government was completely corrupt and there was no leadership. Sarith knew about the corruption—as did everyone—but didn't know what to do about it. He never used any of the money for himself, but he couldn't halt the constant and sordid flow. (When the Khmer Rouge finally took over the government in 1975, only 366 out of 1,000 soldiers were left, but Sarith's uncle and the other generals were pocketing the salaries for all 1,000.)

Lon Nol himself acted paralyzed, waiting for America to tell him what to do. The only Cambodian who was able to talk to Lon Nol was his father-in-law, Thy San. Thy San offered sixty-year-old Lon Nol his sixteen-year-old daughter in marriage. (She presently lives in California with two children she claims are by Lon Nol.)

While with Nol's army, Sarith kept in occasional touch with his family; however, all communication was severed in 1972 when the Khmer Rouge took over Tasoum. In Cambodia, one's home village is central— no one chooses how to think, politically, alone. The village gathers food and works together, so if the village is taken over by the Khmer Rouge, then all the villagers became Khmer Rouge. When Sarith left his village and joined his uncle on the Lon Nol side, he was effectively cut off from his family in Khmer Rouge-controlled Tasoum.

Sarith was never to see his parents again. Unbeknownst to him, both parents would die prior to 1975 from illness and old age.

When the Khmer Rouge invaded Phnom Penh, Battambang and the other major cities in April 1975, taking control of the entire country, Sarith was on the Battambang base. One of the first orders from the Khmer Rouge was that all Lon Nol soldiers should give up their weapons.

Sarith's uncle said to him, "Stay with me and we'll go back and farm together. We'll give up our weapons—the Khmer Rouge won't kill us because they're under the control of Prince Sihanouk."

Sarith said, "No, I don't think so. I spent six months with the Khmer Rouge and they hate the prince. I can't believe they're going let Sihanouk rule and I don't think they're going to be good rulers."

But Sarith's uncle didn't listen because he considered Sarith to be young and foolish. They argued about which course to take.

Finally, Sarith said, "I'm leaving."

His uncle said, "Well, if you don't want to stay with me, that's your choice."

On April 17, 1975, Sarith left the base and struck out toward the Thai border. Since the Khmer Rouge were concentrated in Phnom Penh, as well as various strongholds around the country, the border wasn't protected and he was able to cross into Thailand. Once in Thailand, he began to hear the first terrible stories come trickling back of how the Khmer Rouge were emptying the cities and forcing the inhabitants to walk to the countryside. Three days later, he heard that the troops and officers of Lon Nol had been executed. A total of 106 officers were executed at the

Battambang base alone, including his uncle. Sarith knew that if he had stayed he would be dead.

Sarith was picked up by the border police and driven a half day's journey to Chon Buri, where he was given a trial and sentenced to 150 years in prison for "illegal crossing." The police threw him in Chon Buri prison, a huge place crammed with prisoners. Sarith was put in a room with many other prisoners. Guards entered twice a day and set down two bowls on the floor, one of soup and one of rice. The prisoners crowded around and stuck their fingers in the bowls, grabbing at the rice and slurping the soup. Sarith, repulsed, didn't eat for three days until his hunger grew so strong that he had to shove his fingers in with the rest.

After thirty-one days, the guards entered and grabbed Sarith. Sarith grew cold with fear and thought, "Are they going to kill me?" The guards didn't kill him but took him to another building, where he was given a second trial. At the end of the trial, he was told he couldn't stay in prison any longer because there were so many Cambodians entering Thailand every day, escaping from the Khmer Rouge.

The guards released Sarith from prison and sent him and a few others to the Thai Buddhist temple in Aranyaprathet for temporary shelter. There, Sarith lived with seventy others inside the pagoda—although not a house, it was sanctuary and had a roof.

Every day more refugees were sent to the temple until there were 600 people sleeping under the small pagoda roof. It was too crowded but the group was told to be patient as a new refugee camp was in the process of being built. Soon the new camp was finished and Sarith and the others were the first refugees to enter the Aranyaprathet refugee camp on the Thai border. Sarith stayed there for some time, building up strength and recovering from all that had happened in his short life.

After a period of recuperation, Sarith found himself at twenty-six, young and strong and ready to fight. He had always avoided fighting but thought perhaps the time had come where fighting was the only way to accomplish certain goals. He wanted to fight against the Khmer Rouge, but didn't want to fight for Lon Nol because of the corruption. At the Thai border he found another escaped high-ranking officer from the Lon Nol army and together they formed a guerrilla army to fight against the Khmer Rouge and the Vietnamese.

Their guerrilla army grew to several thousand troops. Because they received support and backing from France, and because they were a substantial army, they planned to take over Cambodia in a year or two.

"At twenty-six you're scared of nothing," Sarith says now. "I traveled back and forth into deep Cambodia on spy missions and was never scared."

Sarith and his guerrilla fighters kept encountering refugees who had escaped from the Khmer Rouge and heard firsthand the horror stories of the Khmer Rouge and their killing fields. Sarith decided he wanted to go to another country.

But he continued to lead the group and go on spy missions for two more years, as more and more people joined their army. Eventually Sarith decided that without strong outside support, there was no long-range success ahead.

So in 1977, Sarith fled to a camp that had been recently built in the Thai border area. He moved on to another border camp called Surin in 1978, where he met a young Thai girl named Teant in one of the neighboring villages. They were soon married. Two daughters—Davy and Davun—were born in the Surin camp. Because of the primitive medical facilities at the camp, their first daughter, Davy, was born hydrocephalic and thus retarded. (Today, at twenty-three, she can read and write her own name, but nothing else. She works two hours a day at a restaurant, washing dishes and doing light cleaning. She will always live with her parents, a visible reminder of the war that devastated their countries.)

Sarith and Teant began applying to go to another country; their first choice was the United States. After a while, they were approved to go to the U.S. but had to wait until a sponsor was found, and were moved to a holding camp in Bangkok. Sarith knew it would be a long waiting period and hated being idle, so he found a job at the American volunteer agency at the camp, where he worked from 1978 to 1979, helping other refugees find sponsors and fill out applications. Grace Lutheran Church of Cambridge, Wisconsin, finally agreed to sponsor the Ou family, but they stayed on longer for a total of two years in the holding camp.

In November 1979, Sarith, Teant, Davy and Davun boarded a plane in Bangkok and flew to Tokyo, on to California, and from there to Madison, Wisconsin. As the plane was descending into Madison, Sarith looked out the window and observed that the trees had no leaves. He thought how odd this was, then decided that maybe the trees in America didn't have leaves. The Ou family deplaned, where some members of the church were waiting to meet them. It was very windy outside and the Cambodians were cold; Sarith and Teant wore plastic sandals and the girls had no shoes. They all wore thin shirts.

The church installed the family in a two room trailer house. After two weeks, Sarith got a job in a furniture factory in a town ten miles south of Cambridge. He rode to work with a man from the church who worked at the same factory. Sarith began to study English at night in nearby Fort Atkinson. Teant, at home with the girls, eight months and one and a half years old, was finding it hard to adapt to the new culture.

In 1982 Sarith was laid off at the furniture factory. He knew he wouldn't be able to get a job suitable to his qualifications—although he could read and write English adequately, his pronunciation was very poor and he spoke with a heavy accent. He decided to try welding, which was good pay but didn't require much English. He studied welding for six weeks with another friend and began work at a welding factory in Janesville, Wisconsin. The friend took to it but Sarith didn't, so Sarith transferred to the machine shop in the same company and worked there until 1986.

In 1986 the family moved to Madison and rented an apartment in the city. In this way, Sarith could obtain more schooling. He took yet more English classes and got a job translating for a public health nurse in Madison. During this time, he developed the habit of working days and studying nights; he got his general education diploma this way. After that, still working days translating, he went to Madison Area Technical College for two years, transferred the coursework and began attending Edgewood College, a private liberal arts college in Madison.

In 1986 Sarith got a job using more of his administrative abilities as a bilingual specialist with the ESL program in the Madison public schools, the job he still has. He enjoys the job, and feels it uses some of his talents, but his real passion is helping "his people": Cambodians in America and in Cambodia. In 1979 Sarith joined the Cambodian Association of Dane and Rock counties and began working with the people of the Cambodian diaspora—all the Cambodians who have fled Pol Pot and his Khmer Rouge and settled in Wisconsin. Soon after joining, he was elected a board member and then chairman in 1983. He stayed on as chairman for ten years but finally retired due to the large amount of work involved with the job.

The Cambodian Association contends with many struggles involving cultural adaptation. The Khmer American children raised in the United States encounter issues that their immigrant parents never faced. Forming solid relationships is a problem. The children marry young, have a couple of kids, then find out they can't live together and split up, leaving the kids with the grandparents. Sarith has seen it happen again and again, both with marriages inside and outside of the community. Divorce was never a problem in Cambodia; the divorce rate in Cambodia before the autogenocide being probably two to three percent. He, along with many other Cambodian refugees, can't understand why it is such a persistent problem in the next generation here.

Sarith graduated from Edgewood College in 1993 with a degree in political science. His background in Cambodian politics had prepared him well for this major. During his years in the U.S., Sarith's army in Thailand had continued to grow until it was 10,000 troops strong. Sarith supported the army financially from the U.S. until 1993 when—after the U.N.-organized election in Cambodia—many of the guerrillas took leadership positions in the Hun Sen government. It was at this point that Sarith realized he no longer believed that fighting would accomplish anything.

In 1994 Sarith went back to Cambodia for the first time. Before his trip, he had a message broadcast on the radio announcing that he was looking for any of the Ou family. In this way, he found two brothers, one sister and their families still alive. Two sisters and their entire families, including the children, had died during Pol Pot's time. Another younger sister's death had not been confirmed, but no one had seen nor heard of her since the late 1960s.

Sarith traveled to Cambodia with the International Grant Foundation of Baraboo, Wisconsin, and thus had a chance to work with the current Cambodian government. He spent three weeks working with Hun Sen's party, an experience that illuminated the enormous corruption within the party. At the end of the three weeks, Sarith obtained an appointment with U.S. aide Edward H. Greeley, executive assistant at the American Embassy. They spent forty-five minutes talking about the problems in Cambodia today.

Sarith said he had worked in every area of the Hun Sen government and had found many examples of rampant corruption.

"It's corrupt all the way through," Sarith finished.

The aide listened for forty-five minutes, then asked, "Do you want me to give you some advice?"

"Yes," said Sarith.

The aide said, "I think you are too democratic—you cannot come to Cambodia yet."

Sarith had watched carefully as Cambodia held free elections in 1993, supposedly upheld by the United Nations. When the votes were counted, the Royalist party had won. Hun Sen didn't like this outcome so he simply grabbed the power with both hands and ignored the election results. The U.N. stood by and did nothing.

Sarith believes that the best leader for the Cambodian people is Sam Rainsy, known internationally for his competence and incorruptibility. At the current time, Sam Rainsy's party holds twenty-two seats in the Hun Sen Parliament. The U.N. trusts Sam Rainsy. Hun Sen tells the U.N. all that he has done to stop the rampant corruption and Sam Rainsy points out why it is not true. Sam Rainsy makes a point of opposing the corruption and sloth every day, and every day Hun Sen gets angry at Sam Rainsy for being such a thorn in his side. In June 2001 at the World Bank meeting in Tokyo the World Bank president invited Sam Rainsy to speak on the corruption in Cambodia. When Sam Rainsy rose to speak, he held twelve prepared pages citing current examples.

Sarith feels corruption is easily the biggest obstacle facing the country. In 1999 the Hun Sen government received $500 million from the United Nations; in 2000, they received $548 million; in 2001, it was $600 million. And yet, Cambodian schoolchildren have no school supplies nor shoes. It's clear that the money is going into someone's pocket: $600 million in 2001—there are only 10 million people in Cambodia! So where is it going? Indirectly—to Hun Sen's government. The U.N. intends for the money to reach Cambodia's many poor people, but it never gets there.

The numbers don't lie: A congressman from the Hun Sen government "earns" $1,800 per month; teachers earn $20–25 per month and a military soldier gets $13–50 per month depending upon his rank. In Cambodia, teachers don't even earn a salary they can live on. Sarith's nephew has been teaching in Cambodia for more than thirteen years. He's single but can't even afford his clothes, much less raise a family, on his salary. In 2001, teachers demonstrated for a raise in salary, but the Hun Sen government responded by threatening all demonstrators with unemployment.

In addition to the gift money from the U.N., the Hun Sen government receives revenue from copious sales and property taxes. Where does this money go? Well, at fifty-two years old in 2001, Hun Sen was the richest prime minister in Southeast Asia. He had no higher education, only elementary school, but then, all the current high ranking officials in Cambodia have only a grade school education. The people with higher educations worked for these elementary school graduates.

Each summer Sarith returns to Cambodia. Beforehand, he raises money from small businesses and individuals to buy school supplies and uniforms for the schoolchildren—Cambodia's only hope. Right now, he focuses his efforts upon the children of his native countryside in Siemreap Oddar Mean Chay, but is planning to branch out in the future.

Sarith also works for the Sam Rainsy Party here in the U.S., writing letters to the United Nations in support of the party. Sarith is confident that if there are ever truly "free" elections in Cambodia and the ballots are counted correctly, Sam Rainsy will win. (He acknowledges that these are big "ifs.") During his travels and work in the Cambodian countryside, Sarith has seen that the nine million people outside Phnom Penh and the Hun Sen government are very unhappy—as well as many people inside. Sarith feels all of these unhappy people would vote for Sam Rainsy in a free election—they want a leader, not a Vietnamese puppet politician.

One day Sarith plans to go back to serve and lead his people, the way his father did before him. He knows his daughters will marry and live here, raising their families in America, but he will return to his homeland and help raise it up from the ashes and ruins left after the Khmer Rouge. This is his calling—and his hope.

15

To Go Forward

Ever since the Nazi holocaust, the phrase "Never Again" has been bandied about like a protective mantra. It's as if the act of saying such definite words will insure against the repetition of that ignominious time. The words imply that as long as people are aware of the enormous horrors of that holocaust, this knowledge will prevent the human race from tolerating any other similar crimes against humanity. In short: Knowledge begets prevention.

Not so. In truth, what is never to have happened again, has happened again and again and again: China during the Cultural Revolution, Cambodia, Mozambique, Burundi, Rwanda, Bosnia and Albania, all examples of genocide and brutal and terrorist acts executed on a mass scale.

America has never taken the responsibility it should for the Cambodian autogenocide. We have never acknowledged our moral accountability for the hundreds of thousands of refugees, for their lost families and for their dead. For the sake of protecting our already tattered national conscience we must ask—as David Frost did in a television interview with Richard Nixon—"If American policy brought Cambodia into the holocaust which created the Khmer Rouge and destroyed a country which might otherwise have survived?"

If we ask that question of ourselves as a nation, I think we will find the answer to be a resounding "Yes." Not only did the U.S. secretly—and excessively—bomb Cambodia in a mistaken effort to triumph over communism, but we then meddled with its economy to ease our withdrawal from that very same war.

Journalist Sydney Schanberg, whose friendship with Dith Pran, a Cambodian journalist, was immortalized in the movie "The Killing Fields," said in his book *The Killing Fields: The Facts Behind the Film* (co-written with Dith Pran): "If you want to be honest, you don't start with the Khmer Rouge in 1975. You start with the secret American bombing of Cambodia that began in 1969 and became public and massive afterwards. And you start with the entry of American troops into Cambodia in 1970 and subsequent American support of a corrupt and venal government, propping them up so they could carry on a war against the communists. Before we started these things, there was no war in Cambodia. Until then the Khmer Rouge had been a bunch of highway-men; they were going nowhere without a war. America created the conditions that allowed these maniacs to take power."

But we are not alone in our desire to forget about Cambodia. The rest of the world also seems to want to forget about this small Southeast Asian country. In 1983, Sir Robert Jackson, deputy secretary-general of the United Nations, said:

> I know of no parallel to the conditions which have been experienced in Cambodia over the past decade to any other experience I have had. In the case of post-war Europe, there is the vast tragedy of the concentration camps ... but thank God, the world had an immediate reaction and to this moment, there has been a sensitivity to events which happened forty years ago. But, in the case of Cambodia, for some extraordinary reason, I am left with the strong impression that the world wants to forget the tragedy that happened in Cambodia—they *want* to forget it.

For many years the United States has accepted the Khmer Rouge as a legitimate political faction in Cambodia despite its ruthless and inhumane actions. In March 1993, the Khmer Rouge went into a Vietnamese fishing village, slaughtered thirty-three fishermen, their wives and children and wounded twenty-nine others. In April of the same year, they entered a video hall and gunned down twenty-nine Cambodians and injured thirty-nine others. That same week they murdered six UNTAC— United Nations Transitional Authority in Cambodia—soldiers and international personnel.

All this took place during the time that the Khmer Rouge were part of the United Nations peace process; they continued to be included despite these serious—and repeated—violations. By recognizing the Khmer Rouge party as the legal government of Cambodia after 1979 and by including its representatives in all subsequent conferences and political settlements, the United Nations has sent the message that a record of atrocities is not a deterrent in the game of world politics.

Until now, there has never been a concerted worldwide effort to bring Pol Pot and his associates to trial. Although the United States has withheld economic aid to Cambodia in the past years because of human rights

Sarith Ou (center) with schoolchildren in front of stupas (Buddhist shrines) in Siemreap Oddar Mean Chey Province. The children each hold a plastic bag containing school supplies donated by Americans. (Photograph from the personal collection of Sarith Ou.)

violations, we have never taken the initiative in pursuing justice for the victims of Pol Pot and the Khmer Rouge.

In *The Killing Fields: The Facts Behind the Film,* Sydney Schanberg says, " ...We Americans say we're different from totalitarian forms of government, that we're human and caring. I believe this to be true, not true in the sense that some yahoo politician says it's true at a press conference, but in the sense of how I understand Americans and what they would like to be in the eyes of the world. Well, if we want to be different and special, then we must behave differently, we can't just make announcements that we care about other people. We have to actually hold ourselves to higher standards. That's the story of Cambodia."

Holding ourselves to higher standards in this case would be to insist upon justice for the victims. In January 2001, the Cambodian legislature approved a tribunal but did not set a trial date; the general feeling was that Hun Sen exercised control over the process which he could delay or derail at any time. The victims understood that a trial was going to take place but wondered if it would resolve anything. The fact that the trial was being held in Cambodia was in itself a sign of bias and made many wonder if the trial could possibly produce satisfactory results.

Preceding the trial, Sophea Mouth said, "The trial is being held for symbolic reasons, for the relief of the emotional distress of the victims and the pain and suffering that they have had inflicted upon them. The trial should show that a murderer cannot go unpunished—or, that at least he is given due process of law and is judged for his crimes."

"Justice for the victims" means that all Khmer Rouge officials still alive from the Pol Pot regime be judged by an impartial tribunal and judge. Although the list of the members of the original central committee of the Communist Party of Kampuchea (Pol Pot, Nuon Chea, Ta Mok, So Phim, Ieng Sary, Vorn Veth, Son Sen and Ta Keu) was culled by its own members throughout the years (Ta Keu, Vorn Veth and So Phim were killed at the orders of their fellow members of the committee by 1978 and in 1997 Pol Pot ordered Son Sen and his family killed, and subsequently either died or was killed himself in 1998) that still leaves three members of that barbarous regime unscathed.

They are: Nuon Chea, Pol Pot's second in command, (Brother Number Two to Pol Pot's Brother Number One); Ta Mok, the one-legged man whose legend is built on extreme brutality; and Ieng Sary, Pol Pot's brother-in-law. At the time of the trial, Ta Mok was currently in custody (along with chief executioner "Duch" from S-21 infamy) and Premier Hun Sen said there would be no problem bringing Ta Mok and Nuon Chea to trial; however, Hun Sen warned of "unrest" if Ieng Sary was tried.

Most likely this was because Ieng Sary, foreign minister of the Pol Pot regime, defected to Hun Sen's government in 1996, bringing thousands of Khmer Rouge soldiers and civilians with him. Clearly, Hun Sen thought it in his own best interest to protect that original member of the genocidal clique.

Hun Sen has been a radical Khmer Rouge Communist since 1970. Although he converted to more conventional Communism in 1977 to escape a Pol Pot purge, the folk saying "A leopard cannot change its spots" leaps to mind. Or, more appropriately, to use a Khmer saying: "The tiger is hiding its claws," meaning although the tiger has claws that are hidden while it is resting and at ease, it doesn't mean the claws aren't there; the tiger has claws it can use any time.

In 1993, when Hun Sen was prime minister, free elections were held in Cambodia. At great personal cost, ninety percent of registered voters went to the polls and elected Sihanouk's son, Ranariddh, and his Royalist party with forty-five percent of the vote. Hun Sen won only thirty-eight percent. This was a surprising outcome as Hun Sen government thugs had murdered about one hundred workers of opposition parties and held rifles to the heads of voters at the polls during the election.

When the election results were made known, Hun Sen leaders made it clear that they would not give up power without violence, and forced Hun Sen and Ranariddh—loser and winner together—to share the top position. Over time Hun Sen consolidated and then kept a tight rein on power, using his murderous tendencies to keep control when he felt it necessary. In 1997 four grenades were thrown into a peaceful demonstration led by Sam Rainsy, former finance minister of the royalist party known for his popularity and personal integrity. The grenades exploded, killing fifteen and wounding more than 200. Sam Rainsy blamed Hun Sen for the carnage; this accusation was shared by most international observers.

At the time of the trial, Cambodians didn't consider the Hun Sen government to be their true or legitimate government since it was not the government they elected in 1993. They were fully aware that the current rulers had not shared their experiences as victims of Pol Pot and the Khmer Rouge but were instead the men who had been regional or local rulers under Pol Pot and had fled to Vietnam when Pol Pot and the party began turning on its own. Since then, they had returned to Cambodia to rule.

Sarith Ou works with the Sam Rainsy party both in the U.S. and in Cambodia, where he returns for a visit every summer.

"The Sam party should have won the election in 1998," Ou says, "but

Hun Sen didn't care. He just grabbed power and ignored the election results. Right now Sam Rainsy has a position in the Hun Sen government and opposes the corruption every day. And every day Hun Sen gets mad. Sam Rainsy is the UN's eyes; Hun Sen will say to the UN, 'We did such and such to stop the corruption' and Sam Rainsy will say, 'No you didn't.'"

Ou's overarching desire is to return to Cambodia to lead and serve in the political arena with the Sam Rainsy party. However, he is well aware that there is no predicting Cambodia's future. Right now there are warring factions and no democracy; whoever has the guns is stronger.

Sam You agrees with this outlook: "Unless someone steps in and stops the aggressor, the fighting will continue. The only deterrent would be for the world to say, 'If you attack we will fight you' but the United States doesn't have the commitment to do that—not to Cambodia. To Kuwait, yes, because of oil. But Cambodia doesn't have anything like oil and therefore isn't a big interest for the United States. There isn't that motive of economic profit."

The U.S. needs to ask itself some difficult questions concerning Cambodia: In our desire not to think about another holocaust after the Second World War—out of our willful ignorance—did we allow Pol Pot to institute his reign of terror? Does our lack of moral outrage on behalf of the nearly two million dead contribute to Cambodia's inability to put this tragic period behind and move ahead?

As part of our conduct and obligation at this point as a nation, we must begin to right our wrongs with regards to Cambodia. We owe it to this small country that we have so often used for our selfish purposes to insist that not only the Khmer Rouge leaders be tried but that the trial bring the victims relief. We must take responsibility for our past and actively work to create a new alliance between the United States and Cambodia—that is, a freely elected democratic government of that country—based on mutual respect and a hope for peace. Only then can we go forward—together.

16

Against All Odds:
The Story of Sophea Mouth

The love story of the parents of Sophea Mouth reads like a classic romance novel, only in prewar Cambodia: two young people flee the provinciality of different villages in the countryside, meet in the big city, fall in love and get married.

Mouth (pronounced "mut") Ouk and Savorn Poeu each left poor peasant villages in order to live and work in Battambang near the western border of Cambodia. Mouth got a job in the military, serving as sergeant chief of logistics and supplies in Sihanouk's Royalist Army. Savorn was educated—she knew both Khmer and French—and had her teaching certification.

They married when Savorn was eighteen and Mouth was twenty-five. Their first house was in the military compound, a typical Cambodian house built up on stilts. Although people in the military didn't make a great deal of money, it was a secure life and there was always enough to eat. Soon after the marriage, a baby girl was born; they named her Sophal. She was followed by a boy named Sameth, then another boy they called Sophea. Sophea was a strong, healthy baby, and noticeably handsome.

As was the custom, Savorn took the children with her every morning to the community basin in the middle of the compound, where she met the other women at the base to wash clothes, to draw the water for daily use and to gossip. One morning Savorn put six-month-old Sophea on the cement wall of the basin so her hands could be free to wash the family's laundry. While she was washing and talking with the other mothers, the baby somehow managed to maneuver himself to the edge of the basin and fall in. After a while, Savorn noticed and pulled him out.

Shortly after, the baby became sick and ran a high fever. Savorn didn't know what to do. Mouth wasn't around; he was often absent for long periods of time because of his work in the army. In desperation,

Savorn found a doctor who gave the baby an injection of antibiotic in the thigh. Either in reaction to the antibiotic or because he had caught polio when he had fallen into the water, both of the Sophea's legs were paralyzed.

When Mouth returned, the distraught parents took Sophea to a *krou*, or folk healer, who made a paste of betel juice, areca nut, lime and tobacco and massaged it on the baby's legs. The *krou* gave a jar of his saliva to Savorn and told her to rub the baby's legs with it every morning. After a period of time one of Sophea's legs got better and Mouth and Savorn attributed this to the healing power of the *krou*.

However, Sophea was left with one partially paralyzed leg. He couldn't walk, so Mouth bought a tricycle that the boy learned to pedal to get around. Meanwhile, other children were born. A girl came after Sophea that died, followed by two more girls, one after another, that both lived.

When Sophea was six years old his tricycle broke, forcing him to learn to walk: he held his hand against his right leg, because his knee was weak, and took a step, thus causing the left leg to catch up. In this way he walked, although it was with a halting, limping gait.

Sophea became aware that people were looking at him differently because of his disability. He heard many comments from strangers: "Oh, that kid is very good looking but there's something wrong with him" or "that boy is so handsome—too bad about that leg." These comments caused Sophea to become more intuitive and read other people's reactions extremely well.

The comments were devastating but Sophea soon realized that he was smarter than the people making the comments—and resolved to use his intelligence to make people overlook his leg. He developed a lifelong habit of making people ignore his defect by using his wit and personality. He also began attending one of the two schools in Battambang for children of military personnel, where he was soon excelling in all subjects.

When Sophea was seven years old, Mouth claimed a piece of land that had been repossessed by the government for nonpayment of taxes. It was a matter of Mouth talking to a government official, paying the back taxes, then filing a claim staking the land as his own.

Mouth and Savorn built a house on their new plot of land and let relatives build houses on other parts of the same plot. Their new house was much improved over the old: it had a corrugated metal roof to keep out the rains and wood slats or siding. Perched up on stilts—long slender columns of wood—like most Cambodian houses, there was a pond in front and a fenced yard lined with a luxurious profusion of flowers and trees in the back.

Newlywed photograph of Mouth Ouk and Savorn Poeu, parents of Sophea Mouth, taken in a studio in Battambang, circa 1960. Mouth Ouk is wearing his army uniform. (Notice the French-style beret, a remnant of colonialism. Photograph from the personal collection of Sophea Mouth. Sophea's father, Mouth Ouk, wrapped this photograph and a few others in plastic and hid them in a tree cavity until the Vietnamese had invaded and the family was ready to escape to Thailand, when he retrieved them and fled Cambodia. They weren't reprinted until 1987.)

Mouth was still absent much of the time because of his job. Savorn gave birth to a boy who died. She became pregnant again, had another boy who got sick shortly after birth and also died. After this last death, Savorn lost all interest in cooking and household chores. Sophal, the older sister, took over the cooking. Mouth began leaving Sophal sums of money before he went off so that she could buy rice and food for the family.

The older children began to notice that their mother was acting in peculiar ways. Sometimes she put on lots of make-up—including many fake moles on her face—and walked around visiting people. Other times she got completely made up and went to a fancy hotel to swim in the pool. When Mouth arrived home on his infrequent visits, he asked a spiritual healer to do exorcisms on his wife, none of which succeeded in making her well. Always, Mouth had to go off on another assignment for the military and leave the children with their mentally ill mother.

The relatives and neighbors were aware of Savorn's condition; they knew she wasn't "quite right in the head" and simply let her be. Nonetheless, it was very embarrassing for the children. Sophea felt embarrassed— and then angry with himself for being embarrassed of his own mother.

One time the children were gathered below the porch of the house, talking together about their mother.

"I wonder if she knows we are talking about her," Sophea said, "and if she does, I wonder if she can understand us?"

They heard maniacal laughter and looked up: their mother's lip-sticked mouth was open wide in an insane smile as she looked down at them from the porch. Sophea grew cold inside.

At the end of 1973, going into 1974, the soldiers brought many dead bodies into the compound, the bodies of Lon Nol soldiers who had died fighting the Khmer Rouge. The bodies that were likely to be claimed by a relative were lined up against the barbed wire fence, while the others were cremated. All day long the families living in the compound smelled the acrid malodor of burning flesh.

Sophea and his siblings were functioning virtually without parents. The older children took turns cooking; Sophal took care of the younger children. Given her homemaker existence, Sophal didn't see the use of going to school and quit.

Every day there were the sounds of guns and exploding shells nearby. The children, along with relatives, dug an L-shaped trench in back of the house for protection, and whenever they heard gunfire, the older ones gathered up the little ones and dashed to the trench and crouched down. Savorn was oblivious to the bombs, so the children watched helplessly from the trench as their mother walked around with bombs exploding on either side.

By 1975, the refugees were pouring in from the countryside and settling along the railroad tracks behind the compound. Savorn began to mingle with these refugees, patrolling in Mouth's military clothes and carrying a stick over her shoulder like a baton. She also began giving herself shots of urine directly into her thigh. (Both she and Mouth had given themselves vitamin shots in the past and had syringes around for that purpose.) Occasionally the area became infected but she always recovered.

On April 17, 1975, word flew around the compound that there was peace! The Khmer Rouge had won the war and now Cambodia would return to its prewar existence. On the base, the feeling was euphoric: It's the end of the war; we will have peace at last; Prince Sihanouk will return and rule again.

The Khmer Rouge marched into the compound and began to loot. They declared: "We are here to liberate you." Sophea had heard stories about them; he and the other boys called them "black crows" because of the loose pajama-like black cotton uniforms they wore.

Sophea, deciding he would check out the new rulers, went up to a soldier, pointed to an AK-47 part and innocently asked, "Does this belong to an M-16?" (Like all boys, he knew the different guns and their parts.)

"No," the soldier said. "That's part of an Aka." (This was the slang word for AK-47.)

Sophea was satisfied that the Khmer Rouge knew their stuff. And they had seemed to be nice enough to him, a little boy.

The next morning a jeep came around the compound with a Khmer Rouge soldier announcing into a bullhorn that everyone had to leave the city within twenty-four hours. "Don't take anything with you," he ordered. "Everything will be provided for you. Just go."

The compound became frantic with activity. Sophea and his brother and sisters didn't know what to do—as usual, Mouth was away and Savorn was wandering somewhere. Relatives and neighbors were busy with their own families and packing. The children began packing their few possessions into a wheelbarrow that their father had made when a neighbor came to the door and asked, "Can I borrow that wheelbarrow? I'll bring it right back."

The children said yes—and never saw the wheelbarrow again. They still had a motor scooter so they decided Sameth would drive the laden scooter and the rest of the children would carry rice, clothing and a few pots and pans. They asked Savorn to go with them, but she replied that she wouldn't leave her property.

The following afternoon the children joined thousands of others leaving Battambang by the main road, heading west toward Thailand. Sophal recognized where they were and recalled distant relatives that lived in the west. The crowd of evacuees walked until dusk but only reached a crossroad outside of Battambang. The children huddled under a tree and unpacked some pots and cooked some rice. The next morning Sophal borrowed a bicycle and rode off to try and find their father.

Meanwhile, on the day of "liberation" Mouth had been rounded up with 5,000 other Lon Nol soldiers to be executed. The Khmer Rouge split this larger group into two smaller ones: those with high rank and those with low rank. Mouth was put with the higher ranking soldiers. This group was being marched to the place of execution when they were stopped by a cadre who said that an order had come from Khieu Samphan that the men weren't to be killed right then, but put into a prison camp and killed later. So Mouth's group was marched back to a camp in Tagnien Takriem, a mountainous area. Mouth was imprisoned here when his daughter rode up on a bicycle looking for him. There wasn't much time for a reunion; she simply told him where the children were and left.

That night Mouth had the first of a recurring dream. In the dream he saw a long and winding road that was very crooked. When he awoke Mouth realized that the dream was telling him that the way to survive was to be crooked, or to lie. From that time on, he did just this—and survived.

A few days after Sophal's visit, Mouth managed to escape. He quickly put on the clothes of a farmer and went looking for his family. He found them camped under the tree at the crossroad and with great relief the children reunited with their father.

The first few days after the evacuation of Battambang, hundreds of people walked past the children but by the time Mouth joined the children, the column of refugees had slowed to a trickle. The Khmer Rouge began bringing in truckloads of Lon Nol soldiers. The jeeps turned off the main road, disgorged the soldiers, then sped back toward the city. Khmer Rouge soldiers stepped out of the forest and shot them. There was no attempt to bury the dead.

Sophea and two of his cousins—a boy and a girl—went to look at the dead bodies and he became very frightened. The next morning, Sophea was playing with his cousins and said that he felt like walking back into Battambang and looking around. His cousins agreed, so the three children set off.

They were stopped at a military checkpoint right before entering Battambang. Two female Khmer Rouge soldiers asked where they were going.

Sophea said, "I'm going to see my mother."

The soldiers said, "Oh, no one is left in the city."

However, they must have felt sorry for Sophea because they put the children on a truck and drove them to the main road in the center of the city and dropped them off.

Sophea looked around him in shock. The city had been completely emptied and looted; there was trash everywhere. It struck Sophea like a blow that he was the first one back in the city. The children left the main road and wandered toward Sophea's house, cutting through a neighbor's yard and approaching the house from the back. The backyard was enclosed with huge sugarcane, papaya and guava plants, but Sophea knew of an opening that he had always used as a shortcut.

The first of the three children, Sophea, parted the sugarcane leaves and looked through—and saw his mother on the back balcony of their house brandishing a chopping knife at two Khmer Rouge soldiers down below.

"If you come in and take my property," she was screaming, waving the knife, "I will chop you to pieces."

The soldiers were bantering with Savorn, amused by the crazy woman. But after a few minutes one of the soldiers got angry and cocked his AK-47 and shot her four or five times in the chest. She crashed onto the balcony railing, her blood dripping onto the ground below.

Sophea still thinks about that moment. For years afterward he had nightmares. Ten years later he was still having the nightmare where his mother wanted him to go along with her into death. Eventually, he came to the conclusion that her spirit had called to him at that time and that's why he had happened to be there at the exact moment of her death.

After witnessing this frightful scene, the children quietly snuck back through the sugarcane to the main road out of the city. Sophea spotted a toy—a play television with a paper screen where the child turns the paper in order to get different pictures—and inexplicably grabbed it.

At the checkpoint, Sophea said to the guard, "My mother is dead and I just saw her being shot."

The guard was suspicious but loaded the children into a jeep and drove them to the family. Mouth was in the process of building a crude hut by draping his military poncho over some sticks. The guard told Mouth what had happened. Mouth stayed very composed and welcomed the children back.

After the guard had left, Mouth gathered all the children and told them of their mother's death. Everyone was very calm. They all knew deep inside that it was better that she was dead or she would have exposed them. Although true, this thinking—and the guilt that accompanied it— would haunt Sophea for years.

Mouth went to the group leader and procured a travel permit. The next morning, he and Sophal returned to the house in Battambang. They took Savorn's body and wrapped it in a military poncho. They were just about to bury her when two soldiers came by and said, "Do you have a permit to bury her?"

"No," said Mouth, "I don't."

Mouth noticed Savorn's ring on the hands of one of the soldiers— a unique ring with a black stone that Mouth had given to Savorn after their marriage. There was no mistaking it. At that moment Mouth knew he was talking to the soldier that had killed his wife.

The soldiers left and Mouth and Sophal approached the house. On the outside of the door, lettered with chalk in Savorn's handwriting, were the words: "Missing all 6 children." This had a double meaning: the children were literally gone, or missing—and Savorn was missing them. These words would be a comfort to the remaining family in the years to come. Inside the house, Mouth and Sophal found disarray and a pot in the fireplace with something in it; Savorn had been trying to cook for herself. After looking around, they left.

The following day Mouth returned by himself and was told that Savorn had been buried in the bombing trench, still wrapped in the military poncho. Mouth couldn't do anything, so he left her like that and returned to the shanty hut under the tree. Shortly after, Savorn's mother— the children's grandmother—died in the night. The family cremated her at the crossroad.

The Khmer Rouge divided the children into groups. The older children—including Sophal and Sameth—were put into a work gang and taken away. Although Sophea was twelve, he was left out of the work group because of his disability. This, and the fact that everyone thought he was a peasant boy, meant that he could stay back with his father, his two younger sisters and younger brother.

Initially, Mouth and the children cooked their own food and were given fairly adequate rations of rice. But after a couple of months, *Angkar*—the Organization, or the equivalent of God in the new society— issued an announcement that everything was to be controlled by Angkar. People were to eat communally because that would save time; food rations were reduced to rice gruel—a watery soup—twice a day.

In 1976, some elderly people—including the *Krou* who had healed Sophea's leg as a baby—were ordered to go and grow vegetables in the jungle. The *krou* had always liked Sophea so he asked Mouth if the boy could come with them. Mouth, knowing that it was safer for a disabled boy to be far away from the Khmer Rouge, agreed, and Sophea set off with eight elderly people.

They hiked sixty miles to a jungle called Kris Klong, where they cleared out a farm in the jungle, cutting down trees and planting vegetable gardens. They built a hut on stilts and Sophea slept on a hammock strung underneath. The jungle was full of wild animals: snakes, deer, rabbits, monkeys and wild dogs that Sophea could hear howling at night. There were also domesticated animals—cows and pigs—that Sophea helped to care for. The group learned to make medicines from the trees and plants and collected coconuts and other fruits such as guava and papaya. They also trapped animals to eat.

In 1977 some Khmer Rouge families with younger children arrived to help with the vegetable farm, so there were other children around. One morning the adults were clearing a field while the children played on the outskirts, when Sophea spotted a man slumped over at the edge of the field. Sophea knew he had to tell the Khmer Rouge leader about the man or the other children would report him, so he went and told the leader.

The leader gathered some Khmer Rouge and told Sophea to come with them. When they reached the man, they seized him so roughly that he dropped his sack and a military compass and cooking utensils fell out, so Sophea knew he had escaped from the military. The Khmer Rouge dragged the man to a clearing where a fire was burning. The leader cut open the man's chest with an ax and pulled out his liver. He handed the liver to the other soldiers saying, "One man's liver is another man's food."

The other soldiers quickly sliced up the liver into a frying pan with some grease. All the Khmer Rouge gathered around and ate some of the liver. Sophea watched the men eating and thought how they looked like animals with their savage faces and bloodshot eyes. When the leader saw Sophea watching them, he told the boy to go look at what was now the corpse. When Sophea went over, the odor of blood was so strong that he threw up.

Later that day, Sophea went back to look at the corpse again—by now loosely buried in the jungle undergrowth. He stood near the body and thought: If you run away, when they catch you they will kill you. This is what happens to traitors.

In 1977, going into 1978, many more Khmer Rouge military families moved into the area. There were so many children that a school was started and Sophea began attending school again. Since the Khmer Rouge families were living and eating well, Sophea, who had been absorbed into the group, was also.

However, others, who were not Khmer Rouge, were not doing so well. One night Sophea made a secret trip to visit his family and noticed his emaciated siblings and the desperation in his father's face. The family was cooking something over a fire and offered Sophea a piece; Sophea took a bite and nearly spit it out—they were cooking a cat. Mouth told Sophea that the Khmer Rouge had tried to take him away several times in order to kill him but he had always gotten out of it by saying that he was sick and couldn't go.

Sophea kept attending school with the Khmer Rouge children. He got along well because the others thought he was a peasant boy who had always lived in the jungle. One day he was called up to the board to read and he pretended that he had never been educated and was learning to read for the first time, and thus read falteringly. The class and teacher were so impressed with his brilliant progress at reading that they made him youth president.

Every night after work the Khmer Rouge held general meetings, where everyone sang Communist songs with rousing fervor. A whole new language had developed; people called each other "comrade" and sang songs about the 17th of April, the day Cambodia was "liberated."

After the songs, the meetings turned into a *kosang*, where anyone could inform on others who weren't working hard enough, and so on. These accusations could be real or imagined, but they were taken seriously; the guilty persons were expected to be very repentant and change their ways immediately.

During one *kosang* a girl stood up and said, "I want to force someone to confess so that they can change. I heard Sophea swear."

Then another person stood up and said, "Oh, I heard him swear too."

Soon so many people were standing up talking about the bad things Sophea had done that everyone began laughing because no one person could do all that. It was all right that particular time because it had turned into a funny incident, but it could be dangerous.

Sophea had been given the job of taking care of the group ox. One afternoon he was so tired that he tied the ox in the long grass and laid down to rest. A Khmer Rouge soldier happened across him and said, "You aren't fulfilling your responsibility in taking care of the ox."

Sophea, feeling a bit sassy, answered, " Oh, I was just taking a break."

This made the soldier angry and he tied Sophea to a pole under the boiling sun. He left him there and red ants came and swarmed over his legs, biting furiously. Finally the soldier returned in the evening and untied him. Sophea was very frightened at this incident and learned his lesson; after this he was more careful around the Khmer Rouge.

In early 1979, unbeknownst to Sophea, the Khmer Rouge regime began to unravel. One night, under the cover of darkness, the original eight elderly people that had come to the jungle grabbed Sophea and left, along with some axes, pots and an oxcart. They traveled for several days, camping out at night. They reached the shanty and delivered Sophea to Mouth. Somehow Mouth had managed to gather all of his children together, even Sameth and Sophal who had been sent off to the work gang.

Sophal, who had always been a little bit plump, was now skin and bones and Sameth had been left to die because his foot was greatly infected.

Immediately after Sophea's arrival, the reunited family was caught in a crossfire between the invading Vietnamese and the defending Khmer Rouge. The Khmer Rouge shot toward the fleeing refugees so they would turn back and be a living shield between themselves and the Vietnamese army. A shell from a grenade launcher landed and blew a refugee family standing near Mouth and the children into pieces.

Mouth decided to head towards Battambang, feeling the Vietnamese who had invaded the city were safer than the Khmer Rouge shooting at them. He led the children several miles into the rice fields and took a detour around a large manmade lake. The children followed him around the lake and fell down exhausted. Before dawn the family crawled through dead bodies lying in the canal, almost suffocating from the stench. At sunrise, they stopped to rest at a big tree where some other refugees were catching fish in the rice paddies. Mouth and his children followed suit and soon had a breakfast of fish and some rice they had carried with them. Sophea thought no food had ever tasted so good.

While talking with the other refugees the family heard that the people who had stayed with the Khmer Rouge had been killed. Mouth went back and saw his brother-in-law, wife, two children and father-in-law decapitated and lying in the dirt.

Upon Mouth's return the family continued on to Battambang. Their former house had been completely demolished so they moved in temporarily underneath the grandmother's house. Mouth wanted to dig up Savorn's body in order to conduct a ceremony but there wasn't time; he had decided the family was not going to stay in Cambodia under another Communist regime. While working in Lon Nol's American-supported army, he had seen the plenitude and quality of American supplies so he determined that the family would head towards Thailand and from there to the United States.

Together they built a cart, dug up some buried money and set out. In a few days they reached Sisophon, where Mouth ran into another officer he knew from the military. This officer said he would get them safely across the Thai border in exchange for gold, so Mouth gave him all he had. The officer took them to a ruined temple, told them to wait and left.

That night bandits came and took everything—which was now mostly pots and pans. Before dawn a couple of guides came up and said, "OK, we're here to take you across the border."

The sun was almost up when the family and guides walked some 500 yards on a jungle path and were ambushed by yet more bandits with guns.

The bandits made everyone strip—even the kids—and give them anything of value. They left, and the group quickly dressed, feeling lucky that no one had been raped or killed.

The guides pointed them in a direction and said, "Go straight on this path, keep bearing left—and watch out for landmines."

Sophea led the way because he knew the jungle the best. After walking a couple of miles he spotted a thin wire a centimeter off the ground that blended in with the sand of the path. It was nearly invisible: a landmine. He pointed it out to everybody else and one by one they very carefully stepped over it.

They walked for several more hours when Sophea spotted yet another landmine—this one was indicated only by a disturbance in the earth where the dry ground had been dug up, the mine installed and the dirt tamped back down. Again he pointed this out and everybody carefully stepped around it.

The family walked several more hours and met a group of Khmer Rouge. Everyone stood still, unsure of what was going to happen. Finally they gave the Khmer Rouge some of their uncooked rice—the Khmer Rouge were starving—and they left. A couple hours later they ran into another group of Khmer Rouge. Again, they gave them some food and were allowed to continue.

They walked for an hour and a half when they reached the Thai border; instantly they were surrounded by the border patrol pointing guns and speaking Khmer with strong accents. All along Sophea had been wearing an amulet of Buddha his father had given him; now he took it off and gave it to the leader.

The leader said, "Oh, we feel sorry for you," and put them in a jeep and drove them across the border to Camp Kokyoung. It was fortuitous timing because the camp had just sent a busload of refugees back to Cambodia for repatriation and these refugees had all ended up dead—either by bombs or by the Khmer Rouge.

At Camp Kokyoung, a holding camp, the family was given food and clothing. After a couple of weeks they were transferred to Surin, the main camp, to wait for sponsorship to the United States. At this point, if a refugee was a former Lon Nol soldier the application was processed more quickly, so Mouth worked diligently and the process went fairly fast. While waiting, Sophea sat in on any English class he could and began to learn the language.

After several months the family received word that a sponsor had been found and they were transferred to a transition camp in Bangkok for medical exams. There was some wondering as to whether Sophea would pass the medical exam because of his leg; some thought maybe he would have to stay behind. Mouth responded that he had managed to keep the family together thus far and if anyone needed to stay behind, he would. Mouth accompanied Sophea to the hospital for his exam, where he passed with no problem.

Next the family met with an interpreter who had been instructed to tell them about their sponsor and the place where they were going.

"You are going to a place in the United States called Wis-ching-kong-sun," the interpreter said.

Ever since the Khmer Rouge had marched into Battambang in 1975, Sophea had felt asphyxiated by a burden on his chest, like he couldn't breathe. This feeling continued throughout the ensuing years and was still there when Sophea prepared for departure with his family. They boarded the plane and lifted off into the sky. During the flight the passengers were served meals of packaged chicken.

The plane landed in Los Angeles and the family disembarked—barefoot, since none of them had worn shoes since the Khmer Rouge takeover. While walking on the airport carpet, Sophea felt guilty, thinking his dirty bare feet would soil the carpet.

The immigration officer looked at Mouth's I-94 Initial Entry permit where his name appeared in the Khmer/Cambodian style of last name first, followed by the first name: Ouk Mouth. So the officer labeled their papers as members of the Mouth family, with Ouk as the head. From this moment on, the family had their father's first name as their last name, akin to arriving in another country and having one's last name changed to "John" or "Fred."

The family boarded a plane to Chicago, where their sponsors Will and Martha Smith* from Lake Geneva, Wisconsin, were there to meet them. The Smiths ran a dairy farm outside of Lake Geneva and had told the sponsoring committee that they had an extra house on the farm where Mouth and his children could live.

When Sophea first saw the Smiths, his impression was that Will was friendly but Martha was cold and unapproachable. The Mouths were loaded into a station wagon and driven to the farm. When they arrived at the farm, the Smiths introduced some of their children: Greg*, who at sixteen was the same age as Sophea but stood six feet two inches tall next to Sophea's undernourished four foot eleven inches; and Phoebe* and Trey*, their adopted African American children. Also part of the Smith family but not present at the Mouths' arrival were Will Jr.*, a practicing

*pseudonym

attorney nearby; Alice*, who was married to Rick Trent*, the man who ran the family's lawnmower repair shop; and twins James* and Joe*. Joe was away in the Peace Corps.

Will and Martha explained to the Mouths that everyone would begin work on the farm the next day. The family could stay in the house free for the first month, after that, rent, electricity, and heat would be garnished from Mouth's monthly wages. (Mouth never saw any money after that first month; the entire paycheck was gone by the time he had earned it.)

It was early evening when the Smiths left. Sophea went out to the porch of the rental farm house and gazed out at the fields. The setting sun was hitting the tops of the corn stalks and turning the fields a golden brown. At that moment the pressure that had been building up in his chest since 1975 simply disappeared. For the first time in years he felt safe and happy.

Mouth and all the children began work on the dairy farm the following morning. Mouth and Sophal and Sameth milked the cows. Sophea also started out milking but couldn't lift or carry the milk cans because of his leg, so the Smiths put him to work in the lawnmower repair shop. Initially he stood around, not knowing what to do, but after a couple months he had learned to take apart engines and clean and fix machines. (After working for four months, he got an engine running for the first time and Rick gave him $20, the first money Sophea had ever had in his life. He promptly went to Kentucky Fried Chicken with Sameth and spent every cent.)

Sophea and the other Mouth children started school. Sophal and Sameth went to an ESL program for a couple hours a day. Sophea was put into the fifth grade because no one believed that he was sixteen on account of his small stature. Consequently, Sophea and Greg Smith didn't have much to do with each other—even though they were the same age—because Greg was busy with high school and the basketball team.

The Smiths introduced the family to American food: spaghetti, macaroni-and-cheese and so on. Martha taught Sophea how to make a tunafish sandwich to take to school. Used clothes arrived in huge bags from the people in the Smith's church; the Mouths didn't know the difference and thought it incredible to get so many clothes at once. At first, Sophea had no idea of how to adapt his clothing to the seasons. He wore only a T-shirt in the dead of winter until someone gave him a jacket, then he began to wear that.

One morning Sophea packed a tunafish sandwich and a can of soda in a bag to take to school. At lunchtime in the cafeteria he opened his

*pseudonym

soda and took a sip. It tasted terrible. Then he noticed that the other students were looking at him and whispering. He had taken a can of beer—Pabst Blue Ribbon—out of the fridge, mistaking it for soda.

Soon everyone knew of the incident. Martha Smith heard about it, the pastor of the church heard about it; everyone was talking about the boy who drank beer in the lunchroom. The Smiths told Mouth but Mouth didn't understand English so Sophea was spared punishment from his father.

Mouth became sick from drinking milk so Martha and Will got a translator to come from Madison, who told them, "These people eat rice." Will and Martha went out and bought rice; unfortunately, they bought brown rice instead of the white rice Cambodians eat. The translator had to come back a month later and say, "They eat white rice." Eventually the family was able to find a kind of rice they liked—Jasmine White Rice—in Madison and buy it in bulk.

Sameth bought a Ford Fairmont from a Cambodian who lived in Madison. He got his driver's license and the family was then free to go places on their own and not depend upon the Smiths for transportation.

After fifth grade, Sophea's teachers took him aside: "Are you prepared to go to high school?"

"Sure," Sophea said, "I'll go."

He began ninth grade the following year. He had no idea of what high school was about, didn't even know what a homeroom was. He was seventeen and everyone else was fourteen or fifteen. No one had been through anything like what he had been through, so there was no one to talk to. There were no other Asians at the school.

He went to ESL class, English class, machine shop class and woodworking class day after day without talking to or connecting with anyone. He became very lonely. The old feeling of being asphyxiated began building up and he had nightmares over and over about his mother being killed by the Khmer Rouge.

He worked at the lawnmower shop a great deal and watched a lot of television. He stopped going to church, which caused some consternation because the Smiths were a strong churchgoing family. He bought Bruce Lee magazines and videos, then ordered *nunchaku*—two sticks connected by a chain—a star, throwing knives and other kung fu materials from the backs of the magazines. He got Sameth involved with the martial arts, causing Martha to worry that Sophea was going to do something violent. Sophea knew deep down that he wasn't a violent person, that the Bruce Lee stuff was just his way of coping; however, he couldn't articulate that to Martha.

One day Sophea arbitrarily sat down at a table in the high school lunchroom, which turned out to be the table where all the rich kids sat.

One of the guys—a big football player—said, "You stupid Cambodian!"

When Sophea didn't respond, he said, "Meet me behind the building after school."

"OK," Sophea said. "Sure."

Sophea knew they were going to fight him. After school he put his *nunchaku* in his waist and went out to meet them. The football player brought his friends. When the row of big guys approached him, Sophea took out his *nunchaku* and spun them in front of his neck and waist a few times. Sophea was good—looked even better—and the football players backed off. Later, they called the principal and said that Sophea had threatened them.

Sophea was called in and he said, "No, they called me stupid."

The minister heard about the incident and came over to talk to Sophea. He told Sophea that the football players had small minds.

"Yeah," said Sophea. "They sure do."

But Sophea was somewhat comforted by the minister's visit. After that, whenever any of the football players saw Sophea in the halls at school, they would make a gesture like they were shooting him with a gun. This happened routinely until the principal saw it one day and called them all in. After that, it stopped.

Sophea made friends with the other high school boy who was working at the lawnmower repair shop—Dan Nevin. They began doing some stuff together, working on dirtbikes, sitting at the same table in the cafeteria at school. They remained friends until Dan moved away after high school.

The farmhouse where the Mouths were staying was owned by the eldest Smith son, Joe, who was away in the Peace Corps. After Joe finished his term and returned to the States, he moved back into his house and lived with the Mouth family. One morning Mouth caught Joe and Sophal in bed together. He attempted both to beat up Sophal and call the police on Joe. Mouth told Joe in no uncertain terms that Cambodian custom said if you slept with a girl you had to marry her.

No one could tell what Joe was thinking, but he and Sophal did get married. The marriage seemed to succeed and they proceeded to have four children. (Eventually they divorced amicably and Joe was given full custody of the children. They both remained in Lake Geneva and neither remarried.)

After two years of working on the farm, Mouth physically broke down. He had worked four years for the Khmer Rouge, which had completely exhausted his strength, and then immediately begun working on the farm so that his body never had a chance to heal. Fortunately, he qualified for Social Security Income because of the mental and physical injuries he had suffered during the Pol Pot regime, and so financially was able to move to Madison with the three youngest children. In Madison, the family lived on his SSI paycheck and Mouth organized and started the Cambodian Association of Madison.

Martha grew so worried about what she saw as Sophea's violent tendencies that she took away the *nunchaku*, star, throwing knives, punching bag—even his Bruce Lee uniform. Sophea begged and begged to get these things back until she finally relented, but said he had to keep them in the car; he couldn't keep them in the house.

After Mouth left with the younger children, Sophea stayed on at the farm. He hung out with the youngest Smith son, Trey, who also enjoyed working on machines. They bought dirtbikes and worked on them together. Trey's dirtbike was a brand new Honda from Will and Martha; Sophea's was a used Yamaha he had bought on the cheap for a couple of hundred dollars.

One night both dirtbikes were stolen from the shed where the boys kept them. Weeks later, Sophea saw a boy riding his bike in a nearby field and went and told the police. The police went to the boy and told him to return the bikes; he did, but in terrible condition—broken and repainted.

The police told Sophea and Trey to go ahead and fix the bikes and to keep track of their parts and labor so they could be reimbursed. Trey didn't bother to fix his bike but Sophea spent many hours fixing and repainting his, then took the estimate to the police.

The police got the money from the thief and brought it over to Martha. Martha took the money but gave only half to Sophea.

"The other half belongs to Trey," she said.

Sophea said, "But he didn't do any work on his dirtbike! I did all the work and that estimate was just for my bike."

Martha went ahead and gave half the money to Trey anyway. Sophea was furious and felt Martha had taken his money but that he couldn't do anything about it. Relations between Martha and Sophea became even more strained. One time she told Sophea that she and Will didn't think he was going to "make it"; they thought he was going to be a mechanic all his life.

During his senior year Sophea bought two guns: a .357 Magnum and a .44 Magnum. Martha became extremely worried but Sophea said he would only shoot targets out behind the shop with Rick.

Rick filed for bankruptcy but Sophea also got along well with the new boss—and began shooting targets out back with him. Sophea taught the new staff everything about the lawnmower repair business: repair, inventory; he had every part number memorized.

As graduation day approached, the local paper listed the seniors graduating with honors. Martha saw his name in the newspaper and came to show him: "Look, you're in the paper for honor roll!"

Mrs. Thompson, the ESL teacher, threw her students a party. Sophal cooked some egg rolls for Sophea to bring. During the party Mrs. Thompson took Sophea aside and told him something that meant a lot. She said he was the smartest in the class because he asked so many questions and encouraged him to pursue more schooling.

Everyone handed around their yearbooks on the last day of school. Many students, as they signed Sophea's, said, "Geez, I wish I had known you all this time—you're a cool guy."

Well, Sophea thought, too late now.

Sophea stayed on in Lake Geneva—living in the farmhouse and working at the lawnmower repair shop—through summer and part of the fall, then moved to Madison to live with Mouth. He was too late to start at Madison Area Technical College (MATC) in the fall but enrolled in a few classes for spring. He didn't do well in the classes because his English writing skills were so poor, so he spent all his free time reading and taking more English classes. He enrolled again and this time received excellent grades.

After a couple more years at MATC, Sophea moved into his own apartment and transferred to Edgewood College, a small private Catholic college in Madison. He was asked to be part of a Cambodian band called "Bayon Dauntry"—named after a scenic region in Cambodia—and gradually worked into disc jockeying at the local clubs.

He got involved in local government—this meant a lot of mentoring of other Cambodians, translating at hospitals and courts. He was asked to be on the Public Safety Review Board, the Dane County Minority Affairs commission with Rick Phelps, and to give talks around the city and at the University of Wisconsin–Madison. He worked with Paul Higgenbotham, now a judge, in Madison.

Sophea wanted justice, he wanted fairness, he wanted to help the down-and-out have access to the system. However, in his Herculean efforts to help others he was neglecting his own life. Looking back, he sees himself as "definitely troubled" at this time and feels that his frenetic schedule was an attempt to escape his own emotional problems.

In 1990 and 1991 while attending Edgewood College, the nuns frequently asked Sophea about his faith and encouraged him to convert.

Several Protestant ministers also approached him at this time. One in particular asked if Sophea had "met" God and when Sophea replied that he was a political scientist and didn't think that way, the man began talking about his daughter, who was the same age as Sophea—did Sophea want to meet her?

Sophea realized that he was neither Christian nor Muslim; he was a Buddhist.

"If they wanted to convert me," he said to a friend, "it backfired, because they convinced me that I believed in Buddhism."

He graduated from Edgewood in 1991 but didn't attend the ceremony. He didn't know what was next. He had thought of working for Human Services in Madison until they said he was too radical because of his speaking and writing against the Gulf War and police violence.

One night in 1991, Sophea went to a Caribbean theme party after deejaying at a club. A girl introduced herself to him, saying her name was Serena* and that she was at the University of Wisconsin–Madison on a semester exchange program from Trinidad. They chatted and danced for a while, then Sophea thought no more of it.

A couple of weeks later Serena called, saying she had gotten Sophea's phone number from someone else. They went out that night, then began dating seriously. During spring semester Serena moved from her dorm room into Sophea's apartment. She said she loved him and he could see this was true. He promised her that after she returned from Trinidad in the fall, they would get married. He didn't think much about this when he said it; he said it more out of compassion than love as Serena wasn't from a wealthy family and needed a way to stay on in the United States.

But living together didn't work out. In a way he couldn't put his finger on, she got on his nerves. He asked her to move out of the apartment a few times but she wouldn't leave. In late spring, deciding he needed a break from the whole situation, he went to visit friends in Pennsylvania. When he returned after a month, she was gone.

During the summer he worked as a deejay and thought a great deal about the relationship. He called her one night in Trinidad and said he wanted to begin seeing other women. She cried and cried, saying that she had already made marriage plans and that her father and others had given her money for the wedding. Sophea told her that he had to think everything over and would call her back in a few days.

Pondering his dilemma, he decided that he had made a promise and

*pseudonym

he needed to keep it. He wanted to bear the burden of his own karma—the karma of his word. In Buddhism if you promise something, you deliver—even if it's at your own expense. So he called her back and told her of his decision. She was ecstatic. He asked when she intended to come and she replied that she was intending to visit New York anyway, so she would fly on to Chicago that coming Friday.

On Friday Sophea couldn't get out of bed; it felt like the end of his life. At last he dragged himself out of bed and drove to Chicago, where he arrived too late—Serena had already boarded a bus going from Chicago to Madison. So he turned around and drove back. Shortly after his return, Serena called and said she was waiting at the University of Wisconsin Student Union and he went to pick her up.

They lived together, paying off debts and student loans, and got married in 1992. Sophea wasn't yet a citizen, but was a legal resident, and thus, Serena could stay in the U.S. Sophea knew that Serena loved him and married him out of genuine feeling and not simply to stay in the U.S.; unfortunately, he didn't reciprocate those feelings.

Sophea began working toward his master's of business administration degree in management at Edgewood College while Serena supported them by working at a restaurant. Serena wanted a baby. Sophea thought he was ready but when she became pregnant, it was difficult for both of them. Serena was emotional; Sophea took over the cooking and cleaning in addition to his schoolwork. He began to see clearly that her personality was too moody for him; even in her happiness, she was too difficult and grated on his nerves.

On August 31, 1993, their baby boy, Sovann, was born. They both adored him and stayed together. Sophea received his MBA and was accepted to go to graduate school at the University of Wisconsin-Madison in Buddhist studies. Serena had also been accepted into the MBA program at UW-Madison. Since they were both in school, Sophea's father—Mouth—took care of Sovann, essentially raising the baby throughout the first years.

Sophea and Serena's relationship became even more tense and strained. Sophea had a lot of pent-up anger inside him but didn't show it. Serena, on the other hand, became violent, screaming at and hitting Sophea. She broke lamps and tried to stab him several times. Sophea didn't worry about leaving her alone with Sovann because she was a very loving mother; the violence was all directed towards him.

In 1995 Serena told Sophea that she wanted him to quit school and go to work full time. Sophea said he wasn't going to do that but promised her that he would finish soon; however, problems kept cropping up and delaying his graduation, namely, one of his professors retired so that he had to wait for a new professor specializing in Southeast Asian Studies and Buddhism to arrive from Harvard.

Finally Sophea decided he had had enough and moved out to live with some friends. He met a Cambodian woman at school named Anny* and they began dating. Sophea occasionally stayed overnight with Anny but always returned to Sovann, who was two years old at the time. Sophea understood that his life was a mess but still wanted to be with his son.

When Sophea moved in permanently with Anny, Serena began to call and harass her, saying things like, "You stole my husband, bitch" and calling her a slut. Despite this behavior, Sophea felt he couldn't divorce Serena until she got a green card and citizenship because only then would his obligations to her be fulfilled.

Once Sophea came by to see Sovann and Serena tried to stab him with a knife with Sovann near by. Another time she tried to beat him with a broom. That time Sophea called the police; when they arrived he told them that he hadn't wanted it to escalate.

By 1998 Anny couldn't take Serena's phone calls and Sophea's indecision and told Sophea he had to leave. Sophea thought of Sovann and how he was neglecting his paternal responsibility and decided to move back in with Serena for a one-year trial period.

It didn't work. There was only more screaming, yelling, and violence. At one point Serena said, "I didn't really want you, I just wanted to break you and Anny up."

Sophea moved out in August 1999 after the trial period was over. Serena filed for divorce in November. Sophea became depressed and avoiding everyone, including his son. He spent a lot of time online in a Cambodian chat room, where he met a woman from Los Angeles. He went to visit her in December but it didn't work out.

Sophea didn't know if he was going to stay in Madison or move to California, so the court awarded full custody of Sovann to Serena. Sophea went online again and talked to a woman named Jacqulyn from Georgia. She had a degree in anthropology but was working as an administrative assistant.

In February he was at a low point: drinking a lot and taking only one class while waiting for the new professor from Harvard. He went back online and started talking with Jacqulyn again. This time she gave him her phone number. He called her the very next day, on February 18, and

*pseudonym

discovered during the phone conversation that she was single, living alone and working two jobs.

At the end of the conversation he said, "I'm coming to visit you." He had not yet mentioned his leg to her.

He wanted to leave the following morning but it snowed, so he waited and left Madison the next day—a Saturday—and arrived in Georgia at midnight. During his visit with Jacqulyn, Sophea found that she had a calm personality that soothed him. Also, she had suffered much in her life, like Sophea. She was born in 1972 and was a baby under the Khmer Rouge, and thus had no memories of that time. In some uncanny links to Sophea's background, she had a mother who was mentally ill and abusive and a father who had been in the military; however, in the reversal of Sophea's situation, her father was dead but her mother was still alive.

Sophea stayed with Jacqulyn for a week and during that week, they fell in love. Sophea knew profoundly that it was a very different sort of love than he had had with anybody else, including Serena; there was a spiritual component present that had been completely lacking in his other relationships. They decided Jacqulyn would come to Madison the following June when they would marry. Jacqulyn called her mother, who was initially happy at the news, but after learning that Sophea was disabled, divorced and had a child, decided that she didn't want her daughter to marry a man with all those drawbacks. However, Jacqulyn remained adamant in her choice.

Sophea returned to Madison after a week in order to go back to school. In June he flew to Georgia and met Jacqulyn's mother, two sisters and the daughter of the youngest sister, all of who were staying with Jacqulyn in order to attend the wedding. Sophea drove everyone back to Madison in Jacqulyn's car where they all stayed in Sophea's two room apartment. Jacqulyn's brother got leave from the army and arrived from where he had been stationed in Germany.

Sophea and Jacqulyn spent most of their time preparing for the wedding. Another sister arrived from Florida. Then Jacqulyn's mother told her that Sophea wasn't the kind of person she wanted for a son-in-law. Jacqulyn didn't respond. This incident ignited a weird sort of war where if Sophea came into the living room, Jacqulyn's mother, brother, sisters and niece would all go into the bedroom. Jacqulyn would remain in the room with Sophea, but then she was also shunned.

Finally Sophea had had enough and told Jacqulyn's mother that he didn't care whether she hated him or not. "I'm used to it," he said, "given all that has happened to me in my background. But the marriage is going to go through."

Jacqulyn's mother cried all night long. In the morning the brother came out of the bedroom and began yelling at Jacqulyn, raising his voice louder and louder.

Sophea said, "Please don't fight in here."

The brother kept on until Jacqulyn's youngest sister got scared and called the police. The police came and said Jacqulyn's brother had to leave.

Jacqulyn's mother said, "If my son is leaving, then I'm leaving too."

Everyone packed up and left except Jacqulyn and her youngest sister with her daughter. It was one week before the wedding. Sophea and Jacqulyn were stunned. They decided to go ahead because all the plans were in place and everyone had already been invited.

Sophea and Jacqulyn were married on July 7, 2000. Sophea's good friends Noeun Has and his wife Mara Roun had offered their house for the ceremony and festivities; they became impromptu parents and gave the bride away. There was an enormous amount of food that Jacqulyn and Sophea had cooked beforehand, along with dancing and musicians. It was a wonderful event; however, Jacqulyn cried once during the ceremony because neither her mother nor father were present.

After the wedding Jacqulyn tried to call her mother several times but her mother kept repeating, "You're abandoning me to a husband." So eventually Jacqulyn stopped calling.

Presently, Jacqulyn is working and supporting the couple until Sophea finishes his Ph.D.; after that Sophea will work as a professor so that Jacqulyn can go back to school. Sophea is close to his goal; he reads English, French, Tibetan, Khmer, Pali, and Sanskrit. Working hard is the key to his academic success, he has decided, which is something he learned from practicing Buddhism. Karma really means action: the Buddhist exerts effort and channels it in the right way. Sophea looks at other people who aren't succeeding and thinks they haven't exerted enough effort.

There is a Cambodian saying: "As a four legged elephant will fall, so a learned scholar will forget." It means nothing is perfect, there is always a problem, everyone has a weakness. Sophea knows this is true. For example, he has always worked from certain weaknesses: his leg, the language barrier, his skin color. But he didn't let any of these stop him; he kept going, using his hands and his mind. He understands where he is working from and thus, where he is heading.

17

Coming Full Circle

In the jungle of northwestern Cambodia lies the ancient stone city of Angkor, built between the 9th and 13th centuries A.D. by Khmer kings in honor of their gods. Laborers crafted the magnificent temples, walls, massive gateways and causeways out of laterite, brick and sandstone. They also dug a vast and sophisticated irrigation system of basins, canals, ponds, moats and reservoirs that conquered the monsoons and enabled the inhabitants to grow two—sometimes three—crops of rice a year.

The stone temple Angkor Wat, masterpiece of Khmer art, sits in the middle of a seventy-five-mile plain surrounded by galleries, courts and towers—every inch ornamented with carvings. The classic temple-mountain, Angkor Wat is triple terraced and intricately designed with cruciform courts and five towering peaks, fitting for the Khmer shrine and symbolic abode of the gods.

When the Khmer Rouge took over Cambodia, all upkeep of the wats, or temples, ceased. Most of the pagodas were destroyed; Angkor Wat was partially destroyed and the last archaeologists and maintenance crews were forced to leave in 1972. Statues and carvings were smashed by artillery fire, defiled with black paint or taken and bartered on the Thai border. Gateways and walls were pockmarked with bullet holes. The untended wats were eroded by the elements and a tide of jungle vegetation flowed into every crevice. Vines twined around the enormous statues, birds cawed overhead and the snakes slithered in and out of temple doors.

At the housewarming party during the summer of 1996, Noeun had seemed to be god of his temple abode and conqueror of his personal and professional life. A few years later, I began to notice signs of decay. Once, in 1998, when I called to talk to Noeun, Prum answered the phone and, as she and I chatted, it was as if she were speaking in code with words having double meanings and nothing meaning quite what she said. Puzzled, I asked to speak to Noeun. She left to go get him, was gone for quite

Children of Sarah Streed and Roger Luhn (left to right): Alec, Theron, Sarah, Drew and Brian, in Stoughton, Wisconsin, taken in autumn 2000. (Photograph from the personal collection of Sarah Streed and Roger Luhn.)

some time, then got on the phone again and said Nouen didn't want to talk to me.

This had never happened before. I left a message and hung up, but the incident troubled me. Why wouldn't Noeun talk to me? And what was that quality in Prum's voice—abject, defeated—that I couldn't place, but knew was there?

More signs of decline appeared: My mother got a phone call from Laurie, the neighbor, who said she was calling on behalf of the children. Many days they didn't make it to the bus stop on time and since Prum didn't like to drive them, they were missing a lot of school. On this particular day Laurie said that Brian's teacher had called her because Brian wasn't wearing socks to school; it being a typical Minnesota winter, the school staff was concerned. Brian's teacher had communicated to Laurie that if Noeun and Prum weren't more attentive, social services would be called. After the phone call, my parents approached Noeun, who brushed it off, saying that Brian didn't like to wear socks.

Around this time, Prum's foster parents—the Larsons—and my parents began discussing the deteriorating situation. Both sets of foster grandparents had observed that Prum wasn't taking care of the children. Noeun was gone at the 4-midnight shift at the factory, then came home, slept for a few hours, and did all the maintenance for kids and house. When Prum came home from her data processing job in the afternoon, she didn't feed the kids, didn't watch them, didn't interact with them. At ages six and seven they were running wild, missing days of school and dressing inappropriately and inadequately. Sarah, their daughter, had cried in front of her teacher because her mother wouldn't fill out the forms she needed to go on field trips.

At Christmas 1998 our family gathered at my parents' house in Excelsior. Nouen and Prum always celebrated with the Larsons, so, as usual, they weren't present. While gathered together, Mom mentioned to us children that Noeun and Prum were having problems and that she and Dad were taking the kids occasionally for a weekend so that, hopefully, Noeun and Prum could work things out.

My mother had also offered to pay for marriage counseling, but Noeun and Prum had refused. This had been the expected—but not hoped for—response, as Cambodian refugees often feel that an American counselor can't help them—both because an American can't understand what they've been through and because of the strong swath of Buddhist determinism that runs through their core: one's current life situation has already been decided by actions in previous lives and accumulated merit.

The family also talked about the possibility of Noeun abusing Prum; a neighbor—not Laurie—had heard screaming one night and called the police. We were worried, the Larsons were worried, but Noeun and Prum were keeping to themselves and pulling away from us all.

Ellyn and I spoke of how we thought the abuse allegation likely, even though it had never been substantiated. I found it difficult to think of Noeun hurting Prum, but then remembered his dark anger when he was a teenager: the black moods that would descend so that I could hardly believe it was the same person who had smiled and joked with me the day before.

Roger and I and our three children left my parents' house before Ellyn and her family did, so Ellyn took the opportunity of those few extra days to call several hotlines and women's shelters in the Minneapolis area. She procured a list of names for Mom and Dad to give to Prum, or to the Larsons, who could then pass it on to Prum. When Ellyn and her family came through Wisconsin on their way back to Illinois, she and I talked for a long time about the situation. There didn't seem to be much that we could do. Ellyn gave me a copy of the list; she was hopeful about one of the contacts, a counselor who had worked directly with Southeast Asian immigrants and domestic violence issues.

Shortly after, the family heard rumors that Noeun had come home from a night shift and found Prum in bed with Lon, his good friend and fellow refugee. Prum took the children and moved to an apartment; the children spoke of Lon being there much of the time.

The Larsons became extremely involved with Prum and the children in an effort to try and help. Jennifer, the Larsons' birth daughter and Prum's foster sister—probably the closest to Prum of anyone—also stepped in. Either Jennifer or her parents would take the children on weekends. The Larsons went shopping and bought the kids the normal accouterments of childhood: bikes, inline skates, videos, clothes and lots of books.

But as the months passed, it didn't seem as if Prum was benefiting from this help. Her typical pattern was to drop the kids off at the Larsons' for a weekend, then not pick them up for two weeks. Or, she left them with Jennifer for the weekend and when Jennifer called her on Sunday night and told her to come get them because she had to be at work on Monday, Prum came late and reluctantly. Then the children hung onto Jennifer's legs, crying and begging to stay with her.

So during the spring of 1999, the children moved in with the Larsons. They and my parents felt that this would give Prum a chance to get her life together. However, the situation only worsened. Prum didn't give any sign of missing her children or wanting them back. Every month or so she and Lon would show up at the Larsons, take the children to a movie, buy them gifts afterward at Wal-Mart, then drop them off, whereupon Prum would cry and tell the children she wished she could be with them, that one day they would be together. The Larsons—trying to remain calm in front of Sarah and Brian—would pull Prum aside and remind her that she could have her children, and that it could be soon.

After this Sarah and Brian were angry and upset for several days, thinking that their foster grandparents were keeping them from living with their mother. They would behave badly for a while, gradually adjusting to life with the Larsons over several weeks, getting back to normal just when Prum showed up again.

Meanwhile, my father was helping Noeun go through the steps of selling the house. The two of them got it on the market and it sold quickly, as it was in an excellent location and still fairly new. Once it had sold, Nouen moved back into his old bedroom at my parents' house. He was in such personal turmoil that he couldn't perform his job of calibrating precise factory machinery, but the management approached him and said they would continue to pay his current salary while he did a much more menial job; they said his original job would be waiting whenever he felt ready to return to it.

After the children had lived with the Larsons for a year, the matter of the children's future became acute. Mr. Larson was retiring and had always planned to move to a warmer state upon his retirement. The Larsons couldn't continue to keep the children but Prum didn't seem any closer to resuming her role as caretaker. Since Noeun and Prum had separated and didn't need to divorce—having never been legally married— Noeun had, against my parents' advice, moved to the East Coast, where he had joined his birth mother and sister in their strong Cambodian community. Jennifer dearly loved the children and would have taken them, but she was single and had a full-time job with lots of travel.

Since it was obvious the children couldn't live with their mother, the Larsons made the next choice of having them live with their father. They enlisted the help of my parents and again the four foster grandparents worked together to help make this transition work.

Phone calls were made; although Noeun wasn't eager to take the children, he was reminded that these were his children and they needed to live somewhere. In the end, Noeun flew to Minneapolis and stayed with my parents for a few days while Sarah and Brian packed for the move. Then the three of them flew out east to start a new life as a family.

Only it didn't work out that way. Various reports began filtering back: the children weren't living with Noeun, but in his birth sister's apartment. The sister was kind to the children, but only twenty-four and starting college, and the grandmother—Noeun's birth mother—didn't treat the children well. She had never liked Prum and had told Noeun not to marry her. She had also been angry at Noeun for continuing to live in Minnesota after she had emigrated to the East Coast. Even though he had finally capitulated—he was living in the same apartment complex— his birth mother remained bitter and unforgiving and was taking it out on the children. There was also a cousin living nearby, a boy of thirteen, who was involved in a Cambodian gang and thus a bad influence on eight-year-old Brian.

It also came out at this time that Prum had beaten Brian at least once when she had been living alone in the apartment with the children. One night she had been drinking and began hitting Brian on the back and the legs with the cord that goes from the VCR to the television—the kind that has a metal plug at both ends. A neighbor lady who saw Brian the next day said that he had looked like a sailor who had been tied to the mast and lashed.

The children couldn't go back with their mother, weren't living or likely to live with their father and were unable to live permanently with the Larsons. My parents, being older than the Larsons, had decided they couldn't raise two young children. Where were Sarah and Brian to go?

The new owners of Noeun's house filed a law suit against him, saying he hadn't disclosed the "snake problem" during the housebuying process. They claimed he had knowingly hidden the fact that the house had snakes in the basement. Noeun insisted that he had never seen snakes in the house nor yard.

When the developers had originally prepared the property for a building site, they had leveled off the land by pushing the extra dirt against the woodsy area that sloped downward to a ravine. This four foot wide berm left along the back of the property line was a perfect place for garter snake dens. There are myriads of garter snakes in the Minnesota woods and after hibernating all winter, they come out in droves every spring to seek the sun, search for food, mate and have their young. Since they have a tremendous homing instinct, every fall they return to the same den.

I don't think Noeun even noticed the snakes because he avoided going near the woods and ravine in back of his house. Interestingly, Noeun, having grown up in Cambodia, didn't like what he referred to as the "jungle" part of his yard and never set foot there.

Two separate trials, many lawyers and a lot of money later, the suit was decided in Noeun's favor, with the jury seeming to feel that the new owners were trying to get Noeun to pay for landscaping work they had done in the backyard. Whatever the truth of how many snakes there were and how often they had come into the yard or house, the judge ruled that Noeun didn't have to pay any damages.

But Noeun's house was gone and with it, the American dream. The ideal life that Noeun had worked so hard to achieve: big new house in suburban neighborhood, wife, kids; it had turned to ashes, and was left to snakes.

My mother called me one Sunday evening in early August 2000 to apprise me on the latest news from Noeun and the children out east. As I was talking, I was looking out the window at our three children who were inline skating and drawing with chalk on the driveway. My mother told me that it was clear Sarah and Brian could no longer stay on the East Coast. Nouen was locking himself in a room every night and talking to himself, then drinking to insensibility. Then she said that he was going to lose his job.

I was aghast. No matter what had happened in his personal life, Noeun had always kept up appearances at work. I asked what was going to happen to Sarah and Brian. My mother answered that the Larsons were talking about foster care as there was no one to take care of them—the attempt for them to live out east with Noeun had been a last resort.

After a few more sentences, my mother said goodbye and we hung up. Roger was just coming in from the back garden, wheeling a barrow full of mulch. I went outside in my stocking feet and met him on the driveway.

"I was just on the phone with my mom," I said. "Things aren't going well with Noeun. He's drinking and is about to lose his job."

"What about the kids?" said Roger.

"Apparently they aren't even living with him," I said, "but with a sister or something."

The words came out of my mouth, casually, not a big deal. "If he sends them back and there's no one else to take them, do you think we should take them?"

I had no idea what Roger was going to say; I had never thought about it myself until that very moment. We had our family of three children and had taken steps to make certain there would be no more. We had never thought of adoption or foster parenting; there had never been a need nor inclination.

Roger looked at me. "I guess we could," he said.

We looked at each other for a moment, then our kids were all around, skating close, laughing, jumping one after another off a chalk ramp drawn down the driveway and out to the street.

"Well, the Larsons will probably end up taking them," I said, shrugging. "Or maybe Prum will decide she wants them after all."

I went back inside while he continued with the barrow full of mulch to the side garden. Little did we know we had just decided the course of our future with those few, simple sentences.

Prum called a few nights later to ask if Sarah and Brian could live with our family. Phone calls went back and forth to the Larsons and my parents before Roger and I decided that we would discuss the matter with our three children. We agreed that if any one of the three was against the idea, we wouldn't proceed. Alec, Drew and Theron were confused at first, wondering why Noeun and Prum couldn't take care of their own children, but eventually all three said in their own ways that they thought it was the right thing to do.

Two weeks later, Sarah and Brian, nine and eight years old, were driven to our house by the Larsons, a transition that would end in adoption and Roger and I as the parents of five children. I can still recall the first few moments of their arrival like a scene from a movie: Sarah and Brian bouncing out of the car with their big brown eyes taking in the house, the gardens, the cats at the window; our three children spilling out the front door to welcome them. There was the noise of car doors slamming and luggage hitting the concrete driveway, then it was as if we were all frozen in time, unable to imagine the rest of the scene. The adults hung back, uncertain. Then Alec, Drew and Theron started talking to Sarah and Brian about who was sharing what room and pointing to the stuffed animals and bikes. The four adults looked at each other and smiled. And time started flowing once again.

The ancient ruins of Angkor have been in peril since the time of Pol Pot and the Khmer Rouge. The social turmoil of the last three decades has threatened the restoration that modern archaeologists and physical scientists began in the 20th century. After the arrival of 70,000 tourists in 1968, Air France had built a second luxurious hotel which was just about to open in 1970 when the Vietnamese Communist soldiers and their allies, the Khmer Rouge, attacked Lon Nol's troops in Siem Reap. From that point on, tourism was finished.

Today, Cambodians, along with several international teams, have joined together to restore Angkor, named on the List of the World Heritage in Danger. The World Monuments Fund has been working at Angkor since 1989 and Cambodian students, local workers and international professionals are now working together to rebuild imperiled structures and regain lost advances made before the political upheaval.

All over the world, refugees are gradually rebuilding their lives in the same way—painstakingly, step by step—in an effort to recover from that same national catastrophe. I think of a ripple effect—a rock thrown in a lake and the water undulating outward in larger, then smaller, waves. Roger and I and our children are part of the ripple effect, the outer lappings of the ever-widening circles that began with the disruption of the placid pool that was Cambodia by the U.S. bombings of 1970 and 1973. Three adolescent boys survived four years of terror, escaped to Thailand and came to live with the Streed family. Now, the two children of one of those boys are part of the Luhn family and the seven of us are trying to build new lives out of the shattered ruins left by Pol Pot and his Khmer Rouge.

So it continues, the quest for restoration. One day we hope to travel to Angkor as a family, to walk on those ancient stones and stroke the ornate carvings on the walls depicting Suryavarman II, builder of Angkor Wat. We will gaze into the all-knowing eyes of the giant stone Buddha who has seen rulers come and go: the Khmers, the Chams, the Khmers again, the Thai, then—after more than four centuries of abandonment to the jungle—the French, the Japanese, the French again, Prince Sihanouk, Lon Nol, and the Khmer Rouge. We will stand under that serene smile and lean in toward the heavy lips which are slightly parted as if about to speak, and possibly, we will hear the secrets of survival.

Cambodia:
A Chronology

1864

France makes Cambodia a French protectorate.

1941

France chooses nineteen-year-old Prince Norodom Sihanouk to be ruler of Cambodia, believing he will be easy to manipulate.
Japan occupies Cambodia until 1945 during World War II.

1946

First Indochina War begins.

1949

Pol Pot leaves Cambodia and goes to study in France.

1951

The Communist Party is founded in Cambodia.

1953

France, in the midst of losing a war against Vietnamese Communists, gives Cambodia its independence.
Pol Pot returns to Cambodia.

1954

Geneva Conference imposes political settlement of First Indochina War that says Cambodia must have national elections within a year.

1958

Sihanouk wins more than 99 percent of the popular vote in elections.

Sihanouk represses local Communists and dubs them Red Cambodians or "Khmer Rouge."

The Khmer Rouge seek refuge in the countryside and form underground resistance.

1960

Twenty-one Khmer Rouge radicals meet secretly to form Workers' Party of Kampuchea (WPK) whose central committee includes Saloth Sar (Pol Pot), Nuon Chea, and Ieng Sary.

Second Indochina War breaks out.

1963

South Vietnamese President Ngo Dinh Diem is assassinated.

U.S. President John F. Kennedy is assassinated.

Sihanouk cuts off American aid, fearing the wars in Vietnam and Laos will overflow into Cambodia.

1965

U.S. combat troops begin landing in Vietnam.

Sihanouk breaks off diplomatic relations with the United States.

Vietnamese Communists create "sanctuaries" in their militarily weak and ineffectual neighbor, thus moving into Cambodia.

Sihanouk reluctantly allows Vietnamese troops in lightly populated areas in the east.

1966

Cultural Revolution takes place in China.

Pol Pot secretly changes name of WPK to Communist Party of Kampuchea (CPK).

1967

Sihanouk represses local Communists.

1968

Tet offensive in Vietnam.

1969

Fearing further Communist inroads, Sihanouk renews diplomatic relations with United States.

America begins secret bombing of "sanctuaries" in Cambodia.

1970

Lon Nol seizes control of Cambodia with a coup d'etat against Sihanouk and establishes a pro-American regime.

U.S. and South Vietnamese forces jointly invade eastern Cambodia, the start of a two-month incursion. The invasion protects the U.S. withdrawal from Vietnam but destroys Cambodian neutrality, and, as Cambodia then becomes part of the Indochina War, starts Cambodia towards its end as a sovereign state.

April 29. In the United States, nationwide protests break out over the U.S. invasion of Cambodia.

May 4. Nixon calls upon National Guard units to quell protests. National Guardsmen fire upon students at Kent State, killing four.

Pol Pot returns from Vietnam and sets up headquarters in Kompong Thom.

To avoid a battle with the Americans at the Cambodian border, Vietnamese Communists move more deeply into Cambodia.

1972

At the Paris peace talks between U.S. and Vietnam, Vietnam agrees to a cease-fire and plans to withdraw forces from Cambodia.

Communist Party of Kampuchea (CPK) refuses to honor cease-fire because they are resentful at being abandoned by Vietnamese.

1973

U.S. bombers drop tens of thousands of tons of bombs on supposed CPK positions, stall CPK offensive on Phnom Penh, inflict thousands of civilian casualties and force tens of thousands of Cambodians from countryside into Phnom Penh and other cities.

August. Congress orders bombing to stop.

1975

January 1. CPK offensive begins. (Khmer Rouge fighting against Lon Nol forces.)

February 5. Communists blockade Mekong River; no food, fuel or ammunition can reach the Cambodian capitol of Phnom Penh.

April 1. President Lon Nol and entourage flee to United States.

April 12. U.S. embassy is evacuated from Cambodia by Marine Corps helicopter.

April 17. The Khmer Rouge capture Phnom Penh. They order immediate full-scale evacuations of the cities ("death march") and state everyone will grow rice in the country. They abolish money, all private property, Western medicine, education and religion.

April 30. Saigon falls to North Vietnam ending the Vietnam War.

May 12. Khmer Rouge capture U.S. merchant ship *Mayaguez*; President Ford and Secretary Kissinger order Cambodia bombed in retaliation.

July. The first of the secret purges takes place in Cambodia, this one killing former royalty and former high-ranking Lon Nol officers, as well as former professional and business leaders.

1976

February 6. Cambodia and China sign secret agreement for nonrefundable military aid.

April 4. Sihanouk resigns his position as nominal head of Khmer Rouge state and spends the next two-and-a-half years under house arrest.

April 14. Khmer Rouge announce new government, Democratic Kampuchea, with Pol Pot as prime minister.

Tuol Sleng (S-21) is opened as an interrogation and torture facility.

July. Second purge takes place in Cambodia against lesser military and government men, the educated and skilled, and those thought to be pro-Vietnamese.

1977

April 30. Khmer Rouge attack Vietnamese border areas.

Photos of Pol Pot in China and biographical information allow outsiders to identify him as Saloth Sar.

July. Another purge in Cambodia; most intellectuals are killed, including those who returned from abroad to help the Khmer Rouge.

October. Vietnamese army launches attacks against Cambodia.

1978

More and expanded purges in Cambodia—especially in the Eastern Zone—including anyone from previous groups who might have been missed.

December 25. Vietnamese troops invade Cambodia; Third Indochina War begins.

1979

January 7. The Vietnamese Army captures Phnom Penh. Pol Pot escapes to northwest where he continues to give orders behind the scenes.

Pol Pot and the Khmer Rouge send Sihanouk to the United Nations to argue on their behalf but Sihanouk defects.

January 8. Vietnam installs Communist puppet regime and changes name of the country to the People's Republic of Kampuchea (PRK).

PRK stages trial of Pol Pot and Ieng Sary and condemns them to death; both men remain untouched in Khmer Rouge jungle encampment near the border.

1981

CPK Central Committee announces party's dissolution but none of its top members resign and Pol Pot retains military posts.

1982

Anti-Communist factions, Sihanouk and Democratic Kampuchea all join together to form coalition government of Democratic Kampuchea (DK).

1985

Pol Pot divorces first wife Khieu Ponnary when she begins to suffer from depression and remarries a woman of peasant background who bears him a daughter.

1988

Vietnam withdraws forces from Cambodia.

1989

Country's name changes from the People's Republic of Kampuchea to the State of Cambodia.
Vietnam withdraws the last of the occupation troops.

1991

Interim government in Cambodia under United Nations supervision.
DK representatives Son Sen and Khieu Samphan report secretly to Pol Pot.

1992

DK faction refuses to disarm and cooperate with U.N. Hun Sen government also stops cooperating with the United Nations.

1993

DK faction boycotts national elections, which are won by the royalist party of Sihanouk's son, Ranariddh (FUNCINPEC).
Hun Sen's party (CPP) refuses to adhere to the election results or give up power so FUNCINPEC and CPP rule together with two prime ministers.

1997

Ieng Sary defects to the Hun Sen government.

Son Sen and his family are murdered under Pol Pot's orders.

March 30. At a rally for the popular former finance minister Sam Rainsy, fifteen die in a grenade attack. Evidence for the attack points to Hun Sen.

Pol Pot is put on trial for treason in a Khmer Rouge encampment. The trial is filmed by U.S. journalist Nate Thayer.

July. Hun Sen attacks all his opponents—Ranariddh, Sam Rainsy and Son Sann; many of their aides are murdered and they all flee for safety. Sam Rainsy later returns.

1998

April 16. Pol Pot dies—either murdered by colleagues or from natural causes—in a Khmer Rouge camp.

Elections are held and Hun Sen becomes "sole premier" with twelve cabinet posts and Ranariddh (Sihanouk's son) becomes president of the Assembly with eleven cabinet posts.

Note: This chronology is drawn from the chronologies in *Brother Number One: A Political Biography of Pol Pot* by David Chandler and *Cambodia: Report from a Stricken Land* by Henry Kamm.

Bibliography

Author's Interviews

Ellyn Bullock, Sinn Lok, Sophea Mouth, Prum Nath*, Nouen Nor*, Sokkhom Ngep, Sarith Ou, Samantha Samreth, Erik Streed, Joan Streed, John Streed, Stephen Streed, Sam You, Sokhary You.

Books

American Psychiatric Association. *DSM-IV: Diagnostic and Statistical Manual of Mental Disorders,* fourth edition. Washington, D.C.: The American Psychiatric Association, 1994.

Arendt, Hannah. *Eichmann in Jerusalem: A Report on the Banality of Evil.* U.S.A.: The Viking Press, 1963.

Barron, John, and Paul, Anthony. *Murder of a Gentle Land: The Untold Story of Communist Genocide in Cambodia.* New York: Reader's Digest Press, 1977.

Becker, Elizabeth. *When the War Was Over: The Voices of Cambodia's Revolution and its People.* New York: Simon and Schuster, 1986.

Bingham, Robert. *Lightning on the Sun.* New York: Doubleday, 2000.

Carney, Timothy. *Kampuchea: Balance of Survival.* Asia: DD Books, 1983.

Chandler, David. *Brother Number One: A Political Biography of Pol Pot.* Boulder, San Francisco, Oxford: Westview Press, 1992.

_____. *A History of Cambodia.* Boulder, San Francisco, Oxford: Westview Press, 2000.

_____. *The Land and People of Cambodia.* New York: HarperCollins Publishers, 1991.

_____. *The Tragedy of Cambodian History.* New Haven and London: Yale University Press, 1991.

_____. *Voices from S-21: Terror and History in Pol Pot's Secret Prison.* Berkeley, Los Angeles and London: University of California Press, 1999.

_____; Kiernan, Ben; Boua, Chanthou, editors and translators. *Pol Pot*

*pseudonym

Plans the Future: Confidential Leadership Documents from Democratic Kampuchea, 1976–1977. New Haven: Yale University Southeast Asia Studies, 1988.

_____, and Kiernan, Ben, eds. *Revolution and its Aftermath in Kampuchea: Eight Essays.* New Haven: Yale University Southeast Asia Studies, 1983.

Conroy, John. *Unspeakable Acts, Ordinary People; The Dynamics of Torture.* New York: Alfred A. Knopf, 2000.

Criddle, JoAn D. and Butt Mam, Teeda. *To Destroy You Is No Loss: The Odyssey of a Cambodian Family.* New York: The Atlantic Monthly Press, 1987.

Davies, Paul. *War of the Mines: Cambodia, Landmines and the Impoverishment of a Nation.* London: Pluto Press, 1994.

De Nike, Howard; Quigley, John; and Robinson, Kenneth. *Genocide in Cambodia: Documents from the Trial of Pol Pot and Ieng Sary.* Philadelphia: University of Pennsylvania Press, 2000.

Drabble, Margaret. *The Gates of Ivory.* New York: Viking, 1991.

Fifield, Adam. *A Blessing Over Ashes: The Remarkable Odyssey of My Unlikely Brother.* New York: HarperCollins, 2000.

Hildebrand, George C., and Porter, Gareth. *Cambodia, Starvation and Revolution.* New York and London: Monthly Review Press, 1976.

Him, Chanrithy. *When Broken Glass Floats: Growing Up Under the Khmer Rouge.* New York and London: W.W. Norton & Company, 2000.

Jackson, Karl D., ed. *Cambodia 1975–78: Rendezvous with Death.* Princeton, New Jersey: Princeton University Press, 1989.

Jarvis, Helen. *Cambodia.* Oxford, England, Santa Barbara, California and Denver, Colorado: Clio Press, 1997.

Kamm, Henry. *Cambodia: Report from a Stricken Land.* New York: Arcade Publishing, 1998.

Kaplan, Harold I., and Sadock, Benjamin J. *Synopsis of Psychiatry: Behavioral Sciences Clinical Psychiatry.* Baltimore: Williams and Wilkins, 1991.

Kiernan, Ben. *How Pol Pot Came to Power.* London: Verso, 1985.

_____. *The Pol Pot Regime: Race, Power, and Genocide in Cambodia Under the Khmer Rouge, 1975–79.* New Haven and London: Yale University Press, 1996.

_____, editor. *Genocide and Democracy in Cambodia: The Khmer Rouge, the United Nations and the International Community.* New Haven: Yale University Southeast Asia Studies, 1993.

LeCarre, John. *The Secret Pilgrim.* New York: Alfred A. Knopf, 1991.

Lyons, Adrian, ed. *Voices Stories Hopes: Cambodia and Vietnam: Refugees and Volunteers.* Victoria: Collins Dove, 1993.

May, Someth. Edited by Fenton, James. *Cambodian Witness: The Autobiography of Someth May.* New York: Random House, 1986.

Ngor, Haing, M.D., with Warner, Roger. *A Cambodian Odyssey.* New York: MacMillan Publishing Company, 1987.

Picq, Lawrence. Translated by Norland, Patricia. *Beyond the Horizon: Five Years with the Khmer Rouge.* New York: St. Martin's Press, 1989.

Ponchaud, Francois. *Cambodia: Year Zero.* New York: Holt, Rinehart and Winston, 1978. London: Penguin Press, 1978.

Pran, Dith, compiler. *Children of Cambodia's Killing Fields: Memoirs by Survivors.* New Haven and London: Yale University Press, 1977.

Safire, William. *Before the Fall.* New York: Doubleday, 1975.

Schanberg, Sydney, and Pran, Dith, personal accounts. *The Killing Fields: The Facts Behind the Film.* London: George Weidenfeld and Nicolson Limited, 1984.

Shawcross, William. *The Quality of Mercy: Cambodia, Holocaust and the Modern Conscience.* New York: Simon and Schuster, 1984.

_____. *Sideshow: Kissinger, Nixon and the Destruction of Cambodia.* New York: Simon and Shuster, 1979.

Sheehy, Gail. *Spirit of Survival.* New York: William Morrow and Company, Inc., 1986.

Sihanouk, Norodom. *My War with the CIA,* as related to Wilfred Burchett. New York: Monthly Review Press, 1973. London: Penguin Press, 1973.

Smith-Hefner, Nancy J. *Khmer American.* Berkeley, Los Angeles, London: University of California Press, 1999.

Storer, Eric, and McGrath, Rae, for Asia Watch, Physicians for Human Rights. *Land Mines in Cambodia: The Coward's War.* New York: Human Rights Watch and Physicians for Human Rights, 1991.

Stuart-Fox, Martin, and Ung, Bunheang. Drawings by Bunheang Ung. *The Murderous Revolution: Life and Death in Pol Pot's Kampuchea,* Australia: Alternative Publishing Cooperative Limited, 1985.

Swain, Jon. *River of Time: A Memoir of Vietnam and Cambodia.* New York: Berkley Books, 1995.

Szymusiak, Molyda. *The Stones Cry Out: A Cambodian Childhood, 1975–1980.* New York: Hill and Wang, 1986.

Ung, Loung. *First They Killed My Father: A Daughter of Cambodia Remembers.* New York: HarperCollins, 2000.

Y, Ly, with Driscoll, John, ed. *Heaven Becomes Hell: A Survivor's Story of Life Under the Khmer Rouge.* New Haven: Yale University Southeast Asia Studies, 2000.

Yathay, Pin, with Man, John. *Stay Alive, My Son.* New York: The Free Press, 1987.

Pamphlets

Cambodian Culture and Beliefs, You, Sam, 1996.

Cambodian Life Before, During and After the War: The Exodus from Cambodia. Ry Mang, United Refugee Services, 1987.

Cultural Survival Quarterly. *Cambodia 1990.* Cambridge, Massachusetts: Cultural Survival, 1990.

The International Rescue Committee. *Children of Kampuchea: Their Nightmares and Dreams.* Thailand: International Rescue Committee, 1982.
To Know a Little of Cambodia. Lor, Saravuthy. Yoshimasa Sudo's Asian Cultures Class, November 23, 1983.

Articles and Papers

Abercrombie, Thomas J. "Cambodia: Indochina's Neutral Corner." *National Geographic*, Oct. 1964, pp. 514–551.
Baron, Roy C.; Thacker, Stephen B.; Gorelkin, Leo; Vernon, Andrew A.; Taylor, William R.; Choi, Keewhan. "Sudden Death Among Southeast Asian Refugees: An Unexplained Nocturnal Phenomenon." *Journal of American Medical Association*, 250 (1983), pp. 2947–2951.
Blair, Robert G. "Risk Factors Associated with PTSD and Major Depression Among Cambodian Refugees in Utah." *Health and Social Work*, Feb. 2000, pp. 23–38.
Carlson, E.B.; Rosser-Hogan, R. "Mental Health Status of Cambodian Refugees Ten Years After Leaving Their Homes." *American Journal of Orthopsychiatry*, 63(2) 1993, pp. 223–31.
Chigas, George. "The Trial of the Khmer Rouge: The Role of the Tuol Sleng and Santebal Archives." *Harvard Asia Quarterly*, Winter, 1999.
Cook, Susan, and Chigas, George. "Cornering the Khmer Rouge." *Bangkok Post*, March 19, 2000.
_____, and _____. "Putting the Khmer Rouge on Trial." *Bangkok Post*, October 31, 2000.
Erlanger, Steven. "The Endless War." *The New York Times Magazine*, 5 March, 1989, pp. 23–52.
Garrett, W.E. "Southeast Asia Ten Years Later." *National Geographic*, May 1985, pp. 574–75.
Kiernan, Ben. "Cambodia's Terror Lords Must Not Evade Trial." *San Jose Mercury News*, March 7, 1999.
Moore, W. Robert. "Angkor, Jewel of the Jungle." *National Geographic*, April 1960, pp. 516–569.
Mydans, Seth. "Praying to Pol Pot, Seeking Health and Good Luck." *New York Times International,* 23 June 2001.
_____. "Split Puts Khmer Rouge Faction in Mood to Deal With Old Foes." *New York Times*, 19 Aug. 1996, Sec. A, p.1, col. 1–2.
Ouellette, Laurie. "The Killing Fields Revisited." *Utne Reader*, Nov./Dec. 1991, pp. 42–44.
Pilger, John. "Pol Pot's Safe Haven." *New Statesman and Society*, 26 April 1991, pp. 10–11.
Sack, William H.; Clarke, G.; Him, Chanrithy; Dickason, Dan; Goff, Brian; Lanham, Kathleen; Kinzie, J. David. "A 6-Year Follow-up Study of Cambodian Refugee Adolescents Traumatized as Children." *Journal of*

the *American Academy of Child and Adolescent Psychiatry*, 32 (1993), pp. 431–437.

Sack, W.H.; Clarke, G.N.; Seeley, J. "Multiple Forms of Stress in Cambodian Adolescent Refugees." *Child Development*, 167(1) 1996 Feb., pp. 107–16.

Savin, Dan; Sack, William H.; Clarke, Gregory N.; Meas, Nee; and Richart, Im. "The Khmer Adolescent Project: III. A Study of Trauma Thailand's Site II Refugee Camp." *Journal of the American Academy of Child and Adolescent Psychiatry*, 35 (1996), pp. 384–391.

"Sudden, Unexpected, Nocturnal Deaths Among Southeast Asian Refugees." *Centers for Disease Control Morbidity and Mortality Weekly Report*, 30 (1981), pp. 581–589.

Tan, Michael. "Bangungot." *Philippine Daily Inquirer Pinoy Kasi*, August 29, 2000.

Thayer, Nate. "Day of Reckoning." *Far Eastern Economic Review*, October 30, 1997, pp. 14–20.

_____. "Forbidden City." *Far Eastern Economic Review*, October 30, 1997, pp. 22–23.

_____. "My Education." *Far Eastern Economic Review*, October 30, 1997, p. 21.

"Update: Sudden Unexplained Death Syndrome Among Southeast Asian Refugees—United States." *Centers for Disease Control Morbidity and Mortality Weekly Report*, 37 (1988), pp. 568–570.

White, Peter T. "Kampuchea Wakens from a Nightmare." *National Geographic*, May 1982, pp. 590–623.

_____. "The Mekong: River of Terror, River of Hope." *National Geographic*, December 1968, pp. 737–789.

_____. "The Temples of Angkor: Ancient Glory in Stone." *National Geographic*, May 1982, pp. 552–589.

Index